ANSELM'S DISCOVERY

ANSELM'S DISCOVERY:
A RE-EXAMINATION OF THE ONTOLOGICAL PROOF FOR GOD'S EXISTENCE

Charles Hartshorne

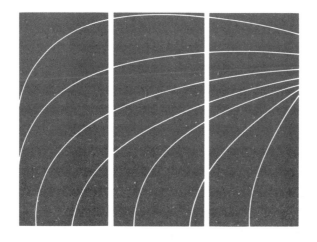

Open Court

La Salle, Illinois 61301

**Anselm's Discovery: A Re-examination of the Ontological Proof for
God's Existence**

Library of Congress Catalog Card Number: 65-3309
ISBN 0-87548-217-1

To Dorothy

Progress is the battle with the experts.

—Peter Schlumbohm

The winning ideas write their own history, and the
history of the ideas over which they triumph.

—Anonymous

He will endow our fleeting days with abiding worth.

—Jewish ritual

Preface

In a thesis written at Harvard in 1923 I termed the Ontological Argument invented by Anselm "an incomparably brilliant and cogent course of reasoning." I was already familiar with Kant's famous refutation. Since that time frequent rereading of Kant and examination of scores of other refutations have failed to convince me that the Argument is a mere fallacy. However, I now think that both the standard criticisms and the older defences, including mine of forty years ago, are all seriously—even disgracefully—defective. In 1923 I had, like so many others, failed to read Anselm with scholarly care; and I certainly took my self-appointed task of rebutting Kant far too casually. Today, instead of brashly asserting, as I recall doing in another student essay, that the Argument "sums up what is most sound in philosophy," I should make a qualified statement. I still hold that there is no shorter way to an understanding of essential metaphysical issues than the careful consideration of the challenge that Anselm issued to his contemporaries and successors. However, I have come to see that the simple acceptance of the reasoning as Anselm left it (were this today still possible) is no better calculated than its simple rejection to give us this understanding. There are ambiguities to be removed and issues to be weighed which have been almost unnoticed by both sides in the long dispute. In this present work I have tried to specify these ambiguities and issues with precision, and to show how, as I believe, they are to be most reasonably overcome or resolved, and with what philosophical consequences.

In Part One a view of the Proof will be presented that is neither simply Anselm's nor that of any of his better-known defenders, but which claims to be a higher synthesis of doctrines, assigning an element of validity to each of the principal attitudes which have been taken on the subject. Whatever its defects, this discussion does take Anselm's proposal seriously and does try to criticize it, partly at least, on grounds which he might conceivably have found pertinent and cogent—as he manifestly did not find Gaunilo's (and probably would not have found most of Kant's). The analysis also takes ancient and modern criticisms seriously in just those respects that are left standing when it is what Anselm wrote and the whole of what he wrote on the subject which forms the target of the criticism. In order to meet these *relevant* criticisms, it is found necessary to revise, not so much the Argument as the precise 'Idea of God' from which it sets out. This revision Anselm might have rejected, but he could scarcely have found it so inconsequential as he (in part rightly) found the counterarguments of Gaunilo. An important point of the analysis is the inadequacy of the dichotomy *essence-existence*. A third term is needed, 'actuality'. An essence exists if there is some concrete reality exemplifying it; 'existence' is only *that* an essence is concretized, 'actuality' is *how*, or in what particular form, it is concretized. The particular form, the actuality, is always contingent—here opponents of the Proof have been right—but it does not follow—and here they have been in error—that the existence is contingent. For existence only requires the non-emptiness of the appropriate class of actualities, and a class can be necessarily nonempty even though it has only contingent members. How this applies to God can hardly be obvious to the reader, unless his training in philosophy has been very unusual. But I hold that it does apply. (See Part One, Sections 8, 11, 23; and Part Two, Section 17.) Essence, existence, actuality—this triad is the minimum of complexity which must be considered if the famous Proof is to be correctly evaluated. As Peirce said, the thinker in mere dichotomies is a crude fellow, trying to make delicate dissections with an ax. So long as philosophers persist in confusing existence and actuality, just so long will they be but bumbling amateurs in a matter in which they have long been claiming competence.

It is hoped that the reader will be brought to a realization of the depth of the issues and the unworthiness of any simple short cut to a definitive conclusion. He will be encouraged to think his way through the Anselmian problem, and not (as is customary) around it, as though the Saint's little book had been lost just after Gaunilo saw it, and we had been dependent upon this one careless expositor for all of our knowledge of the Anselmian idea.

Part Two surveys, partly through substantial quotations, the history of important or representative reactions to the Argument, from Gaunilo's to those of some of our contemporaries, and evaluates these from the standpoint of Part One. The reader of these discussions will have at his command, in outline, something like the entire historical context of a fundamental technical problem in philosophy and theology.

Among other results, it will be shown that most of those who have attacked, and many who have defended, the reasoning of the *Proslogium* have literally "not known what they were talking about" since, according to all probability, they were reacting to a document they had not read, even in a competent paraphrase.

Concerning the length and complexity of my treatment of a well-worn and seemingly restricted topic, some remarks may be in order. I see myself as combating nine centuries of error piled upon error about Anselm, and among these errors is the notion that the problem which he posed is a simple one. In my view it is, like all metaphysical questions, *the* metaphysical question put from a particular standpoint. The defenders of the Proof, if they have understood themselves, have had a metaphysics; and so have its attackers. However, my own standpoint in speculative philosophy has not been expressed in any treatment of Anselm (by others than myself) with which I am acquainted. It is not any of the better-known theistic or nontheistic positions. Several of the more traditional types of metaphysics have been presented a hundred times; students of philosophy are familiar with and influenced by them, whether they know they are or not, and whether by way of rejection or of acceptance. To make headway simultaneously against so many prejudices, some of them reinforced by almost endless repetitions, I have felt forced to put my understanding of what Anselm discovered (and of what he failed to discover) in similarly many ways, and to defend it against many objections. This does not mean that the reader is given but one way of looking at Anselm. Allowing for the greater familiarity, and also greater simplicity, of other views, I venture to think that the main possibilities are here made available.

I am grateful to Dr. Eugene Freeman, Editor-in-chief of the Open Court Publishing Company, for having suggested this commentary, and for his patience as it outgrew the volume for which it was originally designed, *The Basic Writings of Saint Anselm.* For that a much briefer version had to be written. I have also profited by discussions with my son-in-law, Nicolas D. Goodman, which have helped me to mitigate the consequences of my insufficient training and skill in formal logic. I suspect that the future of the ontological problem lies largely in rather technical developments in formal logic (including modal logic or, perhaps I should say, metalogic) or in such studies in the philosophy of logic as only those who know the logic can promote or adequately judge. The stage of mere 'talkietalk' about this matter is probably nearing its close. Those who wish to add something may have to be better equipped than I to explore in a formal manner the logical niceties of the problem of existential contingency and necessity.

C. H.

THE UNIVERSITY OF TEXAS

Contents

Part One

NECESSARILY SOMEHOW ACTUALIZED:

ANSELM'S PROOF IN NEW PERSPECTIVE

PART ONE

NECESSARILY SOMEHOW ACTUALIZED: ANSELM'S PROOF IN NEW PERSPECTIVE

1. *Blunder or Discovery?*

Did Anselm, in his 'Ontological Argument'—about the year 1070—make one of the greatest intellectual discoveries of all time, or did he merely fall into an interesting blunder? Or was there, in this case as in so many others, a combination of discovery and error? We shall see reason to think that there was indeed a discovery, and a great one, but that Anselm was in part mistaken as to its nature. His critics have clarified certain aspects of the problem to which he pointed, but, alas, have also generally obscured the discovery itself. Nor have his best-known defenders understood it much better.

What was this discovery? In crude anticipatory outline, it was the following: Assuming certain 'meaning postulates' (to use Carnap's helpful phrase) concerning the import of 'God' and certain related terms, it follows that the existence of God is a logical or analytic truth. The meaning postulates can be rejected, but the position then taken is not atheism, as commonly understood (or agnosticism either) but positivism (as I shall use this label), the view that the divine existence is logically impossible. The sole alternative to the necessary truth of theism is its logical impossibility. No question of contingent or empirical fact is at stake. Empirical atheism (I shall usually call it simply atheism), holding that there is no objection to the idea of God except that factual evidence concerning it happens to be lacking or negative, is genuinely refuted by 'the Proof' (as I shall call it for short); but equally refuted is empirical theism, holding that although atheism is logically unobjectionable the factual evidence favors theism. Unless Anselm made (as so many, but not this writer, believe he made) a mere mistake, empirical theism and empirical atheism are alike logical blunders. If belief in the divine existence even makes sense, unbelief does not, and if unbelief makes sense, belief does not. The issue between them is not one of fact or contingent truth but of meaning. One side or the other is confused. Obviously this result, if correct, is of great importance for philosophy and religion.

The connection between the idea of God and the inconceivability of nonexistence can be brought out in many ways. Anselm hit upon some of these. For instance, to exist with nonexistence as a conceivable alternative is an inferior manner of existing, compared to existing without such alternative, and hence only the latter mode of existing is compatible with the Unsurpassability (such that "none greater can be conceived") which defines deity. One can read a hundred standard or important philosophical works in which the Proof is discussed and scarcely find even an unclear statement of this point. Yet Anselm himself expresses it plainly more than once and implies it many times. A grosser failure of scholarship will not, I think, be found, considering that it went without effective challenge for centuries.

Anselm assumed as meaning postulate that belief is logically possible, that his idea of deity was consistent. Granted this, he did prove the divine existence. However, should it be granted? Over a thousand years before, Carneades had given impressive reasons for regarding the idea of God as self-inconsistent. Anselm did not refute this contention. Insofar, he did not prove the divine existence.

Here we note another failure of scholarship—or of intellectual perspicacity. To argue cogently for a position is to show the falsity of at least some of its plausible theoretical competitors. A complete demonstration must disprove all of these. Because Anselm failed to accomplish this, it is concluded that he accomplished nothing. But he did accomplish something. He disproved not only atheism but empirical theism as well, and thereby reduced the central religious issue to the forced option, positivism or theism, in either case as logically true or analytic. That he did not resolve this final issue detracts no whit from the accomplishment just stated. One task at a time, if we are serious in our pretensions to sober analysis! The complete justification of theism would require a further argument, that against positivism; but the elimination of two out of four logically possible positions is sheer gain nonetheless.

Since the publication of my *Logic of Perfection,* in which I present several forms of ontological proof, one of the few attempts at rebuttal amounted to this: a premise from which I reason would not be self-evident to philosophers of all persuasions (i.e., positivists would reject it). Is there any piece of philosophical reasoning for an important position which does not depend upon premises similarly open to challenge from some philosophical school? It is an unwitting compliment to Anselm that he is asked to submit to criteria which perhaps no philosopher could afford to accept. An argument is more than a mere mistake if it is cogent against *some* important philosophical position. It is nice to dream of an argument which would be cogent against every such position except one, but we may have to settle for less than this, or give up the attempt to apply reason to basic issues and turn over the field to Zen Buddhism, or some other form of radical intuitionism, fideism, or no less irrational antifideism.

A common method of seeking to trivialize Anselm's claim is to hold that 'necessarily existing' (to use a non-Anselmian phrase) means only, 'existing necessarily if it exists at all'. 'Divinity exists' is perhaps necessary if true; however, it may be false. Obviously, if a proposition p is not true, it is not necessarily true; so there is a sense in which we may sometimes say, 'necessary if true'. But what is the meaning of the 'if . . . then' in such a case? Can it be: If it is contingently true that divinity exists then it is also necessarily true? No, for this is contradictory. But a proposition which could not be contingently true also could not be contingently false; hence the sole sensible meaning of, 'if true then necessarily true', must be, if not necessarily false, then necessarily true. And only of divinity, among distinct kinds of individuals, is there reason to admit that the sole alternative to necessary truth for the assertion of existence is necessary falsity. Moreover, the decision between necessary truth and necessary falsity cannot be empirical or factual but must be logical. So on this interpretation Anselm made a momentous discovery, that one existential question is logical or a priori, not empirical. If this is not important philosophically, what would be?

As an example of this importance, consider the classical argument against theism from the observed facts of evil. If the issue is purely logical, no such facts can be relevant. As we shall see, David Hume conceded this relationship between the Proof and the said facts, though he rejected the Proof itself.

There is, however, another possible interpretation of, 'if true then necessary': 'If it is contingently true that God exists, then it is also contingently true that He exists necessarily'. Since 'contingently' here refers to logical and 'necessarily' to ontological modality, there is no overt contradiction. The one is modality *de dictu* or in language, the other *de re*. Nevertheless, we still have not got rid of Anselm's discovery. For (a) the antitheist has at least been forced to commit himself to a radical disconnectedness between the two kinds of modality (and there are, as we shall see, grave objections to this assumption); and also (b) Anselm himself does not employ the terms 'necessary' and 'contingent', nor is the distinction between *de re* and *de dictu* obviously applicable to his actual procedure. He compares beings whose nonexistence is not conceivable to those whose nonexistence is conceivable and holds that the former must be superior to the latter, from which he infers that 'not conceivably surpassable' must connote 'not conceivably nonexistent'. And since questions of conceivability are logical not factual, Anselm's discovery, as I have stated it, still stands. Atheism is ruled out and only positivism survives as competitor to theism.

The effort to trivialize the great discovery has failed. It must be rejected outright, or its importance conceded. Can it reasonably be rejected outright?

This depends upon what is meant by the Proof. If the standard version, given in countless works of reference and other writings, is the essential content of the reasoning, then

I grant that outright rejection is reasonable. But the reasoning sketched above, which I and others find in *Prosl.* III and later passages, is in no obvious way (I believe in no legitimate way) reducible to the standard version. Therefore, the standard criticisms fail to justify rejection. Generations of philosophers have deceived themselves in this regard. What they disproved was not Anselm's complete Argument, but the simplification and corruption which this suffered in Descartes (especially in the *Meditations*). This corruption was at least threefold. First, *Prosl.* II was taken as the basic text (known to Descartes perhaps only at second or third hand), not the incomparably superior *Prosl.* III. Second, Descartes, by introducing the term 'necessary', raised by implication the issue between logical and real modality which Anselm had avoided. Third, by substituting terms like 'perfect' for the by no means equivalent conception of unsurpassability, Descartes lost one of the best features of Anselm's terminology. The supposition that 'perfect' and 'not conceivably surpassable' are equivalent springs from an illicit conversion. To be absolutely complete or maximal, or to exhaust possible value, is certainly inconsistent with being surpassable. But is being unsurpassable necessarily inconsistent with *not* being maximal or complete? 'What is complete is unsurpassable' may not be convertible. Suppose (we shall see good reason for the supposition) that possible value is in principle inexhaustible, so that the idea of exhausting it is logically absurd. It would follow that either Unsurpassability is likewise logically absurd (and positivism correct) or else Unsurpassability is logically independent of completeness. An advertising slogan quaintly suggests how this might be. "When better cars are built Buick will build them." Insofar as this is taken as absolutely valid for all possible circumstances, Buick cars must as such be unsurpassable, though not maximally good or 'perfect'. Of course absolute validity could not be imagined for a slogan of this sort. Absolutes of this kind cannot qualify ordinary nondivine things. But some such absolute might very well apply to God. It might even be the sensible meaning of 'unsurpassable'. I shall argue that it is precisely that. Clearly 'perfect' is a poor word to suggest this idea.

Anselm himself, it is true, in effect accepted the equivalence of completeness and unsurpassability. It remains a significant fact that his language was wiser than he knew, and that Descartes's language was not wiser than Descartes knew.

I have said that the usual reasons do not justify the rejection of Anselm's Proof. Could better reasons be given? To this my answer is, yes—and no. If by unsurpassable is meant complete, exhaustive of possible value, then it can be cogently argued that neither this nor any other proof is capable of establishing the doctrine. Here I join the critics: Anselm failed to furnish a valid reason supporting his own form of theism. For while atheism cannot fairly defend itself against Anselm, neither can Anselm fairly defend himself against the atheist. Each can point to a fatal flaw in the other's position. Moreover, Descartes and Leibniz were in no better case. Nevertheless, Anselm made a great discovery, and one which can lend valuable support to theism of a different type, not only against atheism, but against Anselm's theism itself. This is the point which has been missed by previous commentators, of no matter what philosophical persuasion, the blind spot for which only the passing of thirty-five generations has brought a cure. Anselm's reasoning, when its logic is sufficiently carefully attended to, illuminates not only the existence but the nature of God. It requires us to reconceive the import of 'divine'.

'Necessary' is sometimes used to mean, upon certain conditions which might or might not be fulfilled. This is conditional necessity, the necessity of p, given q. But there is also unconditional necessity, necessity of p, given q or not q—or as von Wright puts it, "upon tautological conditions." With this latter meaning, it is contradictory to assume that the existence of the thing itself (or the existence of anything else) is condition of its necessary existence, taking 'condition' to mean a requirement capable of being unrealized. It is, from his text, quite clear that the necessity Anselm is talking about is unconditional necessity, and hence considerations which require the necessity to be conditional are not relevant. We have nothing to do here with a necessity obtaining only if the requirement that the thing exists is satisfied (whatever such 'necessity', surely a very odd or tenuous one, could mean).

Any criticism of the argument, to be enlightening, must be more carefully formulated.

Nor is it admissible to settle the question by fiat, that is, by declaring that existence can in no case be inferred a priori. To reply to a man who argues: whereas all other things can be conceived not to exist, divinity, for certain specified reasons, cannot be so conceived, "My dear sir, not only can all other things be conceived not to exist, but—as you simply must admit—even divinity can be so conceived," is childish—or if one prefers, remarkably obtuse. It is mere stubbornness, the method of tenacity. We shall have to do better if we would deserve to be called philosophers. The specific reasons just referred to must be evaluated *before* we could have a right to assert the universal contingency of existential assertions.

Anselm's presentation and defence of his argument occupy slightly over twenty pages, three and one-half in the *Proslogium* (Chapters II-V) and seventeen in the reply to Gaunilo (Which I shall call 'the Reply'). Of those who claim to demonstrate that the argument is a mere sophistry, the majority appear to have read the first page or so (Chapter II), or at least a paraphrase of it in some history, but one would be hard put to it in most cases to furnish evidence that they had read more. Some have perhaps read Gaunilo's reply at first hand, but if they know that and how Anselm replied, namely with care and (in my opinion) lucidity, as well as serene confidence, to the monk's criticisms, they have kept this knowledge to themselves. Even when the *Reply* (he called it his 'apology') is referred to, it is usually the least essential portions which are cited. As Koyré and Barth say, the philosophical world has for the most part simply adopted Gaunilo's point of view, including all its oversights and inability to grasp the subtleties of Anselm.

Does the reader not see a difference which is more than rhetorical between (1) 'that which exists in reality as well as in the mind is greater than that which exists in the mind alone', and (2) 'that whose nonexistence cannot be conceived is greater than that whose nonexistence can be conceived'? This is the point of difference between the reasoning of Chapter II and that of Chapter III. In both cases the writing is almost as lucid as writing well can be; yet one hundred philosophical authors, many of them very famous ones, have proceeded as though it had been beyond their capacity to notice the distinction, although it occurs practically within one page! If a difference between a modal statement (as to what can be conceived) and a simple categorical statement is not important in philosophy, what could be? Had the authors attempted to show that the reasoning of the Chapters (II, III) reduces by recognized logical principles to one and the same, then we might still disagree with them, but at least we should know that they had read the work they professed to criticize. As it is we do not know this, and I personally do not believe it. Or, if the glance of these authors did fall upon the pages in question, then, as Dewey once said of one of his critics, they must have been "suffering from never having been able to learn to read."

Only recently, after Professor Malcolm had called the attention of English-speaking philosophers to the great difference between the logic of *Prosl*. II and that of *Prosl*. III, or between Anselm's 'first' and 'second' ontological arguments, has one begun to meet the contention that the two arguments must stand or fall together. (See below, Sec. 23, and Malcolm in the Bibliography.) But how odd to take nine centuries even to discuss the question! And why is it that specialists in Anselm do not usually take this position? In the effort to show that an obvious textual problem, with which critics should all along have reckoned, is really no problem at all, is there nothing of the 'method of tenacity'? Or, if you prefer, of what may be termed 'the method of convenient ignorance'? It is so much handier to have a fictitious (conveniently simplified and drastically weakened) Anselm to refute than the real one.

If the reader is surprised at my severity, let him hear from two distinguished scholarly specialists on Anselm (Koyré and Karl Barth):

Gaunilo seems to have understood the corrections which Saint Anselm addressed to him; at least, he did not reply. The moderns have neglected this highly instructive polemic, and this is why we have seen them repeating since Gassendi, since Kant, and down to our own time (1923) the same objections, the same errors, as those of the monk of Marmoutiers.[1]

Only fools and their theological and philosophical advocates, the Gaunilos, are capable of supposing that the measure of existence in general is the measure of God's existence, or of either remaining simply entangled in the dialectic of *Prosl.* II, or else of taking *Prosl.* III to be conditioned by *Prosl.* II. But it is altogether otherwise: the existence of God is the measure of Existence in general, and if either of the Anselmian chapters ultimately and decisively conditions the other, it is *Prosl.* III which conditions *Prosl.* II, not vice versa.[2]

To repeat, anyone has the right to argue against this thesis of the logical priority of *Prosl.* III (and many subsequent passages) over *Prosl.* II. But to assume the contrary thesis without argument is what no one who claimed to be a scholar has ever had the right to do. Yet Gaunilo did it, and apparently nearly all followed suit. And they admired Gaunilo for having made things so easy for them!

Perhaps the most astonishing thing of all about this fantastic history is that not only did Aquinas, and many others who rejected the Proof, follow Gaunilo in taking *Prosl.* II as definitive, but so did Leibniz, Hegel, and many others who were sympathetic to it. Rarely does even a friend of the argument clearly appreciate the content of Chapter III; usually he

---

[1] Koyré, (see Bibliography I), p. 225.
[2] Barth (see Bibliography I), p. 178. See also pp. 147, 153.

takes as primary the formula of the previous chapter, and makes no mention of the wide difference between the two forms of reasoning. And Descartes himself seemed to get to his version of the second form only as a sort of afterthought. (Kant, I suspect, did not know this second form in Descartes.) With such minds leading the way, it is perhaps not too hard to understand how an almost rigid fashion became established. The assumption that only *Prosl.* II matters was 'settled' for centuries.

Here is a sample of what has been going on. In a friend's office is a row of sixteen books, some rather old, some recent, dealing with the philosophy of religion. Eleven of these undertake to explain and evaluate the ontological argument, in all but one case mentioning Anselm. These eleven discussions vary greatly in quality, but one thing they have in common: they pay no attention to the chief points Anselm makes in *Prosl.* III-IV and repeats often in the *Reply*. Only the argument of *Prosl.* II is dealt with. One author, W. R. Sorley,[3] terms that argument, 'the sum and substance'—which recalls an old German work in which it was called 'the nerve' —of the Proof. One could hardly imagine more inappropriate phrases. As we shall see in Sections 19 and 20, *Prosl.* II is but a blundering preamble or unlucky false start in the development of the Proof. Its major premise is not even a first approximation to the nerve or substance of the eventual argument, still less its sum. Until such notions are dropped, the philosophical world will not have begun to assume the task laid upon it so long ago, to achieve a collective rational

---

[3] W. R. Sorley, *Moral Values and the Idea of God* (London: Cambridge University Press, 1921).

evaluation of Anselm's claim. It is worth adding that where Descartes is brought into the discussions above referred to he is treated in a similarly—though less obviously—truncated way, ignoring the second form of the Proof given in the *Replies*.

How far can the fallacies of 'straw man' and 'irrelevant conclusion' be carried and still leave a possibility of significant debate? One hundred philosophers (or should I say ten thousand?) collaborate to show that *Prosl.* II does not, without amplification or supplementation, provide a satisfactory account of a valid demonstration. What of that? Was it intended to do this? If so, why did its author hurry on, in the second sentence of the next chapter, to introduce two additional principles from which he reinfers the conclusion that God (necessarily) exists? And why did he repeat the major premise of *Prosl.* II in one short chapter only of the *Reply* II but the principles of *Prosl.* III in the longish *Reply* I, V, IX? And why, whereas *Reply* II merely twice reiterates in perfunctory fashion the all-too-simple notion of *Prosl.* II, do the other three chapters of the *Reply* referred to offer many ingenious variations upon the more complex theme of *Prosl.* III? The intellectual energy which went into the composition of *Prosl.* II and *Reply* II cannot remotely compare with that manifested in the other four chapters. And what have the hundred philosophers to say about the principles so energetically and resourcefully explicated in *Prosl.* III and *Reply* I, V, IX? As a rarely-broken rule, not a single word! For these authors, the chapters might as well have been in invisible ink.

On one conceivable condition the procedure might have been, not justifiable, but excusable: if Anselm had said explicitly that the reasoning of *Prosl.* III required, among its premises, the conclusion of that of *Prosl.* II. For then the two together would prove something only if the earlier chapter proved its point. To be entirely fair, it is possible, on hasty reading, to take the first sentence of *Prosl.* III in this sense. However, closer examination shows that no such thing is unambiguously asserted and that if it had been Anselm would have been mistaken about the logical relations of his two arguments. It should be part of a critic's job to check his judgment on this. Also, and in any case, the intricate, vigorous reasoning of *Prosl.* III (and the portions of the *Reply* which continue its theme) would be interesting in its own right. Unlike that of *Prosl.* II, it turns upon conceptions of modal logic, and deals explicitly with two kinds of existence, contingent and necessary, rather than with existence versus nonexistence, or merely subjective versus objective (as well as subjective) existence.

When a man takes twenty pages to explain an idea (on which immense issues hang), what rule of textual criticism says that the idea must stand or fall by what is said on the first two of these pages? And who could have imagined that seven centuries might pass before the practice of acting as though there were such a rule would even be emphatically called into question? Perhaps, instead of 'emphatically', I should have said 'rudely'. But can one be altogether polite when gentler admonitions are ignored and people persist in acting as though under a spell whose power has scarcely weakened in all this time, or when almost everyone talks confidently about the import of a text the actual reading of which he has obviously left to some other scholar—who has in fact no more accomplished it than he? How is one who sees all this to act? And suppose he has been at least dimly aware of the situation for forty years, and can count on far fewer additional years to convey the message to which, until now, few have been willing to attend. Is not such a one driven to become a bit insistent and dramatic, and not always considerate of everyone's dignity, or of his own reputation for modesty? But indeed, it sets up no claim to extraordinary brightness or painstakingness to have escaped, by some lucky set of circumstances, from a strange fashion, almost like a collective hypnosis, of being, in respect to one subject, exceedingly careless or dull-witted. Or is it, perhaps, naively trusting in relying upon other people to read the book which all discuss, but one does not oneself trouble to read?

If this and similar charges are repeated in this commentary a number of times, let the reader not forget that the practices inveighed against have been repeated tens of thousands of times, until they have come to seem beyond the reach of criticism or change. They must be reached and they must change.

It is staggering to think of the five hundred or more works of reference and aids to students in who knows how many languages which more or less grossly misstate the history of so central a matter as the leading proposal ever made to establish a logical connection between conceptual and real existence, and also, by the most direct route, to show the rationality of the central religious belief! How long will these works continue to misinform their readers? Think of the vested interests favoring such continuance. To repeat, the situation staggers the imagination.

Perhaps the whole modern rejection of metaphysics—or the study seeking necessary truths about existence—rests upon similarly shaky foundations. It ought to be, and it is, dangerous in intellectual matters to attack theories we disagree with only in their weakest form. In that way, we "play the confidence game upon ourselves" (Peirce)—reinforcing our prejudices over and over with never a chance of escaping from them, even when we encounter those who have thought more deeply than we.

2. The Overestimation of Gaunilo

Anselm was a great mind beside whom Gaunilo was not an intellectual giant. Barth will, I think, convince any patient reader that Gaunilo made certain blunders. Indeed, a patient reader of Anselm will also be convinced of this. Yet to many authors Gaunilo was the real hero of the ancient debate. Consider the following:

This argument . . . found an opponent worthy of Anselmus in Gaunilo, a monk of Marmoutiers in Touraine. Gaunilo emphasizes the difference between thought and being, and points out the fact that we may conceive and imagine a being, and yet that being may not exist. We have as much right to conclude from our idea of an enchanted island in the middle of the ocean that such an island actually exists. The criticism is just.[4]

In this summary of Gaunilo's objections, three points are made: the first is compatible with all that Anselm says; the second disagrees with what he says only if it is intended to apply, not to ordinary ideas alone, but to that of God as well, in which case it begs the question; the third is a loose argument by analogy, which will not stand examination. And so the historian, departing from his reasonable schol-

---

[4] Alfred Weber, *History of Philosophy*, trans. Frank Thilly (New York: Scribner's, 1896, 1925), pp. 169-70.

arly role, presumes—with the barest pretence of argument—
to set at naught the chief idea of a great man. And this is a
not unusual sample of the treatment Anselm's *Proslogium*
has received for nine centuries. It depends partly upon the
reader how much longer this state of affairs is to continue.

Has it ever been shown that 'perfect island' and 'perfect
being' are logically equivalent, for the purpose of Anselm's argument? Suppose, for the moment, 'perfect'—or
greatest conceivable—does, as Anselm thinks, imply the necessity of existing; it is also true, according not only to Anselm
but to almost everyone, that 'island' implies contingency. So
'perfect island' implies the contradiction, 'something both
necessary and not necessary'. Conclusion: no island could
conceivably be perfect in that theological sense (if there be
such a sense) which entails existence. And who, indeed,
except to win an argument, would ever have pretended to
know what could make an island the 'greatest conceivable'?
Can it, then, be maintained that the noncommittal term
'being' in 'perfect being' connotes contingency and imperfection as manifestly as does 'island' in 'perfect island'?
Hardly, for whereas nearly everyone expects islands to be
contingent and in many ways other than perfect, the great
majority of theologians have thought that God must be the
perfect and necessary being. So, to assume that this is as
plainly absurd as 'perfect and necessary island' is to assume that theism itself, as usually understood, is an obvious
absurdity. And thus Gaunilo's much admired *reductio ad
absurdum* reduces to a transparent begging of the question!

The brave historian, continuing to condescend to a dead
man long considered fair game, concludes:

Indeed, the ontological argument would be conclusive, only in case the idea of God and the existence of God in the human mind were identical. If our idea of God is God himself, it is evident that this idea is the immediate and incontrovertible proof of the existence of God. But what the theologian aims to prove is not the existence of the God-Idea of Plato and Hegel, but the existence of the personal God. However that may be, we hardly know what to admire most—St. Anselmus's broad and profound conception, or the sagacity of his opponent who, in the seclusion of his cell, anticipates the Transcendental Dialectic of Kant.[5]

Here we have a fourth criticism, borrowed from Kant. As we shall see, what must be inseparable from the idea of God is not His full actuality, but only His bare existence, which is a very different thing.

Weber's admiration for Gaunilo is another echo of a dubious tradition. No one who has ever studied Anselm with care has failed to be impressed with his greatness of intellect and character; but in what sizable group of educated persons will there not be a Gaunilo or two, that is to say, a well-meaning, bright, but rather conventionally-minded fellow, who tends to greet any subtle and unusual idea with a certain commonsense ('empirical') skepticism, and who starts ingenious objections, more or less plausible and more or less relevant, in part understanding the view he is attacking, but in greater part distorting, simplifying, or missing the main point. Every few years, at least, a teacher has a student of this kind. If there is much more in Gaunilo than this, I am not the only reader of Anselm who is unable to see it. To compare such a clever, but essentially commonplace mind with a man of genius seems shocking. And what effort can

---

[5] *Ibid.*

Weber possibly have made to learn *from Anselm's text* how the Saint would—nay, did—answer his critic? Clearly he made virtually no such effort. And why? Because Kant, Hume, Thomas—and Gaunilo (writing before he saw the answer)— had told him to expect nothing valuable there. And so it becomes the historian's job, not to find meanings, but to impute their absence a priori!

Gaunilo's substantial contributions, errors and irrelevancies aside, are: (1) his espousal of what we may today term the 'positivistic' view (largely anticipated by Carneades) that the initial claim with which Anselm sets out, the availability of an at least logically possible 'idea of God', is controversial; (2) his refutation (vaguely anticipatory of Gassendi and Kant) of Anselm's first or preliminary formulation of his proof (in Chapter II), resting as this apparently does on a dubious conception of 'existence' in general; (3) his posing of the quite pertinent question whether the form of the argument, when applied to other topics than the divine existence, would not lead to absurd consequences. What Gaunilo did *not* do (but is generally credited with having done) was to justify the affirmative answer to this, in itself, quite proper question. His attempted *reductio ad absurdum* is easily rebutted. And above all (as Barth remarks) Gaunilo nowhere gives evidence of having got into his head the ultimate form of the argument, which is reached in Chapter III, after a page or two of preliminary skirmishing in the previous chapter. In this oversight his disciples are legion. In view of this long record of haste and carelessness, it behooves all of us to proceed cautiously.

3. *What the Proof Claims to Prove*

First, what did Anselm claim to have accomplished by his Proof? Was it to have demonstrated the existence of God to anyone, no matter what his assumptions? But all proofs, as Anselm knew, have premises; whence the premises? A common answer is, from faith. But in that case, it seems, the proof must be unavailing, except to those who already believe, and for them it should be superfluous! And indeed, if the proof merely derives the existence of God from faith that He exists, it is simply question-begging or circular. Was the thrill of discovery expressed in the Preface to the book concerned with so trivial a matter as that from the premise God exists, one can deduce the conclusion, He exists?

Anselm's discovery was more subtle and complex than any of the above notions. It amounts to this: there are persons who believe in the divine existence, and these, if they understand their faith, are *the only ones who do understand it;* the others, whether they are believers lacking understanding or 'unbelievers', are all people who do not clearly know the meaning of 'belief in God'. They may, if they are 'positivists' (to use a modern word), excuse themselves on the ground that they shrewdly suspect no one else knows the meaning either, because indeed 'God' or 'divinity' has no clear meaning. (However, the understanding believer may think that he knows better.) But if (like the 'fool' of the Psalms) they are atheists, that is, persons who admit that they do find a clear meaning in the central religious question, but yet deny the necessity for an affirmative answer, then, Anselm claims to have shown—and some of us find much additional evidence that he is right—they deceive themselves. What they mean by 'God' cannot be what the self-understanding believer means by the term.

Alas, this is not quite the whole story. Anselm and most believers who have tried to understand their faith have met—like so many human endeavorers—with only qualified success. It can be shown from the Saint's writings that he is partially inconsistent—or else much less clear than he means to be—in what he says about God. But it remains nonetheless true that confusion in ideas is the key difficulty, not the mere failure to consult appropriate facts, or the mere presence or absence of faith. No facts can answer an ill-defined question; especially if, as in this case, when adequately understood, it is a self-answering question. So far as it is self-answering, to answer it is a pure matter of logical insight, not of faith. Also, as Anselm in various places tries to show, logical insight can do something toward showing the propriety and logical validity of the question.

Since Anselm's claim is that only lack of understanding of theistic belief makes possible its rejection, one might have supposed that his critics would have attempted to show that Anselm's own understanding of belief was faulty and would have realized that to do this they must at least understand his understanding, to which a reasonable first step would have been to read what he had written with some care and thoroughness. Is this what happened? Ah, no. From Gaunilo down through a long list of more illustrious names (including Russell, who was evidently misled by Leibniz) the attitude was: on the basis of the first seven lines of Anselm's statement of his reasoning, and our own assumed equal or superior grasp of the meaning of the religious term 'God', let us reach a definitive conclusion as to his claim concerning this meaning.

Some readers will be saying: for philosophy, the important thing is whether or not the argument is valid or useful for unbelievers; and this it cannot be if one must first be a believer in order to understand it. But (1) to take this way out is to renounce philosophy's most important function, which is to clarify the religious question. Science and practical common sense almost take care of themselves, but in facing life, death, and the everlasting, the first and last or strictly cosmic things, man is in great danger of fanatical faith, on the one hand, and cynical despair, on the other. He needs to think about these topics as wisely as he can, and to do this he must cooperate with others, whatever their beliefs, in mutual criticism. This free mutual criticism is the central task of philosophy. So Anselm's challenge is indeed one which ought not to be brushed aside.

Moreover, (2) it is obvious enough that if, as Anselm holds, the central religious question is self-answering, our whole theory of knowledge must be affected by this truth. We can then no longer assume that the only self-answering questions are trivial or merely linguistic. The general issue of the possibility of metaphysics is here involved. Metaphysical questions are those which, when properly put, are self-answering—and yet are not simply logical or mathematical, at least as logic and mathematics are usually understood and delimited. (Whether they ought to be so understood and delimited is a related and important subject for inquiry.) Metaphysical questions are indeed logical questions, questions essentially about ideas; but since an idea about nothing is not an idea, unless the very idea of 'nothing' itself, to say that logical questions are 'merely' logical, and therefore 'not about existence', is an antimetaphysical dogma, not a self-evident truth. If Anselm is right, it can be shown to be incorrect. All logical questions (and indeed all questions) are about existence, though not all are equally directly and significantly so. Those logical or self-answering questions which most directly and significantly concern existence are at the same time 'metaphysical' questions. Anselm discovered one of the most important of these—does divinity exist? What Anselm proved was the contradictoriness of the negative answer. To reject the positive answer therefore amounts to rejecting the question itself. But the believer is likely to remain serenely confident in his realization that the question is inevitable—on some level of consciousness. It can only be repressed, not rejected.

Such was Anselm's gift to faith—and not only to faith, to philosophy, which cannot evade its responsibility to deal with faith. That the gift has rarely been accepted proves little, so long as it remains equally true that it has rarely been examined in anything much like the form in which it was offered.

Let us proceed with our own examination.

4. *The Definition of God: a Dilemma*

The next point to be clarified is the way in which the term *God* is being used. For a premise of the argument is that even the 'fool' who denies God knows, or thinks he knows, the meaning of the word. He is to be confuted by this very meaning. But what is the meaning? Anselm replied with great simplicity: to be God is to be such that 'none greater can be conceived'. And if you ask about the import of 'greater', the reply is, x is greater than y insofar as x is, and

y is not, something 'which it is better to be than not to be'. Greater thus means superior, more excellent, more worthy of admiration and respect. Why does our Saint choose this definition? I suppose because he takes it for granted that by 'God' is meant the universal object of worship, and if God could have a superior, then only the ignorant or superstitious could worship Him—not all creatures, nor any reasonable creatures. They might fear or admire Him, but not rightly love Him in the unstinted way which is worship.

But now, if a whole system of thought—and Anselm intends no less—is to rest upon a single definition, expressive of faith, ought not the definition to be scrutinized with great care to ascertain if possible whether or not it is (a) really expressive of faith, (b) free from ambiguity, and (c) free from contradiction? Anselm does not seem to think of the matter in this way. Worship requires the unqualified exaltation of its object beyond all possible rivalry, and just this and only this (he thinks) is the content of the definition. How could there be any difficulty? And if there were contradiction, faith must be simply absurd, which itself, he would think, is absurd. Yet there are difficulties: both serious danger of ambiguity or contradiction and equally serious danger of failing to express faith.

If Anselm largely overlooked these dangers, his critics—those who were in such pell-mell hurry to refute him that they could scarcely pause to read even the four pages of *Prosl.* II-IV in which the argument was originally presented—these fast-moving critics were not the ones to see the dangers clearly either. Rather it was Leibniz, a defender of the argument (in its Cartesian form, however, or perhaps as reported by Thomas from *Prosl.* II) who brought out the likelihood of contradiction in 'greatest conceivable', and who also made the best start toward clarifying the ambiguity.

Take any conceivable number. A greater can be conceived. How do we know this is not true of 'beings'? So much for the possibility of contradiction. The conclusion Leibniz drew was that 'greatest' must be taken to mean a purely qualitative, not a quantitative, maximum. Or, as he put it, only those properties can be attributed to God which (unlike quantity) admit a maximal case. The others simply do not apply. Hence the ambiguity in 'Great' is to be resolved by the sheer exclusion of quantity. It was, after all, commonplace among the followers of Plato, beginning with Aristotle, and going on through Philo, Plotinus, and Augustine, that deity transcends magnitude altogether. Anselm takes this for granted. God is Great in that He is "whatever it is better to be than not to be." And better than any size, or number of parts, is being immaterial, simple, and immutable .

What is insufficiently noted here is that quantity may, after all, have a value which is not attainable without it. This consideration is simply ignored, not disproved, in *Proslogium,* Chapter XVIII, last three paragraphs. The Greek habit (so apparent in Plotinus) of glorying in mere unity (as though absence of contrast were not in principle as deadly as confusion!) is perfectly apparent here. The contention that all having of parts must mean corruptibility is of a piece with certain antitheistic arguments, which Anselm has to combat, against the divine necessity. All existing, his critics say, is contingent existing; similarly, all complexity is disruptible complexity. In both cases, Anselm should have said, the true rule is less simple. It depends upon the kind of thing and its appropriate manner of existing, or of having parts. If there can be an eminent, necessary manner of existing, why not an eminent manner of having parts? And we shall see that, in one sense, God may have absolutely no parts while in another sense having more of them than any other being. The old sledgehammer methods in metaphysics need improving. There are ways and ways of having parts, as of existing. So far from its being obvious that the absence of parts is a merit, one of the normal procedures in estimating value is to compare degrees of complexity arising from parts. Beauty of all kinds is unity in variety, and the greater the variety, the greater the value of the unity. A musical chord is as unified as a symphony, but its lack of complexity, its poverty of parts, limits its value most severely. Yet, on the other hand, what could be meant by 'greatest conceivable variety'? It must mean, all possible variety; and if this is to be unified to constitute a 'beauty than which none greater is conceivable', we run into trouble. 'All possible variety' is no definite variety at all, but confusion, full of mutual incompatibilities. For, as Leibniz put it, "not all possibles are compossible." So 'absolute beauty'—the great Platonic vision—is to all appearances a contradiction.

5. *Neoclassical Resolution of the Dilemma*

Is there any escape from the dilemma that 'greatest conceivable quantity' is impossible and greatest conceivable quality devoid of quantity is, for all we can see, likewise impossible? Fortunately there is, and to find it we need not abandon Anselm's definition of deity. We need only note the following ambiguity: 'None greater can be conceived' may mean, 'no greater individual' or it may mean, 'no greater thing or entity'. If the latter, then not only can no other individual be conceived superior; the same individual cannot be conceived superior to itself—that is, all increase is, by definition, excluded from deity. This was indeed the old Platonic argument: the perfect, being complete or maximal in its value, could change only for the worse; but the capacity for such change being a defect, the perfect cannot change at all. This argument, and others like it, all characteristically Greek, became almost the real deity of Christian philosophers. Anselm accepts this Greek doctrine. But therewith the guarantee that the definition expresses faith is gone. We are then interpreting Greek philosophy, not faith. To worship God is indeed to exalt Him above all possible rivalry *on the part of other individuals;* they must not be able conceivably to surpass Him. (It is unnecessary to say, 'must not be able to equal Him', for 'two equal but not conceivably surpassable beings' leads to contradictions.) On this condition all may look up to God and worship Him. But if God surpasses God, that does not of itself imply that another individual can surpass Him.

If God is surpassable, even though only by Himself, then He can include quantity in His quality, without the quantity being that presumably impossible thing, an unsurpassable quantity. The divine quantity will be surpassable, but only by God Himself. Now we have none of the contradictions we have been worrying about. God need not be that apparent impossibility, a quality wholly independent of quantity, nor that other impossibility, an unsurpassable quantity. Nor need He actualize all possible value. Yet He can still fully deserve worship by surpassing all conceivable rivals to Himself.

This resolution of the double ambiguity inherent in the definition of Greatness is what I call 'neoclassical theism' (since as a technical doctrine, it is largely a creation of the last four centuries), while Anselm's (or Augustine's or Philo's) essentially Greek way of resolving it fits the label 'classical theism'. I believe that the issues Anselm raised cannot be clarified except in terms of the contrast between these two kinds of theism.

Which form of theism best expresses faith? The classical form is certainly intensely Greek. At least, its authors were all saturated with Platonism. This alone does not show the theory to be incompatible with faith, but it suggests that it might be. And there are strong reasons for accepting the suggestion. A God unsurpassable, even by Himself, is a pure 'absolute', wholly unreceptive or insensitive toward the world. He is anything else than a God of love, if the word has even a glimmer of meaning in this usage. We shall see the unfortunate consequences, for all his doctrine, of Anselm's Hellenism, his substitution of the philosophical absolute for the God of religion. Here, not in the Proof, was the essential flaw. True enough, Philo and Anselm developed Greek theology beyond Plato, Aristotle, and the Stoics, but only by going further in a direction already set. What was needed was a new direction.

Our Saint's bold invention in his Argument had two aspects. (1) He would be the first to deduce, from the definition of the God of faith, not simply God's existence, which would be trivial enough (for of course, faith means by the all-worshipful, all-important being an at least existing being), but to demonstrate rather his *necessary and therefore unique mode of existence (Prosl.* III), *his inconceivability as nonexistent.* But (2) Anselm intended also to deduce all the knowable attributes of God from the same definition. No philosophical theist ever had a more original and brilliant project. (Beside it—oh well, let us not praise one man by disparaging another!) The trouble is that the definition's ambiguity—and the implicit contradiction of Anselm's Greek way of resolving the ambiguity—must dog his steps from beginning to end. However, in that age, one had to philosophize in largely Greek fashion. Anselm did what he could. And his very formulae, interpreted by philosophers not under that compulsion, can, with few changes, be made to express a view less Greek, more Christian, and—so far as has yet been shown—more consistent.

The sources of classical theism are well known: in Anselm's case, primarily Augustine, back of him Plotinus, back of Plotinus, Philo, and back of all, Plato. The negative theology (from which classical theism cannot consistently distinguish itself) is reasonably complete in Philo. With him the pattern was approximately fixed for a long time to come; the submission of religion to the Greek mode of mysticism lasted unbroken for over a millennium. True, Philo put into the tradition religious feelings which were not Greek, and even an idea of divine and human freedom which was rather new. But the logical pattern is still Greek. The exclusion of quantity and becoming from God is decisive. The technical issues are thereby mostly settled; the rest is mainly an emotive difference. Also Augustine had a more nearly Greek theory of the will than Philo, whose great vision of creativity in God and man paled rather than grew brighter in the Christian. A 'process philosophy' of universal creativity had to wait a millennium and a half for its opportunity.

In considering the relation of the Argument to the two forms of theism it is important to realize that these are not simply different or opposed; they have an area of overlap in which they entirely agree. For, as Leibniz said—and the neoclassicists can say no less—those attributes which are capable of maximization must be maximally present in God (otherwise he would not be unsurpassably Great). However, the newer form of theism asserts, and the older denies, that the attributes incapable of maximization must also be in God, provided they are capable of a form which is self-surpassable only, in which form they too describe God. God is, then, absolutely unsurpassable in whatever respects this is possible. Here there is agreement. He is (He is not) surpassable exclusively by self in whatever respects such exclusive self-surpassability is possible—here is the sole disagreement.

We shall see that the area of 'overlap' spoken of suffices to justify Anselm's claim that necessity of existence inheres in the definition of Greatness; while the admission of non-maximal but uniquely self-surpassable properties in God removes the ground from under the strongest of the criticisms of the Argument, the objection that a mere concept cannot entail concrete existence.

It is also important to note that in the 'overlap area' of the two theisms nearly all of Anselm's descriptions of God hold. He has indeed no parts, accidents, changes, or passions—in His unsurpassable aspects; but for all that He can have them in His self-surpassable ones. Thus we can honor our forefathers' wisdom, while not being chained forever to the barren abstractions or negations of Greek philosophical mysticism, which they thought must apply to God through and through.

6. *Existence a Predicate?*

Our next point concerns the logical status of 'exist'. Is 'existing', in general, part of the description of a thing, one of its 'predicates', or is it something quite different from a predicate? If it is a predicate, then hypothetical descriptions are incomplete. "There is a man on this island." "What kind of man, an existing, or a nonexisting man?" No, we do not ordinarily think thus of existing things as a special kind. Any consistently-conceived kind of thing might conceivably exist, no matter what else was true of it. Yet, as Anselm first presents his argument, it appears that he takes existing things to be a different, and superior, kind of thing: hence that which is without conceivable superior must exist. This is the form of the argument which so many, for so long, have triumphantly refuted, on the assumption that it was the essential one. The procedure has this excuse, that not only did Anselm, in his first formulation of the argument (Chapter II), seem to reason in the way just specified, but so did Descartes in his first formulation. (He escaped from it only in dealing with objections in his *Replies*.)

7. *The Second or Strong Form of the Proof*

In both Anselm and Descartes, however, the argument is given a second form which need not assume that existence is, *in general*, a 'real predicate'; moreover, the existence which *in the sole case of God* is taken as a predicate is not simply existence in general, but a unique and superior form or manner of existing. This superior form is necessary existence, or existence *without conceivable alternative* of failing to exist. It may also (*Prosl.* XII, XXII) be termed self-existence, or existence through self—or as Philo had put it, 'according to essence'. In the Saint's words: "Thou dost exist so truly that thou canst not be conceived not to exist." Or again, "Thou art through nothing else than thyself." In other words, ordinary existence is an inferior or comparatively 'untrue' form of existing, existence not through self but through another, always with the threat, the conceivable alternative, of not existing or of never having existed. The existence of all save God is precarious, accidental; and thus to exist is to be inferior to what exists essentially, in its existence beyond the reach of chance or circumstance. This is the Anselmian argument par excellence! The evidence for this is that it is reiterated in a variety of ways (see *Prosl.* III, IV; *Reply* I, V, IX) all incompatible with the customary interpretation that Anselm must appeal to a general principle of existing things being a special kind. The point is rather this: *If God could conceivably fail to exist, He must be something which, "even if it existed," would be less than "that than which none greater can be conceived"; for we can* (it is claimed) *conceive of something such that it cannot be conceived not to exist, and to be thus is better than to be such that the nonexistence of the thing is conceivable; hence that to which no superior is to be conceivable must be conceived as such that its nonexistence is inconceivable. He who says he conceives this but believes that it does not, or may not, exist contradicts himself; for he says that he conceives as possible what he also says no one can conceive as possible.*

The gist of this argument—a stroke of genius if ever there was one—is in the second, third, and fourth sentences of *Prosl.* III, seven lucid lines. Refutations of Anselm which fail—and how many do fail—to quote, paraphrase, or take some account of this short passage (or one of its several equivalents which occur later) may be interesting exercises; they are not, properly speaking, refutations of Anselm!

Our author of so long ago finds it evident—as does this writer—that conceivable nonexistence must be ruled out a priori with respect to Supreme Greatness (we shall sometimes simply say, 'Greatness'). He tries in various ways (customarily ignored, one need hardly add) to communicate this intuition. A Greatest conceivable which existed merely in fact, or so that its nonexistence might conceivably have obtained instead, would not be Greatest, for thus to exist, confronted with the specter of one's own conceivable nothingness, is the abysmal weakness which infects, for example, our own existence. It implies ultimate dispensability: existence might not have included me; I am thus absolutely derivative, owing my existence to a happy chance, or to the choice of another. Thus to exist is a defect or limitation. The superior manner of existing would be 'without conceivable alternative'. So we see that *contingency is qualitative,* a genuine predicate, even though contingent *existence,* as compared to contingent *nonexistence,* is (in a sense, and for the purposes of this discussion) qualitatively neutral.

Among the supplementary arguments by which the Saint tries to support his insight are the following. Where nonexistence and existence are alike conceivable, a transition from the first to the second must also, he thinks, be conceivable. (*Reply* I, IV, VII.) But any existence resulting from such a transition would be incompatible with the status of Greatest. It would imply a beginning in time, dependence upon causes, circumstances, and the like, all of which are deficiencies.

Also, what exists contingently is assembled from elements which previously existed, perhaps, in another combination or arrangement.

Again, Greatness, unlike all other predicates, does not exist by virtue of Being or Goodness taking on some accidental form, called Greatness. God is not merely a particularly good thing but the principle of Good. Were He (*per impossibile*) not to exist, no good thing could either. And as Anselm's teacher, Augustine, said, God is Truth itself; without Him nothing could be true. Hence, 'without Him' cannot express a possible state of affairs.

8. *Malcolm and Findlay: a Fresh Start?*

It is almost miraculous that for so many centuries no one, apparently, was really clear that Anselm had presented at least two ontological arguments, rather than one, and that Descartes had followed him in this. The present writer was perhaps the first to insist upon this distinction as close to the surface in the writings of the two authors mentioned.[6] However, Flint had suggested it with respect to Descartes, and Barth had fully seen it with respect to Anselm. Recently Norman Malcolm (see Bibliography I) has also arrived at it and has presented it so skilfully as to arouse a good deal of interest. (See Sec. 23.)

A few years before Malcolm's essay, Findlay (see Part Two, Sec. 17, and Bibliography I) set forth the following position. Anselm was indeed right in holding that deity

---

[6] C. Hartshorne, "The Formal Validity and Real Significance of the Ontological Argument," *Philosophical Review,* 53 (1944), 225-45, esp. p. 234 n.

must be supposed (if supposed at all) to exist necessarily; for a being worthy of worship could not have the defect that its very existence was contingent or had a conceivable alternative. However, said Findlay, so far from proving the divine existence, by pointing to this requirement, Anselm had really disproved it. For modern logical analysis shows that no existence can be necessary. Concrete or actual existence cannot follow from a mere predicate or abstract definition. Hence divine perfection is impossible.

In my opinion, this criticism was more penetrating than all the classical ones. A merely contingent being would not deserve worship, for we should be revering at most a big and wonderful accident; yet, on the other hand, that a mere abstraction like 'all-worshipful' could necessitate a concrete actuality is a logical absurdity. I call this the Findlay paradox or dilemma. Both horns of the dilemma seem unacceptable. However, as often, it may be a trilemma: there may be a third horn. Must one choose between taking divinity as a candidate for contingent existence and supposing that 'necessary existence' means the necessity of a particular or concrete actuality? Anselm, so far as I can see, overlooks the dilemma and can offer us no escape from it. This was his major error, resulting as we shall see from his Neoplatonism. But his critics seem to have shared his oversight. They have never focused on the real point, the assumption that the existence of an individual must be concrete or particular and can in no case be abstract and universal.

There is another, more commonly-noted difficulty: if divine or necessary existence is a superior kind of existence, what does it have in common with the inferior forms? For if it has nothing, then we merely equivocate when we speak of God's existing. And what can contingent, and absolutely necessary 'existence' have in common? Anselm does not tell us in any satisfactory or clear way.

Is it not evident that an existence which is deducible from an abstract definition—such as that used by Anselm—must itself be abstract? An abstract idea is always neutral as to the particular concrete reality in which it is or may be actualized, and this is inherent in the very meaning of 'abstract' and 'concrete'. Either, then, God's reality is wholly abstract, or He has a particular concrete actualization which is contingent. But if the concrete reality which actualizes divinity is contingent, what can it mean to say that God's existence is necessary? The answer, which cannot be found in Anselm or any of his best-known critics, is as follows: to exist is always, and this is the universal meaning, to be *somehow actualized* in a suitable concrete (and contingent) reality; but whereas in ordinary cases of existence not only is the particular concrete reality contingent, but also it is contingent that there is *any* concrete reality embodying the predicate. In the divine case, however, the predicate is to be thought of as *inevitably* actualized somehow, that is, in some suitable concrete reality. Thus contingency has two forms: either (1) both *that* and *how* the predicate is actualized or concretized are accidental; or (2) only the *how* is accidental, while the *that* is necessary. Existence in general and always means, *somehow actualized* in a contingent concrete form, just *what* form, or *how* actualized, never being necessary. Existence in the superior, or divine form, accordingly, means that the abstract essence (worshipfulness or the impossibility of a superior) is somehow actualized in a suitable contingent concrete form; but here only the *how* of actualization, the particular concrete reality, not that there is *some* suitable actualization, is contingent.

Of course this 'neoclassical' solution implies (what the whole scholastic tradition denied) 'accidents' or contingent properties, as well as essential ones, in God. Yet it is not hard to see that Anselm really needs this distinction, not only for his argument, but for other purposes. Thus he says (*Prosl.* VI, VIII) that God must be a compassionate God, for it is better to be compassionate than not compassionate, i.e., cruel or indifferent to the creatures' sufferings. On the other hand, since there must be nothing contingent, hence no true 'passion', in God, He cannot really be changed by what happens to us. Anselm's solution was that only in His effects upon His creatures is God compassionate, not in His own reality. We receive the benefits which might be expected to flow from His caring about us and being moved to sorrow by our miseries, but really He remains quite unmoved, literally indifferent, or in an identical state of bliss whatever happens to any creature. This is a form of 'as if' doctrine; it is *as if* God loved us in an intelligible sense, but really all that can be said is that benefits flow from Him to us. We may call this the 'benefit-machine' view of divine love. The sun produces crops, *as though* it cared about our hunger and its appeasement; in reality it cares not. So with God. Is this satisfactory?

If the distinction between the necessarily 'somehow actualized' and the contingent 'how' of actualization is accepted, then the necessarily existing God can be genuinely compassionate; and the two paradoxes of a necessary yet concrete actuality and the merely 'as if' compassionate deity are removed at one stroke.

From the foregoing it follows that most of a millennium was allowed to go by before the logic of Anselm's proposal was properly explored. No one was sufficiently willing to admit that his previous views might have been radically mistaken to undertake a free exploration of Anselm's problem. Everyone wanted, in some simple way, to accept or reject the argument, and then go on philosophizing as before in other respects. But Anselm's discovery was too fundamental to make such trivial adjustments finally tenable. What Anselm had discovered, or almost discovered, was that existence and actuality (or concreteness) are in principle distinct, and that two kinds of individuals may be conceived, those whose existence and actuality, although distinct, are both contingent and those—or that one—whose actuality but not existence is contingent, this second kind being superior to all others. According to this view, any individual, no matter how superior, exists by virtue of contingent concrete states; but whereas with you or me it is always possible that there should be no such states at all, with God, though any such state is contingent, that there is some such state is necessary.

If God has contingent states, could we not conceive a greater than He by supposing that His contingent state or states had been greater? But this would merely have been God Himself, in a greater state. That God can surpass Himself does not open up a possibility that someone not God could surpass (or equal) God; and only this possibility conflicts with worshipfulness. God may rival Himself, but that justifies no conceit in anyone else.

It may be objected that a greater than God, as we have defined Him, could still be conceived, namely, a being so great that it could not be surpassed even by itself. But this idea leads, as we have seen, to paradox and insoluble dilemmas, to absurdity. Absurdity cannot define 'x greater than any conceivable y', for absurdity does not define anything.

If the foregoing reasoning is sound, Anselm made a very great discovery, though as so often happens, he only partly understood its nature. His critics saw something of what he overlooked, usually, however, at the cost of missing part of what he had discovered. They realized that nothing concrete, or in that sense actual, can be necessary. Malcolm, to be sure, denies this, saying that it is valid only if by 'concrete' we simply mean 'contingent'. But this will not do. For by necessary we must mean abstract. Let us see more definitely why.

9. *The Necessary Is Abstract*

A necessary proposition is one whose truth is included in that of any other proposition whatever. For, were this not so, it must be possible for the other proposition to be true while the necessary proposition was false. But the hypothesis is that the proposition cannot be false under any circumstances, since what it affirms is necessary. In this sense, then, as C. I. Lewis has pointed out, a necessary proposition is entailed by any proposition.[7] This has been termed a paradox. What has 'it rained here today' to do with '2 and 2 are four'?

---

[7] For an interesting discussion of problems connected with this, *see* N. R. Hanson, "A Budget of Cross-Type Inferences," *The Journal of Philosophy*, 58 (1961), 449-70. [I do not see that the Argument is cross-type; neither premises nor conclusion are contingent. Yet Hanson implies that he has refuted the Argument.] For C. I. Lewis's view, see *A Survey of Symbolic Logic* (Berkeley, 1918), pp. 336-339; also *Symbolic Logic* by Lewis and C. H. Langford (New York: Dover Publications, 1932, 1959), pp. 492-514, esp. 511-514.

More troublesome still, perhaps, is the consideration that many very complex questions of arithmetic are so difficult that prolonged efforts by many mathematicians have failed to furnish answers. If so simple a premise as the one quoted above entails the answer to all questions of necessary truth it is odd that we cannot simply deduce these answers. But then no one will contend that deducible consequences are always easy actually to deduce. Moreover, all deduction involves logical rules or principles, and 'finitary' arithmetic, at least, seems to be inherent in these rules. What follows from a premise is what a person with unrestricted logical powers can arrive at by virtue of understanding the premise. Now from a proposition, say p, a sufficiently logical person can derive $p \lor q$; hence he can also derive $p \lor {\sim}p$. In similar though usually less obvious ways any necessary truth, however complex, should be attainable. All one has to do is to weaken or neutralize the elements of irrelevant logical strength in the initial proposition and reason logically about the results. Two difficulties must be overcome in the process. We must be able to abstract from irrelevancies, adequately neutralize contingent alternatives, and still keep our attention upon the extremely attenuated remainder; and in some cases we must perform very complex logical operations (as in the more difficult problems in theory of numbers).

The sense of paradox connected with Lewis's principle arises mainly from this, that in an inference to the necessary, one does not really utilize the *distinctive* meaning of a contingent premise, but only its nondistinctive kernel. It is a mere illustration, where any illustration we are able to think clearly about would do. Note, however, that even in ordinary inferences we usually discard part of the distinctive meaning of our premises. Thus the full or unweakened conclusion from 'Socrates is a man, all men are mortal' would not be, 'Socrates is mortal', but rather, 'All men, including Socrates, are mortal', or 'Socrates, like all other men, is mortal'. Inference to the necessary is simply the completion of the normal weakening or attenuating process of discarding not-wanted aspects of assumptions. Only rather trivial inferences fail to exhibit such weakening. For instance, in 'x is equal to y therefore y is equal to x' the conclusion is indeed as strong as the premises; but this is exceptional. I submit, therefore, that Lewis is essentially right, and that, just as the necessary is what all possible states of reality have in common, so necessary propositions affirm the neutral universally common element of meaning in ordinary propositions, and accordingly, inferring this element is merely the extreme or limiting case of the attenuation of commitment ordinarily involved in drawing conclusions.

We may here suggest by anticipation how the familiar objection to Anselm that necessity is a matter of propositions not of things, or is *de dictu* not *de re,* is going to be dealt with in this book. If reality is essentially creative process, with an aspect of futurity or partial indeterminacy (as Socinus, Lequier, Fechner, Bergson, Peirce, Montague, and some other 'neoclassical' philosophers have thought), then objective necessity is merely what all real possibilities have in common, their neutral element, which will be actualized 'no matter what' course the creative process may take. This neutral element is creativity in its essential or irreducible aspect, which is inseparable from the necessary aspect of deity. That Anselm had an adequate grasp of this theory of modality can certainly not be maintained. No Neoplatonist could have had such a grasp. But his Proof leads us to it if we follow out its implications sufficiently resolutely.

The reader may well be thinking that the assertion of God's existence cannot be comparable to such necessities as '$p \lor \sim p$', since, in the latter but not the former, only 'logical constants' appear, and since what is not a formality of logic must be empirical, only to be justified a posteriori. *If* contemporary logic were a complete system, with a clearly demarcated boundary, and *if* it were proved that the principle of this boundary coincided with that between a priori and a posteriori, then all would be in order. But who would dare assert that such is the case? How far even set theory is purely 'logical' is a moot question, but more than that, the a priori theory of rational inference should, I hold, include some elucidation of two things, the ultimate or completely general theory of concrete entities as such (from which all abstract entities in some fashion derive) and the ultimate or completely general theory of knowing, experience, or awareness, including a theory of givenness, of what it is to experience something. How can the theory of reasoning be complete until these two conditions are met? Logic, as Peirce said (we might mention Husserl here), should include a general or nonpsychological *Erkenntnistheorie,* theory of knowledge as such. But this is impossible without a theory of reality as such, of what it is to be something knowable. When we have such a completed logic, or theory of the a priori, the idea of God will, I argue, be integral to it. For that idea can be defined with no other equipment than the generalized notion of reality as knowable. God is the X who is not conceivably surpassed, in any categorial way, by another; these categorial ways are all equivalent, so that any one of them suffices to define God. Thus that God's knowledge cannot be surpassed (by another) is enough to distinguish Him from all else. If A knows that p and B does not know that p, then A surpasses B cognitively in this respect; hence the unsurpassability of A by another means that A knows all there is to be known, or that 'p entails A knows that p'. So we have defined deity in purely generic or a priori terms. For what empirical fact would be needed in order to form the idea of knowing itself? One would only have to know something, anything at all, and know that it was known, to have the idea. But then one has only to quantify universally in order to distinguish God from all else. Only God has a *universal* relation of knowing to things. Ordinary individuals differ from one another in that, while (if they are conscious) they know some things and are ignorant of others, it is impossible to define the distinctive line in each case between the knowledge and the ignorance without mentioning particular empirical facts. But where *all* is known and there is no ignorance, one needs only a universal statement: No matter what the facts may be, God is the unique X who knows them all. Thus, perhaps: ⁊ x (z) Kxz. This formula has no special empirical content. Yet it defines deity. (Probably, to be adequate, the formula should be in modal, not extensional, logic.)

Again, take the category of causal influence. Without this idea no statement has a complete meaning, for (to give only one of the reasons) an assertion is what might be believed, and belief with no relation to action, causal influencing, is an empty word. But nothing is easier than to state a definitive characteristic of deity in terms of influencing. If A influences C and B does not influence C, then insofar A surpasses B in causal power. Hence the only way to construe causal unsurpassability is to state as minimum that, for any x, A influences x. It is not hard to show that only God can meet this condition.

Since 'God exists necessarily' means (by Lewis's principle) that the assertion of His existence must be knowable from any fact whatever, or the denial of any fact, it follows that, not only is it definitive of God that He knows all there is to know, but also that He is knowable by all minds with sufficient powers of reflection to interpret their experiences adequately. He is in this sense *universal subject* and *universal object* of knowing. The same conversion can be effected with causal influence: not only is God the unique A influencing all things, but God is also the unique A influenced *by* all things. Thus we have already given four ways of distinguishing God in purely generic or a priori terms. And others are possible. Hence I return to the assertion that the divine existence is entailed by any fact or truth whatever, being as a priori as '$p \vee \sim p$'. And indeed, the notion of infallibility means that p entails, God knows that p, and that $\sim p$ entails, God knows that $\sim p$, so that '$p \vee \sim p$' and 'God knows that p or God knows that $\sim p$' are equivalent. They are equally nonempirical or 'formal', in the most basic sense. To suppose otherwise is to confuse creaturely knowledge, subject for its degree of truth to chance, circumstance, contingency, with the Creator's knowledge, whose truth is infallibly guaranteed.

We see then that the idea of God, 'extralogical' as, by some current criteria, it is, need not for all that be empirical, unless in a Pickwickian or misleading sense. The same result ensues if we adopt Popper's criterion of 'empirical', namely 'conceivably falsifiable'. I have shown in a previous work that theism, by its very meaning, is rigorously unfalsifiable. (Positivistically inclined philosophers will then argue that it can have no existential import. But as an inference this merely begs the question.)

The term 'logic', or 'formal logic', can of course be used in the narrow sense now frequently given to it, and this may be advisable. But then the word 'empirical' should also be defined sharply, and not be used so widely and vaguely as to coincide with 'extralogical'. For it is at least as important to have a clear meaning for 'empirical' as for 'formal', and Popper if anyone has explicated the first of these two meanings. But as so explicated it fails to coincide with 'extralogical', taking 'logical' in the current strict sense. Moreover, until various questions concerning modal and deontological logics (and contrary-to-fact conditionals), at the very least, are much better settled than they are now, it is dogmatism if not obscurantism to identify what can be known a priori with any currently available view of formal analyticity.

I now call attention to a widely—I am tempted to say universally—neglected consequence of the foregoing. That 'any proposition entails the necessary truths' itself entails that any proposition *no matter how abstract* entails such truths. Moreover, since the concrete elements all drop out in the inference to the necessary, one might as well or better start with an abstract premise. Thus instead of arguing, 'this world exists, therefore God, the necessary being, exists', one may take as premise, 'something exists'. For if the conclusion is to be strictly necessary (and if not, the necessary being will be but conditionally necessary and not what the argument seeks), the conclusion must follow just as well from the more abstract premise. And so, 'divinity exists necessarily', if true, must follow from 'something exists'—yes, even from 'either something exists or nothing exists'. (This is the proper form of the cosmological argument, which, as we now see, must be valid if the ontological is so.) But, as is logically self-evident, *from an abstract proposition alone only abstract propositions can follow.* For the more concrete a proposition is, the logically stronger it is, or the more it asserts; and from the logically weaker, the logically stronger cannot follow. Moreover, a proposition can scarcely be weaker than 'something exists'. Hence 'divinity exists', which follows from it, as from any proposition, must be similarly abstract or weak in what it commits us to. In addition, any *necessary* proposition whatever that is true of God must be on the same level of abstractness. Take, then, the proposition, 'God knows that you and I exist'. This proposition has concrete reference and so cannot be necessary; nor can it follow from the proposition, 'God, an omniscient being, exists'. For this might be true though it were also true that you and I did not exist, and obviously what was false would not be known to be true, even—or especially—by God. Thus Anselm, had his mind been free to reflect without fear or favor on the meaning of God's necessity, should have seen that God's necessary existence must be very different indeed from His total concrete or factual reality. The divine necessity is *that* such abstract traits or 'perfections' as 'knowing all there is to know' must be realized in some concrete form, with respect to some concrete world of knowable things, but not necessarily in the form and with respect to the world which actually obtain.

10. *In What Sense the Proof Is Inconclusive*

Suppose that what we have said so far is correct; would it follow that God has been proved to exist? Not quite. The reason was given by Thomas Aquinas and, more clearly, by Leibniz: we have not shown that our definition of divine perfection is more than verbal, or as Leibniz puts it, nominal. Consider the definition: 'necessarily-existing round-square'. To deny its existence is contradictory, for we should be saying that the necessarily true is yet false. However, to assert its existence is also contradictory, for we should be saying that what is round is in the same respect not round. The way out of the maze is to reject the proposed definition as an ill-formed expression, incapable of either truth or falsity. Anselm presents us with this question, Is his definition of God capable of describing anything thinkable? And since, as we have seen, the definition is ambiguous, meaning either 'none greater except itself', or 'none greater *simpliciter*', our question becomes a double one. That Anselm's own meaning, the one last mentioned in the previous sentence, is paradoxical we have pointed out. A paradoxical concept cannot furnish the basis of a cogent argument for the truth of that concept. Whether the alternative construction of the definition can evade the paradoxes, without falling into others of its own, is a question which lies outside the present essay. That it does not face the same paradoxes we have seen.

11. *Predicates, Individuals, and States*

Modern logic has made a point of the distinction between 'predicates', which individual cases may 'instantiate' or 'embody', and the individual cases themselves. The latter 'exist' only in a tautological sense. To be an individual is to exist in the only sense in which an individual can exist. A predicate, in contrast, may have a sort of thinkable reality, and yet not exist, that is, not be instantiated. We are told, accordingly, that we should not say, 'God, or the such and such, exists', for this is empty tautology, but only, 'something is divine', or, 'there is a divine individual'. But here logicians are in danger of confusing two issues. If in the formula '$(\exists x)Dx$' ('for some x, x is divine') the values of the variable 'x' are taken to be individuals, in the usual sense of thing or person, then 'for some x' is misleading, since only one individual could be divine. In other words, '$(\exists x)\ Dx\ \&\ (\exists y)\ Dy$' strictly implies '$(x=y)$'. Moreover, the individuality of 'x' must here be as abstract as the predicate 'D'. Thus the mere formula '$(\exists x)Dx$' is adequate to state the meaning of the divine existence in its concrete aspect only if the values of 'x' are not individuals but rather events or states of individuals. The formula then means, 'there are individual states which are divine'. This still does not say what is meant by 'God exists', unless we further understand that any such state x, and any other y, are necessarily 'genidentical' with each other. (Genetic identity is the relation holding between diverse states of the same individual.) This relationship holds because any divine state must be all-knowing and therefore two such states can have different content only on the assumption that when one, say x, exists, the other, y, does not yet exist, and hence even the all-knowing will not know it; but when y does exist, it must fully know x, and for this and other reasons x and y must constitute successive states of one and the same all-knowing individual.

In addition, we must regard '$(\exists x)Dx$' as necessarily, not merely factually, true. Not that the particular value of x is necessary, but that there must be some value or other. The class of 'values of x', say a,b,c, etc., cannot be empty, though the members of this class might have been other than *a,b,c,*. . . Absolute necessity is always the impossibility that a certain class be empty. This is the same as saying that necessity is always abstract. The class of divine states cannot be empty; moreover, every such state must be in a relation of genidentity with every other, and thus all are states of one and the same necessarily-existing individual. That the states might all have been different does not mean that another individual God might have existed but only that the same God might have existed in other concrete forms.

In a philosophy which, like that of the Buddhists or of Whitehead, takes events or states to be the ultimate units of concrete reality and regards enduring individuals as somewhat abstractly conceived sequences of events, with certain relations to one another, the ultimate values of variables are, of course, events. Moreover, in this sort of philosophy it is rather easy to see that the existence of an individual is always more abstract than the actuality of events. The same individual can exist in a variety of events, and these are never wholly determined by the mere individuality of the sequence. We can know *this man* as such long before we know all of his states, which indeed could not be known until he had died. Yet we must know *something* concrete to identify this man. God, however, is unique in that any state with a certain abstract property of divinity will belong to just the one divine personal sequence and no other. This is the only *self-individuating yet radically-abstract* property. All other individuals are individuated by something specific or relatively concrete. It follows at once that they cannot exist necessarily. By the same token, God can and indeed must so exist.

So again we see what deep implications are involved in

Anselm's supremely great insight, that God and only God exists by necessity of His (abstract) nature. The abstractness as such escaped Anselm, but the terms of his definition make it quite plain. Nothing but extreme abstractions enter into 'that than which none greater can be conceived'. This abstractness is the reason why the similarly abstract truth that the defined predicate is 'somehow embodied' is necessary and also the reason why this necessary existence cannot be the concrete or total reality of God. But little in scholastic philosophy, or in Kant's, was favorable to a clear grasp of these two aspects of the Anselmian principle. This principle, in its implications, bursts the bonds of scholasticism. No wonder Thomas rejected the Proof.

The principle, to state it once more, is the necessary noncontingency of the divine existence. What could not be contingent is either necessary or impossible. Anselm assumed that even the foolish atheist would not take God to be impossible (or 'meaningless'). So he inferred necessary existence. Yet Gaunilo rightly urges (it was not a new contention) the reasonableness, from an unbeliever's point of view, of the positivistic position, as we might today call it. And it is here, as we have seen, that the real issue lies. The Saint's attempt (*Reply,* VIII, IX) to show that his idea of God is produced by quite intelligible procedures, and so cannot be absurd, is insufficient to convince very many of us. Leibniz's efforts in the same direction were also not successful. This is the main unfinished business, I suggest, in this whole matter. *Could* God exist, is *any* idea of his nature intelligible? is the great question. Atheism is no longer a valid issue; but positivism certainly is.

12. *The Role of Faith*

Koyré, Karl Barth, and others remind us that Anselm was arguing not with infidels but with believers. Barth admits that the Saint at times seems to forget or deny that there are or can be any true infidels, and to talk as though his argument should convince anyone. Insofar as it does not convince, it follows—even, I think, from Barth's own exposition—that either the argument has been poorly understood, or the lack of conviction means retreat into the positivistic position, the denial that there is, strictly speaking, an idea of God or a cognitive meaning for 'God'. To dispel doubt on this score an element of faith is perhaps needed.

Before Barth, Koyré had put into full relief the precise sense in which Anselm's argument appeals to faith, and is inconclusive against unbelievers.[8] The atheist, the man who says that we can conceive God but cannot know that He exists, will be "silenced" by the argument, *if* he attends carefully to its structure. For—as Anselm discovered, to his lasting glory—to conceive divinity and *know* that we do so is logically equivalent to knowing that divinity or God exists. But, though the atheist as such is silenced, the unbeliever as such need not be. He has only to shift his ground to the positivistic position: "I do not know that I—or anyone—can conceive God (without falling into contradiction or nonsense)." The moment this happens, the theist must either himself lapse into silence or else enlarge his procedure; he must give some reason other than his faith for supposing that divinity is conceivable. Anselm's other theistic proofs (in the *Monologium*) can be used for this purpose, but none too cogently. Like his

---

[8] Koyré, *op. cit.*, pp. 210 ff.

Proslogium proof they suffer from the classical confusion between concrete and abstract, and they have other defects.

But though the Proof does not refute unbelief of the positivistic variety, it does force the unbeliever to take the radical ground of denying coherent meaning to the religious idea. If the believer in God is sure he understands himself, and does not contradict himself or talk nonsense, he is immune to further attack. This clarifies and focuses the entire problem. And at the same time, it disposes of the claim of sheer empiricism (fairly well represented by Gaunilo) to be an adequate method of dealing with ultimate philosophical issues. Carnap and Wittgenstein are right: the basic philosophical questions are not factual, but semantic. It was Anselm who first clearly revealed this truth. For, as Anselm also knew, divinity is the first principle of metaphysics or ontology: if it is not an empirical topic, neither is anything else that is philosophically essential. When Wittgenstein says, "theology is grammar," he is really agreeing, insofar, with Anselm. The remaining issue is, how correct is the grammar? Here is where an element of intuition, faith, insight, what you will beyond mere formal reasoning, is inescapable. But so is it in mathematics itself (consider Gödel's discovery).

Koyré speaks of the 'fact' that divinity is conceivable. But this is no mere fact, but a necessary truth—or else an impossibility or absurdity. Nothing can merely happen to be conceivable. Conceivability is modal, and all modal classifications (on the purely abstract level here in question) are a priori, not factual in the proper sense. What can be said is rather that the truth or validity of the claim to conceive God is controversial, as between believers and unbelievers. After all, there are controversial topics even in mathematics, in the present state of that science; but they are not questions of 'fact', save in a dubiously extended meaning of that word. They are questions of logic, or of linguistic rules and their propriety. Or, they are questions of what the eternal Mind, merely **as** eternal, does or does not see to be valid independently of all factual circumstances. They are not questions of what happens to exist, or come into existence. They are not things 'made', hence not facts in the etymological, which is also the systematically most clear and useful, sense.

13. *Is the Proof Platonic?*

Just as the truth that Anselm's argument 'presupposes faith' is made untrue by being taken too simply, as though the Proof had no secular philosophical importance, so the truth that he was a Platonist is made into an error unless construed with caution. It does not mean that if we are **not** Platonists we can with impunity ignore the Proof. It does not even mean that the strongest version of the Proof is one with a 'Platonic' setting, if that term is interpreted in the most usual way.

Classical theists are, indeed, all 'Platonists' in a certain sense even if, like Thomas, they are also Aristotelians. They all think that the universal principle of being can be a sort of superconcrete yet eternal reality; an *'actus purus'*, immune to change and becoming, and yet *not* an empty abstraction, inferior in value to concrete manifestations of, or creations by, the principle. They think that 'goodness itself' must be the most good thing, or the absolute measure of beauty must be the supremely beautiful thing. They commit thus a sort of 'homological' fallacy. The eternal and necessary principle is, they imply, in no way abstract or inferior to concrete contingent actualities. Anselm's unawareness of the abstract-concrete paradox was merely one form of this 'Platonic' attitude. (Whether or not Plato knew better we need not here inquire. It is important that many of his followers did not.)

Against this 'Platonizing' procedure, we may argue: if, as seems reasonable, contingency is in the step from universal to particular, or from more to less universal forms, then it is also (for this is the same) in the step from the more abstract to the more nearly concrete. But then the necessary should be looked for in the opposite direction, facing toward the *most* abstract!

Does this form of anti-Platonism (or moderate Platonism) invalidate the Argument? Only if one assumes the extreme neo-Platonic or Classical form of Theism as its conclusion. But then the argument is invalid anyway (Findlay paradox). Suppose, however, we take what is often termed the Aristotelian view of universals or forms, that they are not ultimately and absolutely separable from concrete instances, what then becomes of the Proof? Answer: it takes on a neoclassical form. Universals must have some embodiment (if in nothing else, in some mind thinking them). It follows that contingency cannot have its ground in the mere contrast between 'predicates' and 'exemplified predicates'. For *some* predicates *must* be exemplified, or there would be nothing to talk about, whether universal or particular. The ground of contingency is rather in the distinction between specific and generic predicates, or between more and less determinate ideas. Specific predicates always involve mutual exclusiveness. They are *competitive* ways of specializing more general notions, alternative 'determinates' under higher 'determinables'; but the bare 'somehow specialized, somehow concretized', when applied to the highest determinables, is not competitive with anything positive whatever, but only with the ultra-Platonic negation, 'mere form not specialized, not concretized at all'.

It is one thing to say that each step toward particularity, each increase in the logical strength of our assertions, must involve contingency; it is another, often strangely confused with it, to say that there might be no particularization at all. 'The most general universal is somehow particularized' is a completely general statement, affirming no definite particular whatever. The contingency of each definite step toward particularity only means that, instead of this or that step, other *equally definite* steps might have been taken; it does not mean that no definite step might have been taken. To affirm this last as possible is to attribute complete self-sufficiency to the abstract or universal, as I believe not even Plato did.

Applying these considerations to the Proof, we see that the ontological argument is valid if, and only if, the individuality of God is conceivable as a pure determinable, which, like all pure determinables, by the Aristotelian principle (implied by the extensional assumptions of modern logic?) must be particularized and concretized somehow. Although divinity is truly individual, incapable of coexisting with another in its class, yet (as we are about to see) its bare existence, its being 'somehow actualized', is quite as abstract (in the here relevant sense), quite as nonspecific or noncompetitive, as 'reality as such'. It has the same absolutely infinite range of variations, the same unrestricted flexibility. (This does not make the actuality of deity a flabby characterless thing; for the actuality is the contingent *how* of em-

bodiment, not the bare necessary truth 'embodied somehow'. While God, merely by existing, is not required to forbid this or that nondivine form of existence, by free contingent
decision He can do so.) Deity is individual but, according to
the neoclassical view, precisely the individual whose definitive
functions are strictly universal—such as, knowing everything,
influencing and being influenced by everything, related actually to all actual things, potentially to all possible things,
coextensive thus with modality itself, and so bound to be instanced no matter what more special abstractions are or are
not instanced. None of Anselm's critics, nor yet his most recent
defender Malcolm, seems to have considered this notion of
modal coextensiveness as intrinsic to perfection.

The equivalence of modal coextensiveness with Unsurpassability (by others) is manifest: any supposedly rival actuality must be included in the actuality of Greatness (otherwise God would be but a constituent of the total actuality),
and what any other individual could be is only a fragment of
all that the Unsurpassable could and would be if the other
individual were actual. Thus the necessary aspect of deity is
simply the ultimate determinable as bound to be embodied
in some concrete determinate form. To affirm this inevitability
of embodiment as conclusion of the Proof is not to exceed
the logical strength of the premises, for the conclusion (and,
we shall argue, the whole of metaphysics and pure logic) is
already implicit in the minor premise, 'God is conceivable as
not conceivably surpassed', alone. 'Somehow-actualized Greatness' is quite as abstract or 'weak' as simple 'Greatness'
—the concreteness being here wholly in the *how* of actualization. It is different with 'somehow-actualized black swans'.
For here the kind of thing is itself restrictive or competitive,

an hypothetical or threatened limitation upon the realization of other possibilities; 'somehow actualized' simply affirms the realization of this threat. But Greatness does not, of itself, threaten any possibility whatsoever. On the contrary, it is to be thought of as the very being of possibility in general, the power which any possibility would express if actualized.

The reader may be wondering how an ultimate determinable could issue in determinations: there is the old query, can a thing give what it lacks? Here we have exactly the mistake of Platonism (in the bad sense), the notion that all beauty of beautiful concrete things must preexist, or eternally exist, in the Principle or Source of beauty. The notion that creation consists in the mere parceling out of an already completed value is exactly what philosophies somewhat lacking in religious vision might be expected to have. It is the denial of any intelligible creativity, divine or creaturely. To be creative is to add positive determinations to reality, to enrich the totality of things by new values. The ultimate determinable is the supreme creativity; it *produces* the values, it does not simply pass them out, or down, to the creatures from its own prior possession.

We seem to have shown that in the neoclassical, or 'moderately Platonic' use, the Argument can escape the traditional charges of formal fallacy. True, the acceptance or rejection of either the minor premise (that deity is conceivable) or the Anselmian Principle (existential contingency is a defect, because necessary existence is conceivable and better) will, for each individual, involve, directly or indirectly, an element of intuitive judgment. Is there any argument which will not somewhere require such judgment? Not for nothing is 'counterintuitive' used by logicians. Unfortunately, on some topics the available supply of intuitive comprehension is today not great. Perhaps it never can be great, but it might be increased.

14. *A Theory of Modality*

That ordinary predicates neither exist necessarily nor necessarily fail to exist is inherent in their meanings. For they describe a conceivable sort of world which excludes other sorts likewise conceivable, and to do this belongs to their very function as predicates of the usual type. Similarly, self-contradictory predicates, by their mere meanings, necessarily do not exist. In these two cases modal status inheres in the predicate itself. What then is incongruous in there being a third form of predication which, by its very meaning, neither (1) *excludes* existence nor (2) is *neutral* to it (existing if this possibility, but not if that possibility, is actualized), but rather (3) *requires* existence (exists no matter what possibility is actualized)? No impartial person can, I think, deny that there is a certain completeness about this view which has an intellectual appeal. Modal status, it says, is always a priori or logical; but, of the three forms of modality, contingency alone makes existence a question of extralogical facts. The others make it an a priori necessity, positive or negative.

It might be thought that there are four forms of modal status: contingent nonexistence, contingent existence, necessary nonexistence, necessary existence. But the distinction between positive and negative contingency is not, like that between positive and negative necessity, an affair of meaning alone. It belongs thus to a different logical level. Contradiction *requires* rejection, and the necessary is that whose contradictory is self-contradictory; thus only the distinction between 'contingently exists' and 'contingently does not exist' is left open by meaning, or 'the rules of our language'. It is a radically different sort of distinction, therefore. This corresponds to the logic of the notion of possibility: a predicate which describes *no* possibility cannot exist, one which describes a factor in *every* possibility must exist, and only a predicate which describes a factor in *some* possibilities, but not in others, may or may not exist. These are the relations to possibility as such which a predicate can have. Hence there are three and only three modalities. And all of them are a priori. Only the nonmodal distinction between contingently existent and contingently nonexistent is extralogical or merely factual. It is 'existence' in this sense only which is 'not a predicate', and it is not a predicate precisely because it is this sort of existence. Also the logical structure which explains its extralogical status equally explains the intralogical status of necessary existence.

Why has this straightforward analysis not long ago become commonplace? One reason seems to be this: 'possibilities' are taken to include purely negative ones, like 'the nonexistence of birds'. So, analogously, 'the nonexistence of deity'. And then even 'deity exists' excludes a possibility, is restrictive or competitive. What is overlooked here is that a negative possibility, if genuine, is not a single definite sort of possibility, but rather an infinite system of possibilities which differ positively as well as negatively among themselves. The 'nonexistence of birds' would mean that every part of the world of relevant size and condition was occupied by *something other* than a feathered, warmblooded vertebrate. The varieties of cases here are unfathomable. This consideration, that negative possibilities are only an aspect of positive ones taken wholesale, gives us a criterion for distinguishing genuine from merely verbal negations. The non-existence of a predicate, *H*, either does or does not imply the disjunction of various *positive* forms of possibility any one of which would *exclude* the existence of *H*. If for *H* we put divine perfection, no such forms can be specified. It is the same with all comparably abstract properties, e.g., 'something particular'. No positive possibility is excluded by the bare 'existence of particulars', their nature being not further specified. Universals are not crowded out of reality by there being particulars; on the contrary it is only in particulars of some sort, for instance, particular minds, that universals can be met at all. And there being particulars of a kind not further specified sets no restrictions upon the truth or untruth of more specifically defined sorts of particulars. This absence of exclusive particularization in 'particularization' itself, taken merely as such, is entirely matched by the absolutely infinite tolerance of 'divine perfection exists somehow, in some particular concrete form'. Any imaginable being besides God is quite free to exist, so far as this statement is concerned. To say otherwise is to say that something could exist which God could not know existed, and this is to make the idea of His cognitive perfection contradictory.

15. *Contingency and Observability*

If it be thought arbitrary to take positive possibilities as forming the entirety of possibility, then I appeal to Popper's invaluable if simple lesson, that the useful meaning of 'contingent' or 'empirical' is, "capable of being contradicted by some, but not all, conceivable observation statements, these being always positive—'here is such and such'." True, Popper, for his purpose of clarifying the role of science, limits falsifying observation to the sort that human beings could make, and thus he excludes such a statement as, 'Here is a universe everywhere otherwise occupied than by a four-legged feathered creature' (i.e., there are no such creatures). A human being could not observe this, and so it could not falsify, 'There is somewhere a four-legged feathered creature'. But we can conceive a superhuman mind doing this. It is very different with the statement, 'Here is a universe everywhere occupied otherwise than by a divine being'. For a divine being could occupy no place and perform no function that anything else could occupy or perform. Hence one would have to observe the bare absence of deity, and this no sort of mind could conceivably do. (All observation is of a presence, not of a mere absence.) If, for instance, one observed a disorderly or 'badly-ordered' universe, how, without being divine, could one know that a certain degree of disorder or of evil was more than was compatible with divine rule of a universe of free creatures? Or that creatures should or could wholly lack freedom? (And the disorder and evil must be relative only, or no mind could exist to know it.) Thus the Proof is concerned with a statement which is not, even in an extended Popperian sense, empirical or contingent. Anselm's 'Thou canst not be conceived not to exist' is correct, if to conceive a negative fact is to conceive a positive one incompatible with a given hypothesis.

How could any conceivable experience exemplify 'God does not exist'? God's own experience certainly could not exemplify it. Could any other experience? No, for from the very definition of Greatness, as implying existential self-sufficiency, it follows that God must be able to exist no matter what appears in any experience other than His own. Could such an appearance contradict the existence of God, God would owe His existence, should He exist, to the absence of the hypothetical experience containing this appearance. This contradicts His independence of existence from all special conditions. So we have rigorously shown that the nonexistence of God has no conceivable experiential meaning, in terms of divine or nondivine experience. Either then 'conceivability' has no essential relation whatever to the testimony of possible experience, or the 'nonexistence of God' is inconceivable.

Has the 'existence of God' an experiential meaning? ('Experiential' is not the same as 'empirical': the latter connotes, 'compatible with some, but *not all,* conceivable experiences'; the former, 'confirmed or manifested at least by some, perhaps by all, conceivable experiences'.) Clearly, God could experience His own existence, if He could do or be anything. And also, in principle, nondivine experience could imply, and hence know, God. For, just as it follows from the idea of Greatness that its existence must depend upon nothing else, so it follows also that the existence of other things must depend upon Greatness; and, if all things require God's existence for their own, the occurrence of anything whatever—and so of any nondivine experience—implies the divine existence. Accordingly, whether or not in such experiences there is consciousness that God exists depends only upon the level of self-understanding of the experiences. The logical basis for the consciousness is given in the definition of Greatness. So, while the nonexistence of God cannot be experientially significant or genuinely conceivable, his existence very well can be. Hence, the impossibility of significantly denying 'Greatness exists' appears not to be nullified by any comparable difficulty in asserting it. And of course many mystics claim to experience God. Since their claim is compatible with the conception of God, and the claim of falsification is not thus compatible, Anselm's Principle seems to be vindicated. Greatness is conceivable only as existent, by the very criteria which allow us to conceive either the existence or the nonexistence of any island, dollar, devil, you please.

16. *The Proof and Logical Rules*

The basic pattern of attacks upon the Argument is this: however exceptional God may be, He cannot be an exception to the ultimate rules of language or of meaning. But this is also the pattern of many positivistic attacks, not simply on the Argument, but on the idea of God itself. Thus God could not be infallible, for to perceive or know is to experience things in a perspective which is bound to put some things in clearer light than others: He could not be both perfect and 'living', for to live is to have an environment whose features set limits to the actions of living organisms. In short, God cannot be a sheer exception to the rules governing the meaning of the terms applied to Him. Just so, the anti-Anselmian is sure that God could not be an exception to the rule governing 'exist'—that it is always an arbitrary or contingent determination of the disjunction: to exist or not to exist. So sure is he of this that he does not even need to read and rarely does read—or at least remember—even the four pages of *Prosl.* II-IV in order to know how wrong they must be. And what is the critic so sure of? Unwittingly or wittingly, of this: God is logically impossible. For His very definition requires Him to be an exception to the alleged rule. That this discredits the idea is a conclusion capable of plausible defence—if the critics would but defend it and not confuse the issue by pretence of neutrality concerning God's logical possibility.

God is by definition an infinite exception! Until this is seen and admitted by all parties, debate concerning theism is essentially in the dark, and about no one knows what.

But the subtlety of the matter lies of course in this: that if God's existence simply violates rules, there can be no rational approach to it whatever. Indeed, either there is a sense in which 'God' fulfills, rather than violates, the normal logical rules, or the positivist is right and the idea is nonsense. The function of the idea of God must be to 'fulfill, not destroy', to constitute the meaning or rationale of things, to establish universal sense, not universal nonsense. Either there must be a more truly universal Rule, which illuminates the lesser rules, and explains why they not only admit but demand an Exception, or else the idea of the Exception is against all logic.

Here again is where classical theism fails. It does not exhibit such a Rule, in appropriate relations to the lesser rules. For instance, it does not clearly say *why* and *how* existence is generally but not in the supreme case contingent; or why and how life is generally but not in the supreme case dependent upon an external environment. Yet a rule which does this is nonetheless conceivable. We have indicated it in various ways. To exist *competitively* is indeed to exist contingently; hence to exist noncontingently is to exist noncompetitively. Again, to exist with but limited capacity to respond or 'adjust' to things is to be able to achieve clarity and coherence only by responding more to some things and less to others in a graded perspective, and this is precisely what it means to be 'localized'. But localized beings are competitive; where one is another cannot be. By the same token, to exist with infinite capacity to respond is to have no external environment and no limiting perspective or competitive locus. The rules which set the limitations also prescribe the rule for the absence of limitation. Thus, for instance, to be *completely* 'adaptable' is to be able to exist in *any* state of affairs; hence to exist wholly noncompetitively or all-tolerantly, i.e. (by the very rule which explains ordinary contingency), noncontingently.

In classical theism one cannot proceed in this way. Not infinite or perfect power of adaptation belongs to God, but simply the *absence* of any need or capacity to adapt or respond to things ('impassibility'—an Anselmian doctrine); not perfect love or compassion, but only an 'as if' simulation of this, so far as effects upon others are concerned. Here the exception to the rule is not, as in neoclassical theism, built into the rules—it is a sheer violation. Rather than positing infinite adaptability in God, one says rather that God has no need to adapt at all and that what world exists simply makes no difference to His actual state. Thus, one by one, the concepts in terms of which something might be said about God are discarded. He is not the Exceptional fulfillment of the concepts, rather He is their exceptional—indeed absolute—unfulfillment. That this is the way to lose the game of talking with meaning about deity appears especially in this, that one rule which is as surely logical as any, the rule that the necessary must be abstract, empty, entailed by all concrete or actual details of existence, but entailing none, is set aside in classical theism by a mere fiat. God *must* be actual, not a mere abstraction, and yet also wholly necessary. For *this* exception no rule is possible, and by it no lesser rule is illuminated. This is the real flaw in the Argument as used by nearly all who have employed it.

However, this flaw was not accurately seen by any of the critics either! Or, at least, it was not seen (by Findlay, for example) in conjunction with the relevant consideration that perhaps God need not be taken as simply identical with 'necessary being'; for while His individuality or essence must be thought of as necessary, *how* the essence is actualized in actual states of experience or consciousness may yet be contingent. This conjunction of ideas—which preserves as without exception the grand rule that the actual or nonabstract is contingent—was overlooked by nearly all parties alike. Why? Because their approach was unwittingly dogmatic. They had a rigid element of belief that was not subject to revision: e.g., that no form of existence could be necessary, or that no aspect of the divine existence could be contingent; or that theism could not be rationally known as true in *any* form; or that it was known (or should be believed) to be true in some classical form (including classical pantheism or its equivocal derivative, Hegelianism). The parties scarcely open to conviction on one or other of these points divided the field. They still do largely divide it. But the rigidity seems to be giving way. This is the promise of the present situation.

The promise will be fulfilled only if we become aware of the devices to which tenacity resorts when its beliefs are threatened. We shall be told (probably by some nontheists as well as theists) that neoclassical theism is 'anthropomorphic'. As though infinite adaptability to all possible worlds were not separated by a literally infinite gulf from human adaptability to some things in this world! To put man (and any other mere creature) in his proper place there is no need to allow him to usurp and exhaust categories like adaptation, passibility, change; this is just the way to give man undue importance. For then all that is left as God's province is the emptiness of eternal necessity, void of true freedom and all concreteness! The negative theology was not nearly so modest as it appeared to be. It put God behind the beyond, where He could do nothing and be nothing intelligible to us. All the more freedom for us to attend to our affairs, without relating them positively to God!

If Anselm's formula, 'God is whatever it is better to be than not to be', had been strictly conformed to the negative theology, it would have run, 'God is not what it is worse to be than not to be'. Would this have improved it? I submit: we do not worship God because of the defects which He does not have. We worship Him for His positive and all-encompassing love and beauty.

The use of the Argument by proponents of the negative or classical theology has not been a grand success. The proposal to empiricists that they should use the Argument has caused them to be unable to read. Perhaps another possible use is worth looking into, that by neoclassical theists, those who admit knowable and positive—though extremely abstract—divine properties, as well as largely unknowable concrete divine actualities.

17. *Anselm's Appeal to Rules*

Suppose we can without contradiction conceive that there is a unique x which is unsurpassable, and suppose we can also without contradiction conceive the negation of this. Then either supposition is the notion of an *absolutely* inexplicable brute fact. Ordinary facts may in a relative sense be inexplicable, but in a relative sense at least they are always explicable. They have causes which at least partly explain them. Even if determinism is, as I confidently believe, a false doctrine, still, every existing thing of ordinary kinds has come into existence thanks to causes which made the emergence of some such thing when and where it did, if not inevitable, at least more or less probable. But to be unsurpassable a being must exist thanks to no cause whatever, and without ever coming into existence or being capable of ceasing to exist. An uncaused being such that it might have failed to exist, yet incapable of coming into or going out of existence could only be, in the most absolute sense, inexplicable, a wholly and simply irrational contingent fact. No antecedent fact would illuminate it, and by hypothesis no abstract principle of logical necessity would either. It would just be so. Unlike ordinary ideas of chance, such as those of Peirce and others, which always set limits to the inexplicable aspects of things, we would here have an existence through and through *pure* chance, in the strict logical sense of having no aspect derivable either from necessity (as in pure mathematics) or from antecedent fact or cause. All else, then, would exist as at least partly explicable, but the inexplicability of this existence would be infinite and total. God exists, He might not have; He does not exist, He might have—whichever is true, there can (according to the thorough-going empiricist) be no aspect whatever of reason in its being true. It just is.

Thus, whereas the usual view is that Anselm is breaking all rules to establish his case, it is from some points of view his critics who break rules, among them the notion that a contingently existing thing should have some explanation for its existence. Everywhere else mere chance, as entire account of a being's existence, is ruled out; here it is admitted! Anselm commits no such violation of ordinary principles. He rejects the contingency hypothesis as applicable to this case, holding that in the existence of God there is neither cause nor chance, but the impossibility, inconceivability, of an alternative. *God is* states the only possible truth about the divine existence; hence there can be no question of why, or how it came about, that God does, rather than does not, exist—except in much the sense in which we may ask why five and seven are twelve, rather than some other number. The sole and sufficient reason is that it must be so; there being no possible alternative, the nonrealization of any such alternative calls for no explanation. How different with contingent facts!

In final metaphysical analysis: that acts occur for which there is no *complete* causal derivation is not 'irrational' if the *essential* function of reason is to explicate and serve cretivity (rather than to foresee its results); deity, however, cannot be conceived as a mere product of creativity, but only as its supreme and indispensable aspect, whose flexibility is coincident with possibility itself, and is thus on both sides of every contingent alternative, hence itself not contingent but necessary.

Anselm's critics, we see, have not been the only philosophers who appeal to the opponent to acknowledge rules and abide by them. Anselm himself made such an appeal. Thus it is a rule that contingent things (generally admitted to be such) go into and out of existence, have parts, depend upon causes, and suffer limitations of capacity inherent in the circumstances of their coming to be, or in the particular parts and causes involved. Adhering to these rules, the Greatest thing, which must at least exist always and could not require for its existence any particular set of parts (for a Greatest set has no meaning) or depend upon any cause for existence, since to depend for existence upon something else is a defect—such a Greatest thing cannot be contingent. Here it is the critics who want to waive the rules. They want to regard *one* concept, lacking in any of the features found in all the things whose logical contingency is noncontroversial, as nevertheless purely contingent in its actualization.

Moreover, it is no mere inductive generalization that all contingent things have the features specified (and still others of the kind); there seems to be an intelligible connection between these features and their contingency. So, approximately, Anselm thought—and wrote. His arguments on this point have been ignored in more than nine-tenths of the refutations and but carelessly criticized in the others. This is all part of the great master lesson in how not to criticize a philosopher.

And yet, inefficient as the process has been, it has—after quite a while!—produced some results. It is now possible to see a good way around the situation that Anselm brought about, to relate it not only to Anselm's form of theism but to the chief logically possible forms, to remove the ambiguity in 'none greater' and compare the two ways of doing this, to see clearly the distinction between atheism and positivism as alternatives to theism, to generalize the problem of contingency with respect to alternative criteria for the division between necessary and contingent propositions and to relate these to various language systems and their rules. We are, in short, in a position to *inquire* in this area, rather than merely to debate. So, on the whole, we may after all be at least mildly grateful to those whom we have been viewing with such severity. And certainly we should be grateful to Anselm. He did for us not exactly what he hoped to do, but in some ways far more than he could have dreamt of doing.

18. *Refutation of Some Refutations*

Gilbert Ryle tells us that the Argument rests upon the use of a 'systematically misleading expression'. In 'x exists', existence is only a 'bogus predicate' and that of which it is asserted only a 'bogus subject'. And "if existence is not a quality it is not the sort of thing that can be entailed by a quality."[9] Another author says that the verb *to exist* "takes us right out of the purely conceptual world," and therefore "there can never be any logical contradiction in denying that God exists."[10]

In these charges I find unwitting instances of the 'bad

---

[9] G. Ryle, "Systematically Misleading Expressions," *Proceedings of the Aristotelian Society* (1931-32); also in *Logic and Language,* eds. A.G.N. Flew and A. Macintyre (New York: Philosophical Library, 1951), pp. 15, 17.

[10] *New Essays in Philosophical Theology,* eds. A. G. N. Flew and A. Macintyre (London: SCM Press, 1955), p. 34.

grammar' or bad logic of which Anselm is accused. First, the notion that 'existing deity' is formally analogous, say, to 'existing tiger' violates the grammar or logic of the character 'divine'. Multitudes of theologians have for centuries given reasons for denying that the nature of God can consistently be viewed as a universal 'predicate' capable of embodiment in this or that 'individual'. Thus for instance it was said over and over that God "does not have but is his being or his goodness." In other words, the unique excellence of God implies a *logical-type difference* from all other individuals, actual or possible. How often (in old-fashioned language) this sort of thing was repeated! Second, the notion that even the divine existence is entirely extraconceptual is the very one that the Argument, fully understood, purports to disprove; and thus the quoted objection is merely the unsupported denial that the reasoning is valid. Likewise, to suppose that it makes sense to speak of a 'purely conceptual world', in the application which the phrase must here have, begs the question.

Ryle analogizes 'God exists' to 'Satan exists'. Thereby he misuses either 'God' or 'Satan'.[11] For, though 'Satan' is indeed "not the proper name of anything," what the Argument shows is that 'God', by its whole meaning, either stands for no logically possible conception at all, or is the name of an existing individual. It is no proof to the contrary that there is a *verbal* analogy between 'Satan exists' and 'God exists'. The question of the logical propriety of the analogy is merely one of many ways to put the Anselmian issue. If Anselm is correct, the verbal affinity is indeed 'systematically

---

[11] Ryle, *op. cit.*, p. 16.

misleading'. The phrases, 'Nothing is both devilish and alone in being devilish'[12] and 'Nothing is both divine and alone in being divine', are *not* logically akin, for all their verbal similarity! For, whereas only one conceivable individual could be divine, its individual uniqueness being thus specifiable by a pure concept, there is no correspondingly definite and self-individuating concept of devilishness. For instance, only one being could know or love all things; but 'hater of all beings' has no clear, coherent, and unique meaning. Without some self-love or love of others there is no self at all.

When Professor Wisdom entitled his essay on the divine existence "Gods," he was exhibiting very bad grammar indeed.[13] Only an idol, not God, could be one among a variety of conceivable gods. It is comic—and also sad—to see how easily prejudice, rather than an alleged principle of method, in itself not unreasonable, may tilt the balance in philosophy. Let us by all means talk grammatically or logically about deity. But who that has read much in the history of religious metaphysics will suppose that this is among the easier tasks of 'analysis', to be accomplished by selecting logical devices which have been arrived at in dealing with nondivine things, and blandly applying them to deity as merely one more topic of discourse? This is exactly what Anselm and many others have claimed to show it cannot be!

Do any of the authors discussed in this section show the least inkling of the content of *Prosl.* III? Or of the *Reply* to Gaunilo? Or even of the corresponding passages in Descartes

---

[12] Ryle, *loc. cit.*

[13] John Wisdom, "Gods," *Proceedings of the Aristotelian Society* (1944); also in *Philosophy and Psycho-Analysis,* pp. 149-68.

(or Bonaventura)? Must I answer? They do not. The point that, whereas ordinary contingent existence is not a predicate, contingency as such and its negative, necessity as such, are predicates is simply omitted from the discussion.

The admirable clarity of much contemporary British philosophy makes it no great trick to show exactly where it misses the Anselmian point. Using Ryle's excellent phrase, we may admit that it is a 'category mistake' to treat ordinary existence as a quality, deducible from a quality. But has he never heard the saying, virtually as old and persistent as theism itself, that God "transcends the categories," that they do not apply 'univocally' to God? What categories, then, are being mistakenly applied? If it is a category mistake to treat 'existence' (in the ordinary contingent sense) as a 'quality' (again, in the ordinary restrictive or competitive sense), how does it follow that *existence in the ostensibly extraordinary sense appropriate only to God* is not a quality, in an equally extraordinary and uniquely appropriate sense? The contrary might very well follow: it might very well be a category mistake *not* to treat divine (necessary) existence as a divine (nonrestrictive) quality.

The reasonable questions are, can there be such an extraordinary sense of the categories as theism requires and can this sense be reasonably related to the ordinary senses? But these questions concern primarily, not any argument for theism, but its logical possibility. Why has Findlay been almost the only critic of the Proof who has seen this and has put his cards on the table?

He who attacks the argument can do one of two things, but not reasonably both at once: he can grant, at least for the sake of argument, that 'God' means what theists say it means, that is, 'an individual' who yet is not *simply* an individual, whose 'nature' or quality is not *simply* a quality, and who 'exists', but not *simply* as other things exist (Tillich overstates this by holding that 'God exists' is an inadmissible, atheistic expression); or second, he can refuse to grant all this, and can even contend that an idea which thus violates or 'transcends' the basic categories of thought cannot have a rational content. But then he must not say that the argument is illogical because it applies categories in violation of their rules. For the categories, in their usual meaning, with their usual rules, have been explicitly set aside. They are not being applied and hence are not being misapplied either! The words may still be used, but with a frankly distinct meaning. To take God to be simply an individual, simply having a nature or quality, simply existing, is certainly a category mistake, if ever there was one! Deity must itself be a sort of category, and the supreme category, and until *its* rules have been investigated, there can be no demonstration that any relevant rules have been violated.

From the above the critic may plausibly draw the conclusion: 'God' is an illogical term. He cannot, however, prove this from the assumption that it claims, but fails, to be a case under the ordinary categorial rules. For it makes no such claim. Rather the critic must attack the legitimacy of the pretension (inherent in theism as such) that each category has two levels of possible meaning, the ordinary one and the extraordinary one applicable only to God. And to reject this pretension is to reject theism, rather than just the Argument. Except for Findlay, critics have been playing a game without specifying its rules, and the fact that the game has been played for nine centuries does not provide it with rules, nor make it any the less in violation of reason. (Rather, the offence against reason is made the worse by this exhibition of tenacity.) If the usual categorial meanings have their rules, the unusual ones may have theirs. (See above, Secs. 16, 17.)

Another illustration. Wisdom says that the question about the divine mind has two components, a metaphysical, "Can we know other minds than our own?" and a factual, "Is there a special sort of other mind, the divine? (analogous to, Is there a special sort of mind, that of plants?)."[14] Now this is a category mistake. For 'divine mind' cannot be a special sort of mind, a factual, competitive particularization of 'other mind' in general. It is the supposedly universal medium, creator, sustainer of all minds whatever and all things whatever, the transfactual source and bearer of fact as such. Is the "creator of all things, visible and invisible," in other words, the ground of the possibility of whatever is possible, but one special sort of possible thing? The whole point of what Anselm discovered, if anything, was that the mere 'existence' of God is entirely metaphysical, not factual. Findlay draws the plausible conclusion that God is therefore no conceivable actuality, but only an empty or absurd abstraction. Classical theism cannot, I hold, fairly rebut this charge. Neoclassical theism, however, distinguishes existence and actuality, and does this in reference not only to God but to all things. What is exceptional about God is that in Him alone is it possible to treat existence as not only different, but different *modally,* from actuality, i.e., so that the one is necessary, the other contingent. The 'actualized somehow' here covers such an abso-

---

[14] Wisdom, *op. cit.,* pp. 151 f.

lute infinity of variability in the particular possible hows of actualization that all possibility is included, and hence there can be no possibility that the divine existence will be simply unactualized. This may or may not be a defensible position, but if it is defensible then the usual criticisms of the argument are woefully, ludicrously, beside the point.

The appropriate question is, What categories, if any, apply to God? or How, in what extraordinary manner, do categories apply? not, What follows from the assumption that ordinary categories apply in the ordinary manner? For this assumption renders contradictory the theism supposed (for the sake of argument at least) to form a logically possible position. An atheistic attack on the Argument is one thing—there are rules for dealing with it. A positivistic attack is quite another, and the rules cannot be wholly the same. An attack which hides its affiliations is appealing to no appropriate rules at all. No wonder the debate has lasted so long and has had so little to do with what Anselm actually wrote!

(It is to be noted that atheism has two forms, (1) dogmatic and (2) agnostic: (1) God does not exist, (2) for all we know, God does not exist. Both are excluded by Anselm's discovery. But there remain two forms of positivism: (1) 'God' lacks consistent, cognitive meaning; (2) for all we know, 'God' lacks such meaning. Both remain open so far as the argument, taken by itself, and at least as used against unbelievers, is concerned.)

A favorite attack on the Proof is the pronouncement, 'only propositions, not things, can be necessary'. Very well, but still, what about the proposition, 'Greatness exists'? If that is necessary, then the proof is granted; if not, it cannot be on the ground that only propositions can be necessary. For this is a proposition! And moreover, why not define necessary thing as 'that the existence of which is affirmable in a necessarily true proposition'? But there is still another weakness in the objection. If a necessary proposition is one which is entailed by any and every proposition, then, since this implies that the meaning of the necessary proposition is included in that of every proposition, we may by legitimate analogy define necessary thing as that which is contained in any and every thing, actual or possible. True, a universal constituent of everything can only be something very abstract, but, as we have seen repeatedly, although Anselm could not have conceded this, in a different type of philosophy from his the implication of abstractness can be accepted.

Another familiar but weak objection is that necessity is always relative to premises or conditions and has no meaning when taken as unconditioned, as it must be taken for the Proof. The objection is weak because the proper meaning of 'unconditioned' is, on any conditions you please, or on no matter what conditions, i.e., on 'tautological conditions' (von Wright). It is neutrality as between all possible alternative premises or conditions. God's existence follows necessarily—from what? From any statement, or the denial of any statement. Just so '2 and 2 are 4' follows, not from nothing, but from any assumption whatever. The statement is true if it is raining and also if it is not raining. Absolute necessity is that which requires no special assumptions or conditions rather than any others. Thus the notion that 'necessary' means necessitated *by* something in particular is groundless. To be necessary is merely to be common to all possibilities, hence neutral as to which possibility may be actualized. Of course *some* possibility will be actualized in any case, and so, therefore, will the common factor in all possibilities. The notion of something special behind the necessary pulling it invincibly into existence, or holding it there, is an inept analysis. There is no constraint upon possibilities in ensuring the necessary, for the latter is the principle of possibility itself, the creative ground of alternativeness in reality by virtue of which alone there is any contingency. It is not an iron control, but an infinite flexibility, which can stretch as far as possibility itself, without losing self-identity.

No matter what world exists, or what other world instead, God exists, unsurpassably knowing that world. He can accept *any* world into His knowledge. He can know any truth; hence His own nonexistence is not a possible truth.

Among the anti-Anselmian fallacies which usually go unchallenged is the bold transition from Greatest (or Perfect) entity or individual to Greatest or Perfect 'of its kind', as though what followed from the first must also follow from the second! (I am quoting from conversation with a well-known logician.) This nicely misses the point of the Argument, which is that, for the inference to hold, Greatness itself must be the kind. Otherwise, we have specialization or restrictive limitation, which is always competitive with alternative specializations or restrictions, hence contingent. The very absence of 'kind' in the usual sense is what distinguishes Greatness. The necessity that *Greatness itself must be the kind* rules out, not only 'greatest island', but also (in spite of Bertrand Russell, in one of his reckless moments) 'greatest devil'. Anselm generally chose his words carefully: he said, not greatest god, but greatest something ('that'). (He should perhaps have said greatest individual or being, but this is still not to specialize or restrict.) Divine capacity can take a form corresponding to any conceivable restriction, and therefore is itself unrestricted. What else could 'infinite' cognitive or creative capacity mean?

Special kinds of individuals have special capacities and special limitations of capacity; Greatness is *omnicapacity,* in whatever sense this is conceivable, ability to experience, know, or deal adequately with quite literally anything—in a uniquely strict sense, 'a heart for any fate'. Obviously the individual's own nonexistence is not included in the possible fates, since one can deal with or know that only in restricted ways. Thus, once more, the idea of the 'nonexistence of the omnicapable' is not consistent.

Perhaps someone will persist in urging: even an individual of a certain kind would, by Anselm's reasoning, be better if existing necessarily than otherwise, and hence the 'best conceivable individual of each kind' must exist. What this shows is simply that 'best conceivable of a certain kind' (no matter what kind, if it is different from Greatness as such) is without consistent meaning. A self-contradictory thing is not a better thing than something else, for it is not a thing. There is, in truth, no absolute ideal for any special kind of thing that one individual could unsurpassably realize. What could be meant by 'human being than which none could conceivably in any respect be greater'? By contrast, God could and as conceived would possess every positive value which anyone possessed, and hence His capacity for value is not conceivably surpassable. He would unfailingly participate in all joy, all knowledge, and all reality; and thus His actual feeling and knowledge would include and surpass that of every other individual, and be conceivably surpassable only by Himself, i.e., it would meet the requirements of neoclassical Greatness. But that the requirements should be conceivable, also the least infringement of them inconceivable, and yet the very nonexistence of the being meeting the requirements should be conceivable, this is a jumble of ideas with no intelligible coherence. Nothing could explain or reduce to logical rules such a combination of absolute accident and absolute necessity. Is it not the opponents of Anselm who, at least as much as anyone defending him, lack respect for 'rules'? Seemingly they do not care how anarchic thought about God may be, so long only as it is not to be taken as more than a dubious proposal with little or no chance of finding rational support. They perhaps do not want thought about God to be intelligible; the less so the better. By this method, one may be certain of never learning how far intelligibility can go in a given subject.

Still another refutation echoed from book to book is that the Argument establishes only conceptual existence, not real existence. But what either *Prosl.* II or III proves, if anything at all, is that, supposing Greatness to be conceivable, its failure to have existence in the fullest sense is inconceivable. Not merely that when we think Greatness it must be an object of our thought, as 'fairies' are objects when we happen to think about fairies; but that we must think Greatness, if at all, as somehow actualized or really existent. The Argument proves this, or nothing! And when some persist: but still, do we need to think Greatness, existent or not? part of the answer (the full answer would be all the theistic proofs put together) is: at least, no one can be an atheist who does not think about God, so at any rate we are rid of trouble from that quarter! As for positivism, or the denial that we can genuinely think divine perfection, this remains a plausible contention, which Anselm does not very seriously try to refute. Here he relies chiefly upon his faith. Still, not exclusively, and with subsidiary arguments one can make a good case against positivism. Granted that, as Kant held, the other theistic proofs need help from the ontological, the reverse relation may also obtain, and this without vicious circularity. If the ontological proof by itself refutes atheism, another argument might refute positivism, without leaning on the ontological for that particular accomplishment.

It is a merit of Neoclassicism that, while accepting the Proof, it can nevertheless admit an element of truth in the distinction between merely conceptual and real existence. Here, as everywhere, it softens the clash of extremely opposing opinions by a more moderate or balanced view. It holds that for an idea or essence to exist is for it to be actualized somehow; but that the actual *how* is never capturable in a concept. The *how* is the particular actuality; only percepts can exhibit it, never mere concepts. And, except in the case of Greatness, neither a kind of individual nor an individual can be subject to the requirement, '*necessarily* actualized somehow'. But this is because ordinary kinds of individuals involve restrictive or competitive characteristics; they are not all-tolerant in their requirements for existence. Only the nonrestrictive essence can be 'necessarily actualized somehow', since any positive state of affairs will do (and a merely negative state is a pseudoconception). But the particular actuality which does the actualizing is indeed a 'real existence' which no concept can specify. It is restrictive and contingent. Fortunately, to know that the actualizing must in any case be done *somehow* is all that we need for knowledge that God exists.

In the foregoing we have vindicated, but not on his classical ground, Anselm's proposition: we can conceive that God is greater than we can conceive. Any concrete reality whatever is greater than we can exhaustively conceive. This is so, in a radically unique sense, with the divine actuality, for it is the adequate integration of all actuality as so far actualized. Thus we need not leave it to the classical theist to stress how little we can comprehend God.

It has been said that Anselm's proof takes existence to be an attribute, "whereas it is the bearer of all attributes." This, however, not only does not refute, it can be used to express, the Anselmian principle. For the character or status, 'bearer of *all* attributes', must itself be an attribute, at least if it could describe an individual. And God or Greatness can be conceived only as this very individual. Any realized predicate whatever must be describable as a predicate of deity, in the form: God knowing that S is P. God is thus the universally presupposed subject of all predication, and his own nonexistence is therefore an impossible predication, or if you prefer, an impossible state of affairs. His mere existence is the essential element in all existence (and nonexistence) whatever. Hence his existence is not possibly unreal.

19. *The Argument of* Proslogium III

Everyone who has attempted to analyze the logic of informal arguments knows that the explicit premises from which a conclusion is alleged to follow are often insufficient to establish it, but that additional premises which may have been intuitively or confusedly intended can sometimes be supplied from which the conclusion does follow. If, then, a man of integrity and keen intellect claims to have proved something, ought we not to make some effort to discover all the premises which he was in a position to appeal to, whether or not he stated them in the very paragraph or two in which he first introduced his proof? And if the man wrote several additional pages, further explicating his thought, and later a few more in reply to objections to his argument (an argument which, if valid, must be highly important), is it a great deal to ask that his reasoning be taken to have at its disposal any additional premises introduced and shown to be reasonable in these two sets of pages?

Suppose, however, that the first commentator does not follow these sound principles, but makes everything depend upon the initial statement given in the first page or so. And suppose his report as to the structure of the entire argument is widely accepted, a structure which fails to supply clear and, upon careful examination, credible premises from which the conclusion logically follows, what is likely to happen? Obviously many will treat the reasoning as a mere sophistry. Thus we can understand Gaunilo's myriad followers. But then there may also be those who greatly respect the man who made the original claim, or who feel (as mathematicians often do) that some such proof should be possible. They will grope about until with luck they may find the missing premises, or something like them, or at least intuitively supply them without quite knowing that they are doing so. Thus perhaps Descartes and many others who accepted the Proof but show no signs of knowing *Prosl.* III. Then after many centuries comes another and far greater Gaunilo, David Hume, and still another—whose name needs no telling—of extraordinary intellectual, personal, and literary power, who points out once more the gap in the argument, as it is presumed to stand, and having—at this stage in his career—no feeling that such a proof should be possible, rather very much the opposite attitude, he drops, and virtually forbids for all time, the effort to find any missing premises; instead, he drives through the 'gap' with all possible energy and éclat. After him come the tens of thousands of Gaunilos in nth degree, and how triumphantly they march through the now—as they feel—comfortably widened breach.

Finally, at long last, more than a century later, the secret begins to emerge (a few had known it long before; for instance, Bonaventura): there were additional premises all along, and not unreasonable ones at that. They were actually stated—briefly but with considerable clarity—in the second sentence of Chapter III, and brilliantly elucidated thereafter, best of all in *Reply* I and V.

This approximately is the story of Anselm's argument.

One thing is left out in the above account: the reason which made some think that an ontological proof should be possible. My view is this: the more fully one understands the great Definition, or any reasonably equivalent explication of the religious idea, the more one is put in possession of all metaphysical axioms. The more powerfully intuitive the mind, the shorter the step to the 'missing premises' in question, indeed to any metaphysical premise whatever.[15] The premise, 'God is conceivable as not conceivably surpassed (by others)', is implicitly the whole of metaphysics. This is what Anselm proved, when all the implications of his reasoning are thought

---

[15] C. Hartshorne, *The Logic of Perfection* (LaSalle, Illinois: Open Court Publishing Co., 1962), chapters 3-4.

out. So of course some minds would in effect bridge the gap in the argument of *Proslogium* II, a gap which is greater the more purely verbal one's understanding of the Definition happens to be. And, equally of course, others would not bridge it. Anselm bridged the gap easily enough; he knew that there were not two conceivable states, existence and nonexistence, to be considered for Greatness, but only the one conceivable state. But if Anselm bridged the gap, he also sensed it; and that is why, after having, virtually in the next breath, supplied a new premise (two premises really: that we can conceive of necessary existence, and that this is superior to nonnecessary existence) which bridges it explicitly, he gives perhaps nine subsequent formulations of his Argument, only two of which are of the *Prosl.* II form, all the others being of a form either identical with, or closely related to, that of *Prosl.* III. Does this account not make sense out of the textual and historical facts? Has the reader one which makes better sense? If so, I hope that I shall learn what it is.

The principle of *Prosl.* II is, as all know: to exist is better than not to exist. Let us call this the 'false' Anselmian Principle. Of course it is indeed somehow 'better to exist than not to exist' (unless Schopenhauer is metaphysically right); but to define the 'best possible' being, and therewith assert its existence, is apparently to make optimism true by definition, not a very impressive procedure. "*If* God is God, He, being best, must at least exist." But if God does not exist, then 'He' is neither God nor anything else, for there is no 'He'.

The true Anselmian Principle, which so few know, that of *Prosl.* III, is, *To exist without conceivable alternative of not existing is better than to exist with such alternative;*

hence Greatness is incapable of the latter. Since contingent nonexistence (or 'merely mental existence') is here simply excluded, the comparison of it with objective existence—apparently the very basis of the False—is actually ruled out by the True Principle. The comparison is not only irrelevant, it is inconceivable. And one has not, in this version, put 'existence', *in the usual sense,* inside a definition. One has rather described a different kind of existence, a kind which resolves no such disjunction as 'to exist or not to exist', but transcends it as here inapplicable.

Will any man of sound mind ask us to admit that the False formula is an adequate version of this True one? With a touch of genius, with some luck, and more than a touch of good will, one may possibly succeed in reconstructing or guessing the True from the False Principle; and accordingly, the latter can perhaps be viewed as a crude, distorted simplification of the former. But this is about the most which can be said for it. Yet practically the entire learned world has taken—and takes—the False Principle for the essential form! With what authorization? (a) Gaunilo & Co. so took it; (b) *Prosl.* II comes before *Prosl.* III; (c) the False Principle is much handier to refute; yet (d) in refuting it we also refute the 'True', since if 'existing' cannot be a predicate neither can 'necessarily existing', which includes it. These are the reasons that I can imagine for neglecting Chapter III. They are all poor ones. Only (d) even deserves further consideration, and it is fallacious. The 'existing' which can be proved not to be a predicate is 'contingently existing', the ordinary mode of existence, and that this cannot be a predicate (in the sense required for an ontological inference) is a simple tautology, from the meaning of 'contingently'. (It is a more subtle, implicit tautology from the meaning of 'ordinary' or 'imperfect'.) But *this* mode of existence is certainly not included in necessary existence. Hence (d) is a fallacy of ambiguity. (See below, Sec. 23, (a) and (n).)

To have prefaced his great third by his so inferior second chapter was indeed a sad blunder of Anselm's; but need it deprive us of our intelligence or our scholarly conscience? A man who discovers a basic logical principle involved in the most important of all ideas can be allowed some initial groping, one would think, without all the world groping with him forever, merely saying 'no' where he said 'yes'.

In Ueberweg's *History of Philosophy* (the most learned, or at least detailed, of all), the two Principles appear in their Latin texts; so far so good. But THE FALSE PRINCIPLE IS PUT IN LARGE LETTERS, thus delicately showing that the point of neither had been grasped, and that the editor was thinking with other peoples' minds rather than his own—or Anselm's. I am asking scholars to laugh, for it seems hopeless to try to be merely solemn about so ludicrous a collective mistake. "This king is naked"—the king being Gaunilo, enthroned in majesty for an amazingly long reign to which his original title was decidedly doubtful—if not wholly 'illegitimate'. If the true title, that of the author of *Prosl.* III and the *Reply,* were at last recognized, we might begin to understand that most brilliant philosophical product of the Middle Ages, the *Proslogium!*

In fairness to countless people it should also be said that a combination of bad management and very bad luck built a trap for human nature in the Anselm case. It was bad management of Anselm to make his opening and most dubious step in the exposition of the argument appear to be the argument itself, or at least, an element upon which the whole must depend: when in truth, if *Prosl.* II has any point at all, it is only as a loose analogy to the definitive and independent reasoning of the next chapter. (Doubtless Anselm partly deceived himself, as well as others here; he did repeat the *Prosl.* II reasoning twice in the *Reply,* where, however, that of *Prosl.* III or some related argument occurs seven times! and he never seemed clearly to see its weakness—or its triviality, if it only means that, of course, the worshiper cannot take what he worships to be a mere fancy.) It was very bad luck that the first critic should have been so careless a man that he could virtually ignore two-thirds of the very short text he commented upon and that the prejudices of this critic should have been just the ones which would make him seem an oracle to those who had not yet learned the very lesson Anselm wanted to teach. So they did not check his scholarship and forgot to exert any of their own. The lesson was thus cut off at the root, as it were. After a few more reiterations, scarcely anyone suspected there could be doubt, at least as to the main outline of the argument.

Add to all this that Anselm could not well have broken the hold of Greek thought upon his own thinking sufficiently to solve the abstract-concrete paradox by which the credibility of his reasoning was menaced. Here was more than a 'gap', to be filled in perhaps by adding a premise; here—unless one took great care in how he resolved the ambiguity in 'none greater'—was a contradiction, beyond remedy by any mere addition. The critics were not wrong in thinking there was a grave error or danger of error somewhere, but they were too Greek themselves to guess accurately what it might be. When they were not Greek metaphysicians, they were (like Hume)

Greek skeptics; whereas Anselm's discovery called for something different from either form of classical thought. The last one hundred years have brought it about. It is the conscious emergence of a theism which can admit the abstractness or inactuality of the merely necessary or eternal, without giving up the notion of the all-surpassing and necessarily (somehow) actualized God.

Anselm's argument, in *Proslogium* III and thereafter, has (if the implicit is made explicit) something like the following structure. One and only one of four views must be correct:

A) The property *G,* of being such that none greater is conceivable, is itself inconceivable (There is no 'idea of God').

B) The property *G* is conceivable, but only as not existing.

C) The property *G* is conceivable as existing, and also as not existing.

D) The property *G* is conceivable, but only as existing.

Since A), B), and C) are absurd, D) must be true.

A) may be called 'positivism', B) seems to have no name, C) is 'empiricism', D) is 'a priori theism', (in contrast to A) and B), which are the two forms of 'a priori antitheism').

Anselm took A) to be counterintuitive; he also had an argument against it (in the *Reply*).

B) apparently did not occur to him. It might perhaps be illustrated by Kant's doctrine of the merely regulative use of the Ideal of Reason. Anselm's main effort was to refute C) as absurd. He has two lines of reasoning, at least, to which we add a third (still others are possible):

1) Since 'inconceivability of nonexistence' (necessary existence) is conceivable and must exalt what has it above all else, G must imply it.

2) If inconceivability of nonexistence were not conceivable, neither would G be conceivable (to Anselm it seemed evident that both are conceivable).
Conclusion from 1, 2: C) is absurd, whether inconceivability of nonexistence (necessity of existence) is or is not conceivable, hence in any case;

3) Besides, the nonexistence of G has no empirical meaning; yet, by C), it has no a priori meaning either; hence again C) is absurd.

As to 1). Inconceivability of nonexistence guarantees eternity, indestructibility, self-sufficiency, independence of causes of existing; whereas conceivability of nonexistence (contingency) makes any such guarantee unintelligible; hence such contingency is a defect and contradicts G. Therefore, if the nonexistence of G is conceivable, whatever hypothetically may be supposed to exemplify G must at the same time, and contradictorily, be thought not to exemplify it. This point is made over and over again in the *Reply,* Chapter I, and Chapter V (4th and 5th paragraphs). What is conceivable as nonexistent would be surpassable 'even if it existed'; for the conceivability of nonexistence must remain, and could not be altered by the fact of existing. Facts do not determine conceivability, modal status is independent of them. Thus, as Aristotle in effect argued long ago, such status can only be necessary. This is the anticipatory rejection, and legitimate rejection, of the stock anti-Anselmian phrase, 'exists necessarily-if it exists'. The 'if', as such, implies the very conceivability which one resolution of the alleged alternative must contradict; accordingly, as Malcolm correctly says, the phrase contradicts itself. True, six times in the paragraphs referred to Anselm uses an equivalent of 'if it exists'; but always, note well, as a step in a *reductio ad absurdum* argument against the notion that an *if* can here properly apply. The fifth paragraph sums it up with lucidity. It is not Greatness to whose existence the 'if' is relevant, but a fake substitute, some inferior sort of being whose nonexistence may indeed be conceivable, but whose existence as perfect would be contradictory. It is Anselm who seems to me to have thought clearly at this point, not his critics.

As to 2). G must at least entail eternity, indestructibility, self-sufficiency, and these, the inconceivability of nonexistence; hence if this inconceivability is not conceivable, neither is G.

Therefore, be the inconceivability of nonexistence conceivable or not, G cannot be conceived as in C).

As to 3). To conceive something as existent is to have some idea of an experienceable state of affairs in which it would exhibit itself as existent; to conceive something as nonexistent is to have some idea of an experienceable state of affairs in which its nonexistence would be exhibited. But no experience could establish even the slightest probability of the nonexistence of God, because, since any state of affairs which would amount to the nonexistence of God would be a possibility which must be prevented from realization for God to exist, his existence would thus be made in conception to depend upon the nonrealization of this possibility, a dependence which contradicts the existential self-sufficiency entailed by G. Thus to admit such a possibility is to admit that G's existence is impossible, contrary to C).

As to B). In spite of Kant, I do not believe an ideal can have a clear and consistent meaning, yet be (for all we can know) incapable of existing. I believe that there are ambiguities or inconsistencies even in the regulative use of the classical idea of God which cannot be overcome without at the same time removing the grounds for denying a constitutive use also. And in fact neither science nor philosophy has found much regulative use for Kant's version of the idea of God.

A version of B) is the notion of a 'limiting concept' (like 'perfect lever'), an approachable but unreachable limit of thought or action. But the divine perfection, as Anselm defines it, cannot even be approached. There remains always an infinite gulf.

I submit: D) is the most intelligible of the four ways of classifying the property *G*.

A common objection is, Yes, *if* we think God, we must think Him as existing, but must we think Him? Well, if we are like the animals and do not even raise the question of God, then of course we need not answer this question; but if we are philosophers, we will raise the question, and then only one answer is logically tenable, the affirmative one. In addition, even the animals, though they cannot explicitly 'think' God, must in some way (this follows from the definition of *G*) relate themselves to Him, and they cannot relate themselves to *G* as nonexistent, for this is nonsense. So this objection, which Windelband, for example, seems to plume himself upon, is not so very cogent, after all. It is obvious from reading them that both Anselm and Descartes were in a position to deal with it.

Anselm's greatest weakness is his failure to dispose of positivism, A), in satisfactory fashion. And with his Neoplatonic view of the meaning of G, he could not have been cogent at this point.

Here is another version:

(1) It is possible consistently to conceive of an individual ('God') as such that none greater can be conceived.

(2) It is possible to conceive of an individual which could not conceivably have failed to exist.

(3) Such an individual (as in 2) must be greater than one which could conceivably have failed to exist (Anselm's Principle).

(4) It is conceivable that no God (defined as in 1) exists.

(5) Hence the idea of God (defined as in 1) becomes the contradiction, an individual such that (1) none greater can be conceived, and yet (2, 3, 4) such that a greater can be conceived. But according to (1) the idea is consistent. Hence the four premises cannot all be correct.

(6) To escape contradiction, at least one of the premises must be negated.

Negation of (1) and/or (2) constitutes positivism; negation of (3) conflicts with the intuitive discrepancy between contingent existence and unsurpassable excellence. On this intuition there has been, through the ages, a large measure of agreement among theologians. Thus negation of (3) is implicitly positivistic also. Negation of (4) is a priori theism. It removes the contradiction. Premises (1) and (2) are theistic 'meaning postulates'; they postulate only conceivability. Premise (3) is a corollary of a metaphysical meaning postulate explicating part of the content of 'contingent existence', that it connotes dependence, insecurity, surpassability.

To insist upon (4) is to render theism unintelligible. Meaning postulates in this unique case cannot be neutral to all individual existence; they make the divine existence either necessary or impossible. (4), though atheistic, implicitly begs the question against the conceivability of God, and thus the distinction between positivism and atheism cannot be maintained, except in this sense: atheism is the naive or unwitting form of positivism, positivism the sophisticated form of atheism.

The most crucial phase of the argument is what I call 'Anselm's Principle', the incompatibility of Greatness with conceivability of nonexistence, i.e., with contingency. This may be symbolized as

$$N(p^* \rightarrow Np^*) \text{ or } N\sim(P^* \& \sim Np^*)$$

> The proposition affirming the existence of the unique x which is Unsurpassable strictly implies its own necessity; it cannot be merely contingently true.

This principle is affirmed and justified in the first two sentences of the great third chapter. The point is not simply, "Thou dost in fact exist, and therefore also necessarily," but rather "since the only form of existence appropriate to thy definition is necessary existence, therefore [barring an irrational, though in our time fashionable, assumption that necessity *de re* and *de dictu* are radically independent, an assumption which makes sense at most where conditional, and not as here unconditional, necessity is in question] the only kind of truth which the central religious belief could have is necessary truth." From this it follows that necessary falsity is the only way in which it could fail to be true if it has any meaning at all.

It has been asked whether $N(p^* \rightarrow Np^*)$ means that the necessity of p is deducible from p. It is certainly deducible with suitable meaning postulates, and without some such postulates one has no determinate proposition to deal with. To explicate the meaning of 'Greatness exists' is to rule out the notion that its nonexistence is conceivable. A proposition whose denial is not consistently conceivable is a necessary proposition, and no proposition is consistently conceivable if what it asserts is inconceivable.

Another, more modern, way, less close to Anselm, of putting the point is this: the statement, *Deity exists,* implies that we are all God's creatures, and even possible worlds are merely His possible creatures; hence the statement, *Deity does not exist,* implies that we—and possible worlds—neither are nor could be anything of the kind. These, therefore, are not two factual hypotheses—they are two languages, two systems of metaphysics, two competitors for the task of elucidating what we can and cannot mean by any of our basic conceptions. They concern, not 'what are the facts?', but 'what is it to be a fact?'. They concern what Heidegger calls Being, the 'ontological', not the merely 'ontic'. The category of fact, not any particular application of the category, is the issue. *Prosl.* II is a poor text for this reasoning. I even think it difficult to imagine a much worse one. A greater blunder by so great a man might be hard to find.

It is worth noting, as Koyré remarks, that we have no knowledge whatever of Gaunilo's judgment after he received the *Reply.* (How many textbooks and histories fail even to tell us that there was a reply!) For all we know, Gaunilo changed his mind concerning the force of his objections.

20. Proslogium II, III, *and Anselm's Principle*

Of all the men of genius who have tried to divine Anselm's essential point from *Prosl.* II alone, not one, it seems, has ever arrived at the true formula, the genuine Anselmian Principle, that *what is conceivable as nonexistent is inferior to what is not thus conceivable.* The derivation might run as follows. *If* one accepts *Prosl.* II as valid, i.e., admits that what exists is greater than what does not, and that therefore absolute Greatness must exist, one may then go on to argue that an existence which is thus deducible must be necessary existence, since otherwise one would have something both logically necessary and logically contingent, a contradiction. To suppose the validity of *Prosl.* II is therefore to admit that the existence, lack of which would contradict Greatness, is not simple, but necessary, existence. Hence 'the existent is better than the nonexistent' must *in this case* become, 'the *necessarily* existent is better than the nonexistent'. However, Greatness must equally be better than the contingently existent, since contingency of existence is a defect. So what we really have is that the necessarily existent is better than the contingent, whether existent or not, and also, as is obvious, better than the impossible, or necessarily nonexistent, since anything is better than the last. Thus the distinctive point about Greatness is that it is better than anything contingent can possibly be. This is the principle of *Prosl.* III, the essential principle of the Proof. It is derivable from *Prosl.* II *only* on the supposition that the reasoning of *Prosl.* II is *valid;* and yet to see this validity one needs the Principle. Until we know that God's existence is deducible, we do not know, from anything said in *Prosl.* II, that it must be necessary existence which is in question; and until we know this we cannot know that it is deducible. Deducibility and necessity come to the same thing. Hence we must have necessary existence in mind throughout. This, however, is the procedure of *Prosl.* III.

If the preceding paragraph is correct, the historical procedure of making *Prosl.* II the definitive statement of the Proof was an excellent way to make reasonably sure that the main point of the two chapters taken together would be missed! To refute *Prosl.* II, taken by itself, is easy enough, since so taken it seems to misuse the idea of existence; yet this does not refute *Prosl.* III, which turns not upon ordinary or contingent existence, but upon a contrasting modality of existence. And no parade of ordinary things, as existing nondeducibly or contingently, has any direct relevance, save by contrast, to the question of the extraordinary thing of which it is known that it could not exist merely contingently, because we can see, directly and indirectly (and in many ways), that this is a defective and limiting mode of existing, incompatible with Greatness.

Was there any justification or excuse for the implied claim of nearly all the Argument's opponents that by refuting *Prosl.* II, they had disposed of *Prosl.* III? They might defend themselves as follows: "You seem to say above that *Prosl.* II is valid if and only if *Prosl.* III is so; but then their validity is equivalent, and to disprove one is to disprove the other." My answer: I am not speaking in both cases of formal validity but, with respect to *Prosl.* II, of cogency relative to the meanings which key terms are likely to be given. If existence means general existence, it cannot as a universal rule be taken as a conceptual predicate. One must discern in 'divinity' the requirement for a formally, i.e., modally, unique type of existence in order to grasp the unique deducibility of existence in this case. It is not that God is conceived as too good to be nonexistent, but that He is conceived as too good to be *conceivably* nonexistent, to be *capable* of failing to exist. With all other individual things this impossibility of failure to exist does not come into question at all; only with God. It does indeed follow that if one adequately understands the meaning of Greatness, one understands that God is conceived, if at all, as too good not to exist, but only because He is conceived as too good to be even possibly nonexistent, and what could not be so is not so. However, all this is contained in *Prosl.* II only through an aspect of the meaning of Unsurpassable Greatness which is not in that chapter explicated for the purpose in hand. *Prosl.* II, therefore, could have put the critics in touch with the points they had to refute only if they were already aware of all that *Prosl.* III makes explicit (even then, not fully explicit, since the *Reply* carries the explication further). But if the critics had seen all that, they would also have seen the irrelevance of their contention about (ordinary or simple) existence not being a deducible predicate. Of course it is not; Anselm in effect not only admits but insists upon this.

As someone has remarked, the reasoning of *Prosl.* II suffers from the ambiguity in 'X is thinking of something Unsurpassable'. Does this mean, he is thinking of something which *is* Unsurpassable—in which case, is not existence presupposed rather than proved? Does it mean, he is thinking of something which *would,* were it to exist, be Unsurpassable? In that case, that the something does not exist seems no contradiction—at least, not for the mere reason that the something lacks a certain merit attaching to existence *in its merely ordinary meaning.* For why not take the Unsurpassability as hypothetical, a characteristic which something might have were there to be such a something? If there is no such something, then indeed nothing *is* Unsurpassable, but still we have, it may be claimed, the consistent idea of what it would amount to if something were of this kind. *Prosl.* III, however, shows that this hypothetical way of dealing with Greatness is illogical, since even the bare conceivability of not existing is a defect, and one which *could not be removed by existence,* for *what is conceivable remains so, no matter what exists.* Thus the modal argument of *Prosl.* III protects the apparently nonmodal reasoning of *Prosl.* II, but only by showing that it is implicitly modal.

Even an admirer of Anselm ought, I think, to admit that *Prosl.* II was, at best, a highly misleading first presentation of his case. Contingency is a weakness in a much clearer sense than is mere nonexistence. Unless a thing exists, there are no properties of the thing; and while we may say that at least the idea is there, and that the nonexistence of its object is a weakness of the idea, the trouble is that we seem then to be talking about the properties of the idea rather than of its object. We seem to be committing the 'homological fallacy', making the universal an instance of itself. (However, see Part Two, Sec. 21.) But taking contingency as the defect, we can then compare in thought a necessarily-existing and a contingently-existing thing, and decide which must be greater; then, seeing that the former is greater, since (among many reasons) its existence involves no dependence upon anything but its own essential nature, we deduce that if the Supreme is conceived as existent at all, it must be conceived as necessarily existent, i.e., as *not conceivably* nonexistent. But if we try to add, 'yet perhaps it does not exist' we are simply saying, "perhaps the inconceivable is true." And then indeed we are talking nonsense, or at least we are using 'inconceivable' in a loose sense, whereas the strict sense is what the reasoning requires. For the merit which the Supreme must be conceived to have is strict impossibility of nonexistence, not some fake substitute. Anything with less than this strict impossibility will be inferior to anything with it, and so its denial is incompatible with Greatness.

Thus the reasoning of *Prosl.* III is incomparably more powerful—though less simple—than that of *Prosl.* II, and, therefore, the *'locus classicus'* for the Argument (to speak with one of the many reference works whose miserable treatment of this topic I have had the misfortune to read) is precisely not the earlier but the later chapter.

Detached from its context, *Prosl.* II seems at best no more than an inconsequential truism. The God of religion cannot by the worshiper as such be taken as nonexistent: for to worship something and yet recognize it as a mere fancy is not possible. But this by itself is trivial enough, for perhaps one need not and if intellectually honest will not worship at all! It is quite another thing to discover that not simply the supposition of the *actual* nonexistence of 'God' contradicts the religious use of the term, but even the supposition of the conceivability of this nonexistence does so. For then, not only can the person with faith not conceive the unreality of the object of faith, *no one can do so,* with or without faith. What a world of difference! (And think of taking nine centuries to arrive at what Anselm had said plainly enough.) The worshiper can know that unbelievers cannot be discussing the idea of God at all. They may be using the word, but they cannot have the idea. For the idea forbids the value *false* and admits only the value *necessarily true*. One may deny that there is any such idea, may—with Gaunilo—say that there is perhaps but a word (or an emotive meaning only), but the moment one goes beyond that, and tries to separate the idea, admitted as such, from the truth of the idea, one is in Anselm's grip, so long as logical rules are obeyed and one understands his definition.

Moreover, since the existence of God is the existence of a universal power, infinitely important to all that is or can be, the discovery that this existence is either necessary or inconceivable means that an entire system of metaphysics is the one or the other. Any corollary of the existence of God is also necessarily true, or else necessarily false (or nonsensical). But these corollaries are the whole of metaphysics, the basic axioms of philosophy. This, too, the magnificent doctor saw, or partly saw.

The notion that we can find God, or the absence of God, by picking among the stones of particular facts, is on the face of it foolish; but Anselm found the precise logical reason: God is not conceivably a fact at all (so far as the bare necessary truth that he exists is concerned). The facts are by definition neutral to this—as to any—necessary truth. (Only the actuality of God is factual. But it we could not expect to prove or disprove since it is incomparably richer than all we can distinctly perceive or imagine.) The evidence for God's existence is then wholly intellectual and spiritual, not sensory. Anselm proved that it must be so, and that, in consequence, the whole of metaphysics must derive its logical structure from this necessity. Has there ever been a greater discovery?

If there be a way of rescuing *Prosl.* II from the charge of grave ineptness, if not sheer fallacy, I have not in almost a lifetime of reflection been able to find it. Here I agree with Malcolm. But the modal argument of *Prosl.* III seems to stand entirely on its own feet, and to need no help from the previous chapter. Here also one may agree with Malcolm. There remains, however, the Findlay paradox, and the necessity of resolving the ambiguity between 'none greater' and 'nothing greater'.

The best that one can do with the *Prosl.* II version (taken by itself) seems to be as follows: to think of Greatness is to think of something as *at least* as superior to any unactualized possibility as the corresponding actualized one is. However, this is but a rough analogy, since the sense in which a contingent actuality can be superior to its unactualized possibility is not at all the same as the sense in which the necessary existence of deity is superior to any unrealized possibility, whether that of deity (which would be contradictory) or of anything else. Rather, deity surpasses all other things by the very sense in which its logical 'possibility' is to be taken—namely, as equivalent to its necessity. And the reason, not quite seen by Anselm, is that *this* individual existence is expressible purely conceptually or abstractly. Only God could 'adequately know all things', for example. In this abstract idea, the uniqueness of the divine existence is already contained.

But, on that basis, we cannot well deny that either (Findlay paradox) the divine reality is itself abstract (logically empty) or else (solution overlooked by Findlay) it is not exhausted by its mere individual existence, but has a further definiteness which is genuinely additional to its logical possibility and is therefore contingent. And so it appears once more that

Anselm's main mistake is in his idea of God itself, not in his proof.

Moreover, Anselm cannot escape the difficulties of his Neoplatonic idea so easily as Barth seems to imply when he argues that Greatness is not a description of deity but a mere rule for our way of thinking about deity, a mere negation that anything could conceivably be greater. For the positive nature of God which escapes us not only cannot be known by us to be necessary, it cannot even *be* necessary. The only rules that make sense about 'necessary' imply that its referent must be abstract, so that even the 'description' which God Himself could give of His 'essence' must be logically weak. Hence the *admission of divine accidents* is obligatory.

There is another consequence of these rules: if God, merely as such, merely as omniscient and the like, can be necessary because—though only because—of His extreme abstractness, then so can 'world as such', as merely 'whatever, other than Himself, God knows'. For this is equally abstract. Thus the 'contingency of the world' would become that of this world, not of there being *some* world or other.

The question of the ontological proof is simply this: what way of thinking about contingency should we adopt, and what are the consequences of this adoption? Our decision will implicitly determine an entire metaphysics. Neither Anselm's way, nor that of most of his critics, has much to commend it, so far as this writer can see. We need a fresh start.

21. *Definite Thought Is about Something*

If a man is thinking about fairies and upon being asked what he has in mind replies, "a mere idea," he may be further asked, of what is it the idea? The man could, however, reply: "I am thinking of the world process as productive of all sorts of things, and of the legends of fairies as views about what this process could be imagined to turn up." The Unsurpassable, however, could not conceivably be turned up, and therefore there can be no factual failure to turn it up, either. There is nothing at all to think about, under the name of God, unless just God Himself. It is a unique case, in which to think (consistently and more than verbally) about a certain kind of individual, and to be in real relation to the one possible such individual, as really existent, is a distinction without a difference. All attempts to find an intelligible difference fail. Few indeed even try to tell us what the intelligible difference might be; they content themselves with repeating the bare words, "God may not exist." In all other cases, we can explain the sort of thing we mean by a negation of existence; here we cannot.

We can, however, explain, in innumerable ways, what we mean by 'God exists'. It means, for one thing, that we are fully known, and cannot in the everlasting future ever be unknown, hence that our previous lives are registered where neither moth nor rust doth corrupt and where thieves do not break through nor steal. To say that this is *not* so, however, has no intelligible meaning, since we cannot conceivably experience the noneverlastingness of the factual content of existence. We have to live and think *as though* the past were indestructibly real, for otherwise 'fact' would have no definite meaning. 'God' merely makes this necessary idea more intelligible, that is all. And so with other ideas which we must have: they are all summed up, focused, united, made sense out of, by the idea of God. What is 'added' is only the more complete intelligibility. God is not (except in the how of His actualization) a fact among facts, but any fact as differing from nothing only through a love which sways and registers all occurrences.

It is to be noted that the only Faith that Anselm's Proof justifies is faith in God as greatest conceivable being. People's judgment as to what exalts God over all others may differ at many points. Our task is to distinguish much more carefully than the Saint did between the truly self-answering religious questions and all others. His glory is to have discovered that there are those of the former type, and that they are all corollaries of two questions: What does 'Unsurpassable' imply? Are the implications consistent and definite enough to be capable of truth?

22. *The Proof and Pantheism*

Is Anselm's argument, as Weber alleges, 'pantheistic'? This much-abused word has a wide spectrum of meanings. If it connotes the Stoic-Spinozistic view that all things follow necessarily from the eternal divine nature, then the relations to the Argument are as follows. If the necessary reality we prove is taken to be God in His concrete actuality, for instance, God as knowing that you and I exist, then so are we (and all things) necessary. For if we could have failed to exist, then God could have failed to know our existence, since one cannot know as existing what does not exist. As Husik has shown, this is why Spinoza, following Crescas, was a Spinozist. The only escape from such Spinozism, while using the Argument, is via the frank recognition of the Findlay paradox, and the acceptance of its resolution in neoclassicism. The

Argument, by deducing existence from an abstract definition, proves that the necessary in God must be but an abstraction from His total reality.

Of course we shall still have another kind of 'pantheism', if the word is used very broadly. God, as knowing all things, includes them somehow as contents of His knowledge. In addition, if things were simply 'outside' God, there would be a greater reality than God, God and the world. (Deny that this is in some way greater and you merely deny that the world has any value whatever. And on that basis you could not know what 'value' means.) Pantheism in this sense is simply theism aware of its implications. But obviously the very point of 'God exists necessarily' is that other things exist contingently; therefore, when Spinoza denies contingency altogether he is not improving upon Anselm, but is merely cutting off the branch of meaning on which the Anselmian idea must perch. However, the abstract-concrete paradox shows that classicism (the denial of contingent states to God) is a logical blunder equally whether it takes the pantheistic or the theistic form. Apart from that blunder, there is indeed no real issue between theism and pantheism. We all exist in the divine being, as St. Paul said. What more could a pantheist want, if he renounces necessitarianism (and determinism)? We are in the free, partly-contingent divine life with our own contingency and freedom. (That this is possible means that the divine life does not consist in mere 'power', mere control, but has also a passive aspect, as all life indeed must have. Lequier, Fechner, Varisco, W. P. Montague, E. S. Brightman, and Whitehead are among those who have defended this view.)

23. *Some Recent Criticisms of the Proof*

The validity of our position may be tested by considering some recent criticisms of the Anselmian argument, particularly as the argument is presented by Malcolm.[16]

(a) The 'second argument' (from necessary existence as a predicate) is held (Allen, Abelson, Penelhum) to imply the principle of the 'first argument', that existence is a predicate, which, as Malcolm himself says, is invalid. Yet that existence *in the one case of Perfection* is a genuine predicate is quite compatible, as we have seen, with its not being so elsewhere. The critics are indeed right in holding that existence must always have a contingent aspect, for it implies a step from the abstract to a particular concrete case and thus a passage from one logical type to another—a passage, moreover, in the direction of greater definiteness, since the concrete instance must have further qualities not specified in the predicate that is being considered. That such a step in its particularity should be entirely necessary would be sheer contradiction. But the ontological Proof, when employed in a neoclassical system, need not take this step to be necessary.

Consider any predicate, H: if it is actualized in a certain way, or by a certain concrete instance, it is always possible to conceive it as actualized in another way, by another instance. If H means human, or 'rational animal living on the earth', there might have been such animals different in each case from any which have actually existed. There might also have been no human animals at all; but this is a further

---

[16] See *The Philosophical Review,* 70 (1961), for articles by R. E. Allen (pp. 55-66), R. Abelson (pp. 67-84), T. Penelhum (pp. 85-92), P. Henle (pp. 93-101), and G. B. Matthews (pp. 102-3).

point which, if we abstract from the sort of predicate being considered, and let H stand for predicates in general, is not deducible from the mere contingency of particular instances.

Thus we have:

(1) H is actualized somehow, it might have been actualized otherwise; also it might have been unactualized.

(2) H is actualized somehow, it might have been actualized otherwise; but it is not true that it might have been unactualized.

What contradiction or absurdity is there in (2)? There are propositions whose denial is inadmissible; how do we know that none of these is existential? It cannot be merely because of the type difference between predicate and instance; for we have just shown that this difference is compatible with necessary existential statements, provided that they limit themselves to saying that their predicates are actualized somehow, without specifying how, or in what particular instances.

That divinity is a predicate with no more than one possible concrete instance, so that the necessity of the divine existence refers to a unique concrete actuality, is indeed logical nonsense. No actuality can be necessary. Findlay is here correct, the conclusion aimed at in the classical proof was in reality disproved. But suppose that 'divine actuality' means a *kind,* not a unique instance, of actuality. Would it follow that God is not individual? Yes, if *individual* means a single determinate actuality. And this is precisely what is at issue between those who hold a substance theory of personality and those who hold the Buddhist-Whiteheadian or event theory. According to the latter, an existing person is a sequence of actualities, several per second presumably (in the human case), not one of which, unless the first one, is necessary to the individual's being himself. (Leibniz held the contrary opinion, but his view has its penalties.) At each moment, I have the capacity to be actualized the next moment in more than one way. And since in the case of an uncreated being there could be no first actuality, we may drop the qualification, 'unless the first one', and say that God could have been Himself even though every actuality in or by which He has existed had been otherwise. (There are, of course, innumerable theologians who deny the applicability of the concept of personality in this sense to God, but there are others who admit it, and a refutation of the Proof can be general and inclusive only if they too are taken into account. This has never been done, to my knowledge.)

(b) Here is the place to consider Abelson's contention that there is not a single idea of 'God', but a loosely-connected family of ideas. This is plausible, but it is also fair to say that only two of these ideas are relevant to the Proof: the paradoxical one which takes the necessary exist-ence of divine perfection to mean a necessary yet unique actuality, and the other which takes it to mean the necessary realization of an individual divine nature in *some* suitable actualities or other, *which* actualities being a contingent matter. Either (1) Divine perfection is necessarily realized in the very actuality, or in the very manner, in which it is realized, *or* (2) it is necessarily realized somehow, in some actuality or actualities able to realize it.

Corresponding to these two views are two concepts of perfection: (1) a being than which none could conceivably be greater, not even the same being in another actual state; (2) a being than which none could be greater except the same being in another actual state. Only (2) escapes the absurdity of a necessary particular actuality, yet it too furnishes a premise for the Proof. For an individuality necessarily actualized somehow is superior to one which merely happens to be actualized. The critics deny this, but on poor grounds. One way to put the Argument is as follows: in religious terms, 'God is perfect' means that He is the appropriate object of total devotion, so that all concern, even all interest, has Him for its object. But the interest in the 'possibility' that He might not have existed at all—does that have God as object? Any interest in a situation alternative to God would violate the Great Commandment of total devotion. So it can only be contradictory to recognize a being as perfect in the religious sense, yet as existing contingently.

(c) One critic (Allen) grants that within religious language it is scarcely permissible to speak of the nonexistence of deity. And he suggests that one might argue that, outside such language, the question lacks meaning and cannot even be discussed. But then he doubts if this proves anything, since we have to have rules for dealing with languages in general, or with language as such. With this last point I agree. And it is possible, as we have seen (Sec. 16) to set up rules for the ontological argument.

Those who say that 'existence', taken on the one hand as a predicate, and on the other as not a predicate, can have no true analogy or common meaning should also, by parity of reasoning, deny that 'truth', as analytic and as synthetic, can have common meaning. The parallel is very close. *Truth* in the one case is a relation of correspondence between language and extralinguistic fact, in the other an intrinsic property of a portion of language itself. For this reason some philosophers do indeed reject 'necessary truth', and offer 'validity' instead. Certainly there is an important difference between the two sorts of correctness of statements. But nevertheless 'correctness' is common to them, and similarly 'actualized somehow' is common to necessary and contingent existence. Both forms of existence imply 'capable of being actualized otherwise', but only in the contingent form is 'capable of being unactualized' also implied.

What logical difficulty is there in this?

Factual truth and validity have this, among other things, in common, that both valid and true propositions are always mutually compatible (both among themselves and with each other). And indeed, valid propositions are virtually contained in every true proposition (also in every false one), and are a part of what is affirmed in them. Similarly, the divine individuality or existence is in some way contained in every individual, affirmed when it is affirmed, but not denied when it is denied. The critics of the Proof must, it seems, reject this analogy altogether. And so far, they do not show any awareness that this is what they are doing. The fault lies chiefly with theologians, or with theists who have failed to furnish a reasonable analysis of 'necessity' which connects it with logical rules exhibiting the relation between necessity in language systems and in reality.

Analytic truth in an extensional or interpreted language is also a sort of correspondence, for it corresponds to every possible object. It is the universally tolerant form of correspondence, just as analytic falsity is the universally intolerant form. The divine existence alone is compatible with any other existence you please, including that of any genuinely conceivable devil.

(d) The plausibility of the Proof is said to depend upon confusing necessity *de re* and necessity *de dictu,* necessity in things and in discourse (Allen). Thus, to exist, God might need to have the property, existing necessarily; but still, the assertion that anything has this property remains contingent. Yet it is arguable that the relation between the two meanings of necessary is closer than is here seen. What can be meant by 'necessary, *if* it exists'? The intelligible meaning for objective or extralinguistic necessity is, 'realized no matter what possibility is actualized'. Thus a "necessary thing" is one required by every possible thing, and this can be so only if it is somehow constitutive of everything. If it be thus universally constitutive, then any language which permits us to deny the statement asserting it allows us by implication to deny simultaneously every positive assertion. And this can only be a defective language. Where necessity is meant, as the Proof intends, unconditionally, there the *de re* and *de dictu* forms of necessity should be taken as coextensive. See p. 122(1).

(e) Someone (I do not now find who) has contended, against Malcolm, that the meaning of existence must remain the same, namely contingent existence, existence as not a predicate, no matter what sort of evidence is relevant to establishing it. Thus 'round-squares do not factually exist' is necessarily true, even though it is known by analysis, not factual observation. But this overlooks the point that contradictions not only cannot be factually true, they also cannot be necessarily true. They are necessarily *neither* factual *nor* necessary. Thus the meaning of 'The contradictory cannot exist' takes 'exist' in a modally neutral sense, not in the sense of 'contingently exist'. This modally neutral sense is precisely that in which the second 'exists' in 'perfection necessarily exists, therefore it exists', takes 'exists'. And the meaning of the whole sentence is, perfection is necessarily actualized, therefore it is in truth actualized, i.e., present in some concrete actuality or other; or equivalently: necessarily (and therefore truly) some actuality is perfect (possesses adequate knowledge of the totality of the actual, and views it with ideally appropriate appreciation, etc.). 'Some actuality' has here a neutral meaning, implying an instance of concreteness as such or in general, which instance is, in addition, an example of the property, 'belonging to the life of a perfect individual, than which none could be greater (except itself), and which could not be unactualized'. Where is there any logical confusion here?

(f) Is existence ever a 'real' predicate? Mr. Allen's rendering of this Kantian expression is, a term which predicates of a thing more than that it is a (concrete) thing. 'Actuality' is surely no such predicate, for it can only say that something actual is actual. But 'actualizes perfection, which in any possible state of affairs is actualized somehow', is a real predicate, for only divine actualities can possess it. And it is inherent in the meaning of divine perfection that there must be some such actualities, correlative to whatever nondivine things exist.

(g) A necessary god, it is held, must be extremely abstract, and so not the God of religion (Abelson). But, since the abstraction 'necessarily actualized somehow', means, necessarily concretized somehow, and since any concrete state embodying perfection must be worthy of worship, the God proved to exist is indeed the God of religion, but the God of the religion of any and every being capable of worship. One's own religion and one's own God involve personal elements extrinsic to every general proof or argument. But it does follow from the sense of the Proof that there must be some such personal elements in every case.

(h) Henle contends in an ingenious way that there is (except on certain Neoplatonic assumptions) no contradiction in combining necessary existence with perfection 'in some respect only' (supposing that there is none in combining it with perfection in all respects). It is clear from what has been said above that this is incorrect. Only that can be necessary which is infinitely tolerant, in *all* essential respects, of alternative possibilities, absolutely free from competitiveness in its requirements for existence. Imperfection (even in some respect only) is always competitive, this degree instead of that, or my imperfect aims prevailing instead of someone else's. God's essential role alone collides with no other. Coincidence with modality itself, flexibility as unbounded as all positive logical possibility, this is the prerequisite if existence is to avoid selecting among possibilities. The assumption here is hardly the 'Neoplatonism' to which Henle refers; for it is not the classical idea of perfection at all.

I am surprised that so thoughtful a writer as Henle could think it significant that Anselm did not bother to explain why Gaunilo's perfect island analogy is irrelevant. What Anselm saw was that God exists necessarily, not because He is perfect in His kind, but because His perfection is His 'kind', and because, being individually unique, divine perfection is not in the usual sense a kind at all. On the contrary, 'island' is such a kind, and because it is, 'island uniquely perfect as such' lacks definite and consistent meaning. Individuals of specific kind, such as islands, have to be identified by relatively specific descriptions, and finally by pointing to some individual taken as given; hence they are all alike wholly contingent. God escapes such sheer contingency because His identifying characteristic is as universally relevant, and in this sense as abstract, as any idea whatever.

The only sense in which the comparison of one individual with another can point the direction toward God's necessity is this: some individuals have greater flexibility, greater capacity for preserving significant self-identity through wide changes than others. Hence their identifying traits can be less specific. But to transcend contingency, the traits must be absolutely nonspecific, and only God has such traits. As for an island, it is scarcely an individual at all; for its identity through change is chiefly a fact for the observer, rather than for the island as a whole, or for the molecules and the like which constitute it. Only by stressing the combination of intrinsic self-identity with flexibility, as a mark of the superiority of (say) high-grade human beings to low-grade, or to any island (unless it be thought of as conscious), can we get any very direct light on the meaning of necessity as inherent in perfection. If the island is conceived as conscious, and this consciousness as individually perfect, unsurpassable, then it will be equivalent to God, save with the addendum, 'composed of earth or rock, or something of the sort, and surrounded by liquid'. And the combination of the two ideas is not obviously consistent. How can an argument be refuted by showing that a vaguely parallel argument from a doubtfully consistent, or even rather obviously self-contradictory, premise would arrive at a doubtfully tenable conclusion? No mode of reasoning could be safe, under such conditions! Only if the credentials of 'divine perfection' to constitute a coherent conception are at least far better than those of 'perfect island' has the argument any cogency. But its credentials are incomparably better. For one thing, we know of innumerable believers in God, and no well-documented instance of a single individual who ever believed in such an island, or gave evidence of seriously thinking it could be believed in. Is this because the islands we know have defects or limitations? Rather it is because simply being an island is already a vast limitation, so that to get rid of defects we must in thought get rid of the character of being an island, or anything much like it.

(i) In spite of Anselm and Malcolm, an eternal reality—it is said—may yet be contingent (Penelhum, Plantinga). We are even told that "for all we know" electrons may always have existed. But physics denies persistent self-identity to electrons! Besides, since there is no conceivable positive empirical test for the capacity to exist without having come into being, nor yet for existing everlastingly, only logical analysis could show this, and according to my understanding, only necessity, the impossibility of not existing, could give support to such notions.

It is worth dwelling for a moment on this matter. Becoming is the pervasive principle of reality; anything which does not become must have some very unusual features indeed, and so must anything which endures forever. The controversy over evolutionism arose partly from the failure on the part of many to see that the burden of proof is upon the assertion of ultimate constancy, not inconstancy. What keeps species stable is at least as much a problem as what makes them change. Natural selection is no less powerful as a conservative and stabilizing force than as a destructive or creative one. But in the end, nothing is simply and always stable, except that which could not possibly be otherwise. To survive change (as an individual or species) requires a positive capacity; to transcend all change (by preceding and surviving each and every change) requires absolutely infinite capacity to resist or assimilate change. And absolutely infinite capacity cannot just happen to exist, for it must be the principle of possibility itself; and since 'principle of its own possible nonexistence' is nonsense, there can be no such possibility. True, these points may seem less than self-evident. But are their denials any more truly self-evident? I am only urging that the Ontological point of view is no mere sophistry, but an important perspective upon the whole of metaphysics.

One difference between philosophers is in what they expect to understand and how much they want to understand it. When told that an ungenerated and everlasting being might yet exist (or fail to exist) contingently, some of us ask, what understanding could one have of such contingency? The ordinary sources of intelligibility for 'contingent' are totally lacking in this alleged case. On a few (to some of us very reasonable) assumptions about becoming or creativity, viewed as the perpetual resolution of the partial indeterminacies constituting the future as such, one can see why all things which come to be must do so contingently. Even the contingency of the laws of nature, as Boutroux showed long ago, can be illuminated in this way. But this mode of rendering contingency intelligible fails utterly with an ungenerated and immortal being. What other mode of explicating contingency have we? So far as I can see, none; we have as sole resource the complete inhibition of all curiosity in the matter. Something might exist always and forever which might also forever fail to exist—period. Ask no further questions. No prior indeterminacy would have been resolved, no choice would have been made, no dice thrown, no random process of nature eventuated thus and thus—no! Merely, it is, perhaps, so, and yet it might always have been otherwise. Is there so much instruction in bare words? They remain merely words, and therefore of no real use, until we can connect the supposed ideas with other ideas in some intelligible way. I suggest, therefore, that if Henle had thought with more acute and persistent curiosity about contingency he would have been able to carry further his generous concession that there *may* be a good meaning in 'necessary existence'. It is that meaning which forms one end of the triple disjunction by which *contingent* is to be understood, the disjunction: totally exclusive, partially exclusive, totally nonexclusive, of (positive) possibilities; or the disjunction: completely intolerant, partially tolerant, completely tolerant, of all specific possibilities. Complete tolerance is the same as absolute adaptability, unlimited power to preserve self-identity and integrity in response to any world whatever. And this is again only a way of looking at cognitive infallibility. Only knowledge can take a form correlative to anything and everything (the strictly unknowable being the same as nonentity). But only states of *perfect* knowledge can fully actualize this principle.

For the reasons sketched, should we not side with Anselm in thinking that only the necessary and perfect can be eternal?

(j) One critic appeared to think that a consequence of this—that nothing eternal can be created—is absurd. But why? True, 'the world', in its most general possible meaning, can be eternal; but in this meaning it is not a particular or individual creature, but merely the bare eternal truth that there are creatures, none first or last in time. And this is an eternal truth only if it be necessary, that is, if God *must* create without a temporal beginning or end of His creation, or if He could not produce a first or last creature. (This contradicts His perfection of power only if some other being could conceivably produce such a creature. But Aristotle may have been right in thinking that an absolute first or last is here unmeaning.)

(k) It is contended that independence of existence is not uniquely good (Abelson). For bare existence substitute 'actuality', or *how* the predicate exists, and Abelson's point is an understatement. The divine actuality must be the most sensitive to influence, and in that sense the most dependent, of all. But for its being somehow actualized, no matter how, divinity must be conceived as wholly independent, and *this* independence is entirely a merit. Maximal independence and maximal dependence, the one for abstract, and the other for concrete, aspects of individual existence, these are essential to the worshipful perfection of deity.

(1) A shrewd point is made by Matthews when he notes that Anselm puts God above anything we can conceive, so that if, as Malcolm does, one identifies 'conceivable' and 'logically possible', then God must be logically impossible. The answer is that God is above the *humanly* conceivable, but not above all conception, including His own. In 'nothing greater is conceivable', however, there is no reference to human conceiving; even God Himself cannot conceive another greater than Himself. Only this second, unrestricted use of 'conceivable' is equivalent to logical possibility.

There is, nevertheless, a danger of injustice to Anselm in substituting for his 'not conceivable as not existing' the Cartesian 'necessarily existent'. For then the query seems to arise, are we here dealing with necessity only *de re* or also *de dictu*? But if the nonexistence of deity is strictly inconceivable, it cannot be legitimate to assert it, and atheism is ruled out. The strictly inconceivable cannot be said to be even possibly true.

(m) A sixth recent critic of the Ontological Proof assumes that by perfection we have to mean an actuality uniquely defined by its 'completeness'.[17] Of course it is easily shown that this leads to difficulties. (See Part Two, Sec. 8.) But we do not need to identify perfection with completeness in this sense. Perfection is *modal* completeness, not actual completeness. No individual actuality can be absolutely complete (exhaustive of possibility), though it can be relatively so, i.e., inclusive of all that is in fact actual, and this by necessity, or in any possible state of affairs. Individual potentiality, however, can be absolutely complete, i.e., inclusive of all that is logically possible, *qua* possible. God's modal completeness means that He *could* have, not that He *does* have, any predicate or compossible set of predicates whatever. In this is no impossibility. (Of course, God does not have the anger of the angry man as the man has it, but He has all its actual value, by intuiting with absolute adequacy the man's experience, and that of those at whom the man is angry. He thus has all, in the way of value, which the man has, and incomparably more. And so with other

---

[17] Leslie Armour, "The Ontological Argument and the Concepts of Completeness and Selection," *The Review of Metaphysics,* 15 (1961), 280-91.

actualized predicates.) Our critic has merely resolved, without noticing it, the ambiguity in 'none could be greater' in favor of the interpretation, 'even itself in another state', rather than in favor of, 'except itself in another state'. The latter interpretation avoids the difficulties to which he points, and actually strengthens and clarifies the connection with necessity. Thus he proves nothing against our version of the Proof.

(n) Still another opponent of Anselm (See Bibliography, Zabeeh) reminds us that if the premises of the Ontological Argument are tautological rather than factual, that is, if they are "true in all possible worlds, then . . . they are vacuously true, since they then tell us nothing particular about our world." He fails to note that by 'the existence of God' is not properly intended a *particular* feature of 'our' or 'the real world', but only the following purely *general* status of any world whatever: if that world exists God created it, and if it does not but could exist, God could create it. Naturally, then, 'God exists' is true in any possible world; this is one of the many ways of putting Anselm's point. The divine existence cannot stand or fall with that of a certain world, a certain contingent thing, for this would mean that the creator was a mere creature! God's mere existence is not, in the proper sense, 'particular' at all, though His actuality is indeed so.

Our author is right in this: the essential question is whether the idea of God, or that of necessary, uncreated, yet individual, existence, makes sense. Anselm frankly assumed that it did. Against the positivistic contention to the contrary a supplementary argument is needed, and here

Anselm was in trouble. But with a different philosophy the supplementary argument can perhaps be provided.

Professor Zabeeh's willingness to beg the question he purports to discuss is rather breathtaking. Thus, leaning on Hume: "it is a brute fact that every object or impression which exists, *could* cease to exist." We have Hume's (and Professor Zabeeh's) word for it. However, I have read Hume, and I find no evidence for the assertion, just the assertion itself (nor does Kant help here). Again, leaning on Ryle: "since things do happen to wear out, it is rational to expect them to wither away . . ." And so the weakness of the creatures is *ohne weiteres* attributable also to the creator! By what rule of logic? It cannot be God who is here referred to!

It is said, rightly enough, that the mere use of a word cannot establish a necessity. However, as Findlay (and others) have shown, it is the meaning not just of 'God' but of the attitude of worship, that it refers to a not conceivably surpassable being. Since no such being could be a contingently existing thing, i.e., a mere creature, either worship is self-contradictory (rather than merely mistaken), or its object exists necessarily.

Still another attempt to throw new light upon the ancient controversy is Nicholas Rescher's argument (see Bibliography) that the real point of the Proof is this: to understand blue one must have experienced blue and insofar must know that there is (or has been) such a thing; similarly, to understand 'God' one must have had religious experience, but then one will also know the reality of the object of the experience. Rescher's proposal implies that deity, like redness, is a special sort of thing, to know which requires a special sort of experience. As though the universally immanent were only in certain corners of reality or experience, rather than everywhere! Also the author suggests that the definition from which the old proof started was insignificant from the standpoint of religion. But the definition grew out of religious experience as such, or as worship. God is defined as worshipful because beyond all possibility of rivalry. Yet this definition (when the false interpretation of 'none other' is corrected) has an intelligible content which presupposes no special sort of feeling or sensation. *Willingness* to consider the definition on its merits, to genuinely inquire into its logical implications, does require that one should *not* be in the emotional state in which many philosophers find themselves. But the analogy with color sense is about as misleading as it well could be. No willingness can help the colorblind man to experience color; but sufficient willingness may enable anyone endowed with intellectual powers to see some point in the modal form of the ontological proof. To appreciate the full value of the Proof *is* a religious experience, but to see that it offers a legitimate, and not merely silly, line of inquiry it is only requisite that one think with honesty and scholarly care about the matter, going behind the textbooks to sources in writers who have themselves really meditated upon the problem, and not merely copied others, and noting how these writers have dealt with the objections which have become standard. Professor Rescher does not show any sign of realizing that, precisely for religion, God is a principle and not a mere fact, the contrast between the creator and the creatures being indeed a supreme abstraction for all religious persons. The more abstract and universal a factor of reality, the less must one have *this* experience rather than *that* to be able to think the factor. And the bare existence of deity is strictly universal, hence any experience will do, if it is sufficiently reflective and unconfused concerning its own content. What Anselm proved and meant to prove is that, assuming that the man of faith understands himself, the Fool deceives himself; not as the color-blind man by being simply unable to encounter the thing, but by being unwilling, or emotionally unable to try, to think a certain concept. God in His bare existence is not a mere special quality, but a Universal of universals, the Form of forms. He is infinitely more than this, true enough, but He is not less than this. And this suffices for His necessary existence. Even Thomas admits that all creatures in some sense know their Good, and that this is God. But man reflects upon his good; he cannot be simply unable to know it. The problem is one of self-understanding on the deepest level. The color-blind man can understand himself perfectly on *that* level.

One final attempt to discredit Anselm's argument as reformulated by Malcolm runs as follows.[18] Malcolm gives the proof in the following steps: (1) If God does not exist His existence is impossible; (2) if He does exist His existence is necessary; (3) His existence is either impossible or necessary; (4) His existence is not impossible; (5) hence it is necessary. Huggett objects: since Malcolm derives (1) from (a) 'If God does not exist, He cannot come into existence'; and (2) from (b) 'If He does exist He cannot have come into existence, nor can He cease to exist'; it follows that (3) has no more force than the disjunction: either (p) 'God is nonexistent and cannot come into existence', or (q) 'He exists and

---

[18] W. J. Huggett, "The Nonexistence of Ontological Arguments," *Philosophical Review*, 71 (1962), 377-79.

cannot have come into existence or go out of existence'. But then one cannot refute (p) by arguing that God's existence is at least conceivable, for (p) says only that *coming into* existence, not that existence, is inconceivable of God. However, the argument has here been oversimplified. Huggett is assuming that what does not exist and could not come into existence nevertheless *might* always exist, need not be logically incapable of existing always. But this implies an ultimately total divorce between modal and temporal status which an Anselmian ought to reject. What does 'might' mean in nontemporal terms? The intelligible reference is to possible happenings, whose antecedent conditions—at least if we go back far enough—do not uniquely determine their specific outcomes. A critic of Anselm needs to show that contingent existence is intelligible in some terms other than those of coming to exist and ceasing to exist. I am not aware that this can be done. A concept whose representation in reality is contingent is one which can be conceived as realized and also as unrealized; but if both these conditions are conceivable, how can a transition from one to the other be inconceivable? You may answer, because the thing is defined as eternal. Yes, but this amounts to conceiving two alternative states of 'eternity', and saying that it is logically mere chance, arbitrary fact, which one is realized. But is it not *in time* that accidents, contingencies, can occur? The theory which the anti-Anselmian is implicitly adopting is that of happenings, accidents, in eternity. The difficulty is not merely etymological. We have no experience of contingency in nontemporal form; the notion is at best wholly controversial. Save to refute Anselm, it performs no function that I at least can see. Hence it is question-begging. Known contingency is confined to things capable of a genesis.[19]

The very meaning of 'eternal' is dubious apart from necessity. Without necessity, nothing could establish the least probability of eternity; one would have to wait, so to speak, forever to see if the thing did always go on existing. Nay more, since the future is potential rather than actual, even God Himself could not know that He would never cease to exist, except by knowing this to be impossible; and how He could at the same time know that His nonexistence was (is?) eternally conceivable is utterly beyond even the vaguest imagining.

Someone may wonder if the foregoing commits us to the view that either the world has had a beginning or it exists necessarily. It does so commit us, but we must not overlook the ambiguity of 'the world'. Either it means the universe in something like its present state, or at least with the same or similar laws, or it means some universe or other (created and nondivine reality) with no matter what laws. The former is reasonably viewed as contingent and also as having had a genesis; the latter I suspect is necessary and has neither come into being nor can cease to be. It is not, however, a rival to God, for it is not save in the vaguest sense an individual, but only the exceedingly abstract class, nondivine individuals in general. The rivalry which the definition of God excludes is with individuals. Besides, the universe is always wholly embraced and surpassed by the divine knowledge. Its eternity only means that God can never lack a universe to know.

Anselm has other ways than the one just considered of

---

[19] C. Hartshorne, "Real Possibility," *The Journal of Philosophy*, 60, No. 21 (1963), 593-605.

discriminating contingent from noncontingent conceptions. Thus if a concept requires a certain composition of parts, how could this be necessary, why not some other parts, in some other arrangement, instead of the specified composition? What Anselm was groping for but did not entirely attain was a theory of arbitrary, exclusive, or competitive conceptions as distinguished from those wholly without arbitrary, exclusive, or competitive features. Becoming as essentially involving real additions to the definiteness of reality must be arbitrary or competitive (why not some other addition?). So with any particular arrangements of parts. So also with any particular degree of imperfection (and all imperfection is a matter of degree). Imperfect things compete for existence, they get in each other's way, to some extent, and their precise degree of merit is always accidental. Their partial intolerance for other forms of existence is one of the implications of their lack of perfection. But absolute perfection (unsurpassability by another) is no arbitrary degree of value, but the measure of all degrees; and its absolute capacity for dealing with others enables it to be the wholly tolerant, noncompetitive accompaniment of all competitive existence (including God Himself in His contingent or competitive aspects).

Huggett's little essay is one more in the long line of melancholy examples of how eager people are to refute Anselm's reasoning, rather than to learn from it.

None of the above-mentioned critics seems to worry about the paradox of a God to whom existence can at best, as they seem to suspect, be imputed by sheer faith, but whose allegedly possible nonexistence must even more definitely remain a matter of sheer unfaith, or negative faith. Obviously God could not know His own nonexistence, and if no one else could either, then it is simply unknowable. It has been proved above (Sec. 15) that an imperfect mind could know the existence, but not the rlonexistence, of a perfect mind.

Nor do any of the critics seem to have a clear notion of why existence is in general contingent, unless it is merely because predicates are abstract or indeterminate and existence is concrete and definite. But it is only actuality which is fully concrete, only the particular how or state of concretization; the mere *that* is always at least relatively abstract, and in the supreme case before us, it is infinitely abstract, and indeed as abstract as genuine or positive possibility itself. Hence the type distinction is here entirely concentrated in the gap between the *that* and the *how*. Like so many dichotomies, that of 'essence and existence' is simple-minded, and obscures a real distinction. 'Existence' is merely a relation of exemplification which actuality (any suitable actuality) has to essence. Thus I exist if my identifying personality traits (gene structure, the property, first-born son of— and—, or what you will) are somehow embodied in actual events, no matter which. Upon the legitimacy of applying an analogous, but even more radical, distinction to the idea of God depends the possibility of an ontological proof. Most theists have not been in a position to make this application. The central difficulty with the proof, the partly unconscious ground of opposition to it, and probably even of the positivistic denial of the concept of God itself, is in the oversimplified form of this concept presented by classical or neoplatonic theism.

Philosophers should, at long last, give due heed to the manifest difference between *existence,* the mere abstract truth *that* an abstraction is somehow concretely embodied, and the *actuality,* the how, of the embodiment. The ignoring of this duality in nearly all discussions of the ontological problem is a marvelous instance of how even centuries of prolonged controversy, involving almost an entire learned world, can still leave a point unnoticed by anyone. The possibility of such collective blindness helps to make intellectual life exciting. There is always a chance of seeing clearly for the first time what implicitly many have been looking for.

The failure to distinguish between existence and actuality seems also responsible for the notion that one might collapse Anselm's second argument into his first, and refute *Prosl.* III by refuting *Prosl.* II. The contention that the second argument presupposes the first has been strongly put in Germany by Henrich (see Bibliography), who, in his detailed and, in some respects, admirably careful analysis of the fortunes of the Argument in modern philosophy, stresses the difficulty of explicating 'necessarily exists' unless it means that (simple) existence is contained in the essence, and hence derivable a priori. But then the first argument should be sound, since simple existence is being treated as an attribute. What is missed is the distinction between being actualized somehow and being actualized precisely thus and thus. The latter can *never* be an attribute, but must be a concrete instance of the attribute, hence contingent; the former can in principle, or in one privileged form, be an attribute, the attribute 'exemplified in any possible case'. This is noncompetitive exemplification. Competitiveness is clearly an attribute (hypothetical dollars are hypothetical competitors, actual dollars actual competitors), and therefore noncompetitiveness, if there can be such a thing, is also an attribute. But, since it is competitiveness which gives meaning to nonexistence, the noncompetitive cannot not exist; it must be actualized somehow.

Henrich wrestles valiantly with the apparent abolition in the Argument of the categorial difference between a predicate and its realization, in other words the abstract-concrete paradox, and reaches the conclusion that the problem has neither been solved nor definitively shown to be insoluble. He is to be congratulated, for he is right on both counts, so far as the philosophers he discusses are concerned. He also lays down three conditions which a philosophy must meet to have the right to employ the Argument. It must have an idea of divine perfection; it must be aware of the radical difference in general between essence and existence; and it must be able to admit a spiritual reality (an *'eidos'*) quite independent of any act of thinking it. That a philosophy exists today which meets these conditions is a fact apparently unknown to this German author, even though, long before Whitehead and certain other non-Germans, some largely forgotten German thinkers (e.g., Fechner) could have met them.

It is strange that the author's otherwise magnificent erudition has not saved him from the traditional fault of limiting Anselm's reasoning to that of *Prosl.* II. For he imputes only the first argument, from simple existence, to Anselm, while the second, from necessary existence as a perfection, he treats as a post-Anselmian achievement! Thus the Gaunilo legend for the thousandth time poses as a piece of scholarship.

Does perfection not entail infinite existential tolerance or adaptability (the infallible can know *anything* whatever), hence absolute noncompetitiveness, hence the exclusion of nonexistence as meaningless or contradictory? If so, the

Argument is valid. Yet it takes no step in the direction of describing how, or in what actual concrete form, perfection is realized. The categorial or logical gap between essence and existence, which Henrich stresses, in the divine case becomes an absolutely infinite gap between abstract essence and/or existence, on one side, and concrete actuality on the other.

The trust in mere dichotomies was effectively criticized by Peirce seven or eight decades ago. But the lesson has yet to be learned. The 'cultural lag' in philosophy is great indeed. (Thus Henrich in 1960 does not know *Prosl.* III.) 'Existence' can have various positions short of full concreteness or actuality, but in one supreme case it must be as abstract as essence, and hence a priori. The comprehensive or universal contrast of idea or essence is with actuality, not with existence.

Against these authors I maintain: Anselm discovered, and really discovered, the modal uniqueness of the idea of God. What he overlooked, and nearly all his critics equally fail to see, is that, since actuality cannot be necessary, there must be a real duality in God, as in no other being, between necessary existence and contingent actuality.

24. *The Proof and the Other Theistic Arguments*

There is a final consideration. Philosophers all know that according to Kant the other supposed proofs for God fail unless they can resort to the principle of the ontological proof (that perfection and necessary existence are inseparable). Kant is believed to have refuted the principle, hence to have disposed of all the proofs in one blow. But did he refute the principle? True, he also accused the proofs of other weaknesses.

But in view of the disreputable history of the criticisms of Anselm, can we trust the criticisms of the other proofs? Admittedly, there is no one *locus classicus* to be compared to the neglected and scorned *Prosl.* III and *Reply to Gaunilo* (though the 10th Book of the *Laws* has perhaps some title to this honor, and it, too, is underestimated). Still, similar prejudices are involved, such as the belief that theism must mean either classical theism or classical pantheism, or the empiricist notion that a proof for God must be a posteriori. From the empiricist assumption it was deduced—essentially a priori and without any empirical nonsense of reading texts— not only that Anselm's proof was invalid, but also that the only hope of a proof other than the ontological would be in an inference from some sort of factual observation. In reality, the ontological is not the uniquely a priori proof; it is but one such proof. All the proofs, properly stated, proceed from ideas; but not all from the idea of God itself. And all show that we must either admit some basic idea to be absurd, or take it to be necessarily true, and admit also that this truth entails the necessary existence of the Greatest being. Unbelief is confusion or else belief is confusion. There is no third possibility.

Belief here of course means only belief in God. No special doctrine of any church or group is involved, unless it, or its denial, is deducible from the conceivability of Greatness. Such matters as Anselm's special beliefs about the Church, the Trinity, and the Incarnation are at best subsidiary to the main religious belief, belief in a God who is unsurpassably all that it is better to be than not to be, just so far as such unsurpassability is logically possible, and who is surpassable exclusively by Himself, so far as this mode of exclusive surpassability is possible. Beyond that, He is what He is, and there is little we can know about it except that *He* knows, and that what He knows is all truth. In what sense does He know? In just the sense in which it is better to know than not to know: infallibly, because this is possible and best, yet not completely and once for all with respect to actualities, because this is contradictory, possibilities for actualization being inexhaustible and therefore never exhausted, even by deity.

To the Anselmian theory that Christ must suffer so that man's offense against God could be pardoned without injury to the divine honor or justice we may object that an author who insists that the divine nature is for us ineffable and full of paradoxes ought not lightly to assume that the values which motivate God in His treatment of man will agree so precisely with the transcendentalized legalistic notions of a certain human society. Medieval notions of 'honor' and 'justice' may be absurdly inadequate or irrelevant to the cosmic and everlasting. God (in His necessary aspect) is 'whatever it is better to be than not to be': perhaps it is not better to be so concerned with legalities and prestige as the deity of *Cur Deus Homo* is represented as being.

Thus a weakness in Anselm's thinking is in the 'human-all-too-human' valuations on the basis of which he applies the above-quoted formula. The formula, however, transcends these applications and may, if properly construed, have independent validity.

Part Two

A CRITICAL SURVEY OF

RESPONSES TO ANSELM'S PROOF

PART TWO

A CRITICAL SURVEY OF RESPONSES TO ANSELM'S PROOF

1. *Anticipations of the Proof*

In a remarkable article, Prescott Johnson (see Bibliography) seems to succeed in showing that Plato's dialectic (in *The Republic*) as means to knowledge of the Good amounts to an ontological argument for the necessary existence of the Good. The lesser ideas are incapable of expressing the principle of order among themselves; in conceiving this order we are conceiving a supreme idea which therefore cannot be lacking in content for our thought. This is—says Johnson—the a posteriori element in Plato's reasoning. In effect, it is his refutation of positivism. The supreme reality is *not* inconceivable. (I would here depart somewhat from Johnson by remarking that the conceivability of something is a necessary, not a merely contingent or factual, truth and that it cannot, properly speaking, be known a posteriori. But I shall not attempt to relate this consideration to Plato's procedure.) The supreme reality is not to be treated as a mere hypothesis. Knowledge of it "requires no assumption," and "makes no use of images, relying on ideas only." In short this knowledge is strictly a priori. And no merely contingent existence could be thus known.

(Nor, I add, would it make sense to say of a contingent reality that it was "superior to existence," as Plato says of the Good. Only a reality existing in an underived and necessary fashion could be to all things as the sun is to life on the earth.)

Johnson correctly defends Plato's procedure against the Kantian criticism that the merely possible and the existent cannot differ qualitatively. In regard to the supreme conception, the *merely* possible is indistinguishable from the impossible. We have not to compare two states of the Good, one as nonexistent and the other as existent; for this is to treat the "beginning" or "principle" of all meaning, value, and reality as a mere possibility which might or might not be actualized. But if it can be so treated it is not the absolute principle at all, and the knowledge of it must be precisely the hypothetical knowledge which Plato contrasts with the highest knowledge.

Johnson does not discuss the relation of the Good to God. This is a difficult topic in Platonic scholarship. Perhaps one is fairly safe in saying that there are grave difficulties in either denying or asserting the identity of the Good with God. Moreover, when in the *Timaeus* deity is plainly under discussion, we again have ambiguity, for there we seem to confront two Gods, the 'eternal God and the God that was to be', or the Demiurge and the World Soul. I wish merely to suggest that Plato is wavering between classical and neoclassical theism, or between the view that deity is pure absoluteness or necessary existence and the view that deity is indeed absoluteness necessarily actualized somehow, but with the particular concrete how or actuality contingent and relative. What in Plato was an unresolved ambiguity, a wise restraint in the claim to settle basic issues, in his followers tended to become a premature and unwise resolution of the ambiguity. This unwise resolution, which oversimplifies the religious idea and gives it a fatal one-sidedness, has exacted severe penalties all through the history of thought. One of the penalties has been the failure to clarify the Anselmian problem in a permanently satisfactory manner.

It was a rather close anticipation of Anselm when Aristotle declared, "To be possible and to exist do not differ in eternal things."[1] But Aristotle came even closer:

For what is 'of necessity' coincides with what is 'always' since that which 'must be' cannot possibly 'not-be'. Hence a thing is eternal if its 'being' is necessary: and if it is eternal, its being is necessary.[2]

No eternal thing exists potentially. The reason is this. Every potency is at one and the same time a potency of the opposite; for, while that which is not capable of being present in a subject cannot be present, everything that is capable of being may possibly not be actual . . . And that which may possibly not be is perishable, either in the full sense or in the precise sense in which it is said that it possibly may not be. . . Nothing, then, which is in the full sense imperishable is in the full sense ['in respect of substance'] potentially existent (though there is nothing to prevent its being so in some respect, e.g., potentially of a certain quality or in a certain place); all imperishable things, then, exist actually.[3]

Some things owe their necessity to something other than themselves; others do not, but are themselves the source of necessity in other things. Therefore the necessary in the primary and strict sense is the

---

[1] *Physics,* III, 4. 203^b, 30. I owe this reference and the literal translation to my colleague A. P. Brogan. Oxford translation, "In the case of eternal things, what may be must be."

[2] *De Generatione,* II, 12, 338^a, 1-4.

[3] *Metaphysics,* IX, 8. 1050^b. 8-18. Trans. W. D. Ross.

simple; for this does not admit of more states than one, so that it cannot even be in one state and also in another; for . . . it would already be in more than one [if it were in all respects necessary]. If, then, there are any things that are eternal and immovable, nothing compulsory or against their nature attaches to them.[4]

Nothing is by accident perishable. For what is accidental is capable of not being present, but perishableness is one of the attributes that belong of necessity to the things to which they belong; or else one and the same thing may be perishable and imperishable, if perishableness is capable of not belonging to it. Perishableness then must either be the essence or be present in the essence of each perishable thing. The same account holds for imperishableness also; for both are attributes which are present of necessity.[5]

Certainly Anselm did reason partly as follows: To exist eternally is better than to exist with a temporal beginning or ending; hence God cannot be conceived in the latter fashion; but only that which could not not exist is intrinsically, or for an intelligible reason, without beginning or ending, secure in its eternity. As a Socinian theologian later put it, "that is eternal which cannot not exist." There is no other criterion for eternal existence, since one cannot wait forever to observe that a thing always goes on existing. Not even God Himself could know it in *that* way.

Actually Aristotle is superior to Anselm in some respects in this matter (save only that he did not turn his insight into a proof). For one thing, he makes a clear, and virtually neoclassical, distinction between eternity or necessity of mere *existence* ('in respect to substance'), and eternity or necessity with respect to *all properties* whatever. The former, he

---

[4] *Op. cit.,* V, 5, 1015^b, 9-16.
[5] *Ibid.,* X, 10, 1059^a, 0-7.

says, does not entail the latter. Precisely, and the neglect or underestimation of the former was the great error of classical theism, an error into which Aristotle himself fell, as is indicated in the next to last of the above quotations. The blunder was natural enough. There are: (a) things contingent or ephemeral both substantially, or as the individuals which they are, and also in the qualities not essential to their individual identity; (b) things (a thing?) existing eternally, necessarily, as the individuals which they are, but not eternal or necessary in all their properties or states; (c) as the extreme or pure case of necessity, things or a thing which could neither fail to exist nor ever in any way be other than it is. The superiority of (b) to (a) seemed clear to Aristotle (as it does to me); he apparently inferred that, by the same principle, (c) must be superior to (b). However, it is not the same principle at all. That it is better to be both contingent and necessary than to be contingent alone does not entail that it is best of all to be necessary alone. It is better for a saw to be both sharp and not sharp, the one in the blade, the other in the handle, than to be not sharp all over; but it is by no means best of all that it be sharp all over and have no handle. To lack necessity even of existence and be therefore wholly contingent is indeed a defect; but this is entirely compatible with its being also a defect to lack all contingent qualities and be wholly necessary. For, if the necessary as such is, as has been shown in this book, extremely abstract, a mere universal common factor, then to be purely necessary is to be purely abstract, totally lacking in concreteness, that is, richness of definite detail and variety.

True, Aristotle seems also to have reasoned: since 'actuality is prior to potency', the supremacy and ultimate priority must belong to a purely actual being devoid of potentiality for further actualization. But we saw in Part One, Secs. 4, 5, that this assumes an irrelevance of quantity to quality and also of incompossible values to the supreme value, which are anything but noncontroversial. I pass over Aristotle's suggestion that the supreme reality must be immune to influence by others, a typical piece of Neoplatonic scorn (is not Aristotle the first Neoplatonist?) for passivity, responsiveness, sensitivity to what passes in others.

In the above quotations the Stagirite not only makes an important distinction between two ways of conceiving necessary existence, but he also (1) gives reasons for identifying modal status with temporally limited and temporally unlimited ways of existing, the contingent having being at most for some time, the necessary always, and (2) with lucid, subtle reasoning shows that such temporal-modal status is itself in all cases necessary, so that the contingent and perishable could not have been necessary or imperishable, and the necessary and imperishable could not have been perishable. This is a form of the modal reduction principle; modal status, including that of nonnecessity, is itself always necessary. And here, two thousand years in advance, is the answer to Kant's charge that the ontological argument must assume that existence is, in general, a predicate, whereas in general it is not. Rather, either contingency (perishableness) or its negative, necessity, (imperishableness) is inherent in any predicate whatsoever: modal status is *always* a deducible predicate. (See the last of the quotations on page 142.) Kant's cultural lag on this point is two millennia. Surely Aristotle would have known what Anselm was talking about at least better than even the greatest of Gaunilo's countless disciples.

Since neglect of the temporal aspect of modality, or the modal aspect of temporality, is a major defect of the European tradition, it is an interesting question, which I hope to pursue elsewhere, why Aristotle failed so signally to communicate his insights at this point.

Of the long and shameful story of the underestimation of Jews by Christians (in our day by communists as well), one of the least shameful but still interesting chapters is the underestimation of Philo. It is easy to say that Wolfson has exaggerated Philo's importance; it is harder to find in medieval scholasticism a single statement about God—apart from the Incarnation and some points about the Trinity—which cannot be matched in Philo's own words. Practically the entire religious metaphysics of fourteen centuries (including both best and worst features) is definitely Philonian. That the divine existence is necessary is repeatedly stated, as follows:

"The virtues of God are founded in truth, existing according to his essence: since God alone exists in essence, on account of which fact, he speaks of necessity about himself, saying, 'I am that I am'.[6]

". . . the God who exists in essence, and who is duly thought of in respect of his existence . . ."[7]

". . . God who exists only in essence . . ."[8]

". . . He is full of himself, and He is sufficient for himself . . ."[9]

Here we have the idea of existence as an identity, therefore

---

[6] *Works of Philo Judaeus,* trans. C. D. Yonge (London, 1890), I, 282.

[7] *Op. cit.,* IV, 283.

[8] *Ibid.,* II, 28-29.

[9] *Ibid.,* p. 243.

necessary. Recognition of existence in this superior form of sheer self-existence is not indeed new with Philo, for—besides being in Aristotle—it seems to be as old as monotheism itself, since Ikhnaton expressed it nicely, "Thou of thyself art length of life, men live through thee." (And not of course men alone, as the grand old hymns make clear enough.) Thus the idea that God's existence could be just another case of existence in general has *always* been a failure to comprehend theism. It is three millennia out of date.

The unsurpassability or perfection of God is indicated by Philo as follows:

> It is impious to conceive that anything can be better than the cause of all things, since there is nothing equal to him, nothing that is even a little inferior to him; but everything which exists in the world is found to be in its whole genus inferior to God.[10]

> . . . the living God . . . is superior to the good, and more simple than the one, and more ancient than the unity . . .[11]

> His nature is entirely perfect, or rather God is himself the perfection, and completion, and boundary for happiness.[12]

I submit that these passages are at least as close to the *Proslogium* as anything in Augustine, who is usually cited in this connection. And they are about four centuries earlier! True, Philo apparently did not see that he had in such considerations the basis for a proof for the divine existence, but then neither did anyone else before Anselm. Augustine's proof from the superiority of reason to all but Truth, and the identity of

---

[10] *Ibid.*, I, 196f.

[11] *Ibid.*, p. 229.

[12] *Ibid.*, IV, 1-2.

God with Truth, is a version of what I call the epistemic or logical proof, not of the 'ontological', which must (if the label is to be of any use) be from the idea of God itself as intrinsically connoting necessity. Nor are proofs, such as Aristotle's, from 'degrees of perfection' to perfection itself ontological. To use the term so widely makes virtually any proof ontological. The essential idea is not of kinds of things, one kind implying another, but of ways of existing, and of one way as self-realizing and self-certifying, and as such alone appropriate to the all-worshipful being, hence either assertible or deniable on grounds of meaning alone.

A third (vague) anticipation, though not in our Western tradition, is found in the Taoist principle that the supreme reality (the Tao) is like water, completely without exclusive form of its own, but able to assume the form of any vessel. This makes deity a correlate of being as such, rather than one form of being instead of another. Such absolute nonexclusive flexibility or absence of competitiveness is, I have argued (in this book and elsewhere), identical with noncontingency. The principle is also suggested in the analogy employed by the ancient monists of India that space can take the forms of all the objects in space, and hence is not itself limited by any of these forms. The important thing is to see that the perfection of cognitive capacity, infallibility, is even more clearly without exclusive form, since by definition it must be able to express any form whatsoever (in knowing it). Anselm failed to achieve clarity at this point, and his Greek cast of mind made this inevitable. He was typically Western in exalting 'masculine' mastery, power, stability, control, being, absoluteness, while depreciating the feminine, yielding, passive, fluid—that is, becoming and relativity.

Taoism and Buddhism are closer to the truth here. But Jesus was perhaps closer still. God's sensitivity registers the fall of the sparrow. This occurrence is a modification of his sympathetic awareness. The absolute responsiveness of universal love is purely noncompetitive, hence in its bare existence wholly noncontingent.

All genuine thought about deity must, indeed, be close to the ontological proof. For it is blasphemous to think of God as merely an additional fact, however great, merely one side of a significant alternative, rather than as the soul of factuality itself and the very basis of all alternativeness, the potential registrant of whatever value or importance *eithe*r side of any disjunction can have, hence not subject to intelligible denial.

Ikhnaton (in spite of associating deity peculiarly with sun and sunlight) clearly thought of God as the strictly universal principle of meaning and value, measuring by His love all the forms of existence. He was the God of absolutely all creatures, not just of some. It is only a clarification of this to see that possibility itself must be expressive of the divine, and hence that the 'possibility of there being no divinity' formulates an absurdity.

The very notion of creator, introduced into philosophy in the *Timaeus*, implies the principle of modal equivalence just referred to. For if the reality of the Demiurge actualized a possibility capable of being unactualized then He must be Himself as much in need of a creator as anything else. Thus the Platonic, which is the oldest, formal proof for God breaks down if Anselm's discovery is a mere sophistry.

And yet no one formulated his Proof or anything much like it before he did. Esser, in his monograph on alleged anticipations of the Proof (see Bibliography), considers a number of pre-Anselmian proofs and rightly dismisses them as not proofs from the mere idea of God. Esser ignores Philo and the most relevant passages in Plato and Aristotle; but I incline to agree with him that before Anselm there was no Ontological Proof.

Anselm's formula for deity is perhaps less novel. Collingwood mentions some precedents in Boëthius, and he should have mentioned Philo and Augustine. (See Sec. 15, p. 250.) Nevertheless, here, too, Anselm remains distinctive. He alone puts sufficient emphasis upon the difference between greatest, or unsurpassed, *in fact* and *not conceivably surpassable.*

No one before Anselm gave so neat a formula for the divine excellence. Correctly interpreted, as to be sure he did not interpret it, it remains without a flaw, precisely as he stated it. I hold that this definition, and the deduction of noncontingency therefrom, constitutes the greatest single step forward in constructive metaphysics taken after Philo and prior to Leibniz. It is also the least understood, the most carelessly treated, by scholars.

2. *A Strange Story*

The history of discussions concerning the ontological argument might have been that of a collective inquiry into the validity of the reasoning of *Prosl.* II-IV, with reasonable account taken of later passages. This inquiry might also, after a few centuries perhaps, have led to the discovery of the abstract-concrete paradox as inherent, not in the Argument as such, but in classical theism, yet made more apparent by the Argument. All this might conceivably have happened.

What we find in fact is rather different: a story of prolonged debate largely, often exclusively, over the thinking of the fictitious Anselm of the Gaunilo tradition, that conveniently naive fellow who made his whole point in *Prosl.* II and added nothing relevant thereafter, in contrast to the historically demonstrable, keen-witted philosopher whose main point first appeared in *Prosl.* III, and was considerably amplified and carefully defended in still later discussions. And the last thing anyone saw clearly was the abstract-concrete paradox, the heart of the whole problem; the problem, however, not alone of the Proof, but of theism itself.

Such is the tale—'stranger than fiction', though in a sense about a fiction—which we shall now tell, partly in the words of some of the chief participants. The story has at least a happy ending, for it seems to show that the long-stretched-out farce is nearing its probable dénouement, and that the unconscious falsehoods about the magnificent doctor can scarcely retain their innocence, which has been their strength, much longer.

3. *Gaunilo*

Whatever the first commentator upon a philosopher may say, be it intelligent or otherwise, he will of course have been the first to say it. Moreover, as human nature is, the chances are that he will be praised for having said it (all the more if there is no other commentator for a hundred years). For his view will probably be a natural interpretation, or misinterpretation, of his subject, and for this reason, and also by the power of suggestion, others will, even more probably, say it after him. But he will always remain the 'discoverer'.

Such are the reasons for the fame of Gaunilo. Any very much better reasons the specialists in Anselm, so far as I know, have not detected.

The many signs of limited perspicacity in Gaunilo have been painstakingly detailed by Barth. I shall mention only some of the most important.

Was it smart, or was it not a little stupid, to 'point out' to Anselm—what the latter had not only admitted but insisted upon as integral to his theory—that all sorts of things can be conceived as nonexistent? Anselm not only accepted the empirical fact that we often think about nonexistent things, he had a theory, which is more than we know Gaunilo had, about *why* all things other than God are thus thinkable, or what constitutes the ground of their contingency. Should one then offer the bare truth of general contingency as basis for rejecting the Proof? This is common ground, and is quite compatible with viewing God as the great exception. By definition God is exceptional. Yet to this day, as in the pages of Gaunilo and Kant, reminders of the universal contingency of existence, apart from God, are supposed somehow—it is never quite explained how—to give the Anselmian pause! True, they might well give him pause had Anselm stopped his exposition of the Proof at the end of Chapter II. For only in III is the uniqueness of necessary existence made explicit.

Gaunilo is the originator of the logically bizarre idea, also still widespread, that the admission of God's existence as a fact must be the premise for any proof that He also exists necessarily. There is, unfortunately, some suggestion of this way of looking at the matter in the opening of *Prosl.* III (following, as it does, upon the alleged proof that God exists in *Prosl.* II): "thou dost exist so truly that thou canst not be conceived not to exist." But later passages, long before the *Reply,* and above all in the *Reply,* make manifest the principle (evident in itself to reflection): facts cannot determine what is logically conceivable; hence it is absurd to talk as though an inconceivability of nonexistence could depend upon a thing's existing in fact. *Necessarily* existing in fact? Then the thing could not but exist in fact, and there is no possible nonexistence to disprove by factual inquiry. Contingently? Then we have a contradiction.

What it comes to is that the idea of unconditional or strict logical necessity of existence never makes its appearance at all in Gaunilo's discourse. Only the words, 'cannot be conceived not to exist', are there, not what the words mean. (Those who have accepted the monk's refutation often fail to include either the idea or the words.) Gaunilo also betrays himself by talking as though the nonexistence even of ordinary things, or especially of oneself, may be inconceivable. This merely confirms, from the other end, his blindness to the modal concepts which are Anselm's preferred intellectual instruments. Of course, if there is no contingency, there cannot in any distinctive sense be necessity either—and vice versa. Over and over Anselm talks in modal terms, while Gaunilo never clearly does so. Where Anselm says, none greater can be conceived, Gaunilo speaks repeatedly about none greater, or greatest, *simpliciter.* He allows God hypothetical preeminence in the realm of actual existence, but not in that of possibility or conceivability. Accordingly, to ask, Does God exist? must be to ask whether or not some possibility logically prior to God happens to be actualized. But the Unsurpassably great, hence all-inclusive of actuality and possibility, self-existing no matter what else does or does not exist, can have nothing logically prior to it. It is that not to think which is to think nothing, and so not to think. This is Anselm's world of ideas. Gaunilo has not entered it, even for a trial run. Nor has he, Samson-like, pulled its pillars down from inside. He has not been inside, but only in a fragile and readily detachable antechamber.

The strongest objection to Anselm's procedure, never clearly seen by Gaunilo, concerns the apparent transition from abstract to concrete, from a brief verbal definition to the incomparable richness and beauty of the divine actuality. The pertinent question is whether or not existence and full actuality are in general coincident and equally concrete; and if not, whether they might not in God be exceptionally distinct and far apart (all aspects of God are somehow exceptional), so that the existence to be established by the Proof would be as abstract as the unprovable divine actuality is concrete. Had Gaunilo the faintest glimpse of this possibility? Have Gaunilo's admirers glimpsed it either? Yet is it not relevant, if our question is not merely, was Anselm justified in using his Proof to support *his* religious beliefs, but rather, could it justifiably be used to support some religious belief or other, and if so what? This is the more general question; intellectual progress takes its greatest leap forward when higher generality is attained. The fate of classical theism may in the long run be a picayune detail compared to the fate of theism as such.

Gaunilo is abundantly justified, and it is his most relevant point, in asking, Do we really have "the *idea* of that than which none greater can be conceived" (rather than merely the words)? We have seen (Part One, Sec. 4) the ambiguities and possible contradictions which must be looked to in trying to adjudicate this question. But these are logical questions and have nothing to do with particular perceptual facts, to the lack of which Gaunilo refers. If God's very existence were relative to particular perceptual facts, then He would not be God but an idol. The problem is one of meaning: is worship self-consistent, or is it either contradictory or too indefinite an attitude even to contradict itself?

Considering the reception which Gaunilo has had to this very day, one is moved to ask: has ever a commentator upon a philosopher so long and so much misled so many?

4. *The Scholastics: St. Thomas*

The reception of the Argument in the twelfth and thirteenth centuries was almost as odd as what happened in its inventor's own lifetime, or in the modern period. (In this section I am heavily indebted—and deeply grateful—to P. A. Daniels. See Bibliography I.) In the twelfth century the Proof was simply ignored, so far as our records go. Three conclusions have been drawn from this: all accepted the Proof, all rejected it, they were unacquainted with it. Daniels shows that the last is the most reasonable. In the next three centuries things were dramatically different. Fifteen authors refer to the Proof, of whom the following ten accept it: William of Auxerre, Richard Fischacre, Alexander of Hales, Bonaventura, Matthew of Aquasparta, Johannes Peckham, Nicolaus of Cusa, Aegidius of Rome, William of Ware, and Duns Scotus. Of these at least four, Alexander, Bonaventura, Nicolaus, and Scotus seem to have some appreciation of *Prosl.* III and of the true Anselmian Principle; the rest seem to be thinking largely or exclusively of *Prosl.* II. Albertus Magnus, Peter of Tarentaise, and Henry of Ghent take no position on the Proof; of these, only the first seems to have read past *Prosl.* II. St. Thomas and his disciple Richard of Middleton reject the Proof; Richard cites only *Prosl.* II, while Thomas refers (in five different writings) sometimes to this and sometimes to the following chapter; however, *where he is explicitly rejecting the Proof* (in the two *Summas*) *he mentions only Prosl.* II; and where he does mention the other chapter he, in my opinion, misconceives the relationship of the two.

We have then fifteen medieval judges, of whom at most five show that they have the Principle clearly and centrally in mind; one or two others exhibit some conception of it, and the rest, little or none. Of the five having the Principle (as Anselm did) clearly and centrally in mind, four accept the Proof, and the fifth takes no stand. Of the other ten, those who seem not to grasp the centrality of *Prosl.* III, six accept, two reject, and two give no verdict. Thus even where the Proof was taken at its weakest, still six found it convincing and but two rejected it; and where it was taken at its strongest, four out of five accepted and none rejected it. This seems to show the power of the Proof even when incompletely grasped, and its much greater power when fully grasped. It also shows the blighting influence of Gaunilo's inability to read beyond Chapter II.

Unfortunately, the example of Thomas has in the end outweighed in prestige all the others put together. Bonaventura's cogent rebuttal of Gaunilo's 'island' analogy has been passed over as though it had never happened, while the objections of Thomas have been treasured. Bonaventura may have been somewhat to blame for this. After grasping the true Principle, he attempted to improve upon it and, by a series of steps, reduced it to 'God is God; therefore He exists', thus, as Gilson says, "Simplifying the dialectic to the vanishing point."

How well did Thomas understand the Proof? He seems scarcely to have seen at all how the essential step of the reasoning is back from *Prosl.* III to *Prosl.* II, rather than, as admittedly Anselm seemed for a moment to think, in the reverse order. The key to the whole proof is the connection between perfection and the unique kind of existence which is essential, necessary, or self-existence. Thomas knows this connection in his own philosophy, but he denies Anselm's right to make use of it for an ontological inference. His reasons we shall consider presently; meanwhile, the point is that to *assume* that this must not be the reasoning is to beg the question. And Thomas in effect makes this assumption. He implies that we must first, as in Chapter II, prove that God exists, and then, as in III, infer that His existence is of the necessary type. But since the first step is not cogent, the whole Proof must be invalid. Accordingly, in refuting *Prosl.* II in the *Summa Theologica* (see below), he thinks he has disposed of Anselm's proposal. But this is not very perceptive, is it? Like contingency, necessity must be a property knowable a priori, the difference being that whereas from the modality 'necessity of existence' existence is deducible, from the modality 'contingency' it is not. How does this depend upon *Prosl.* II? By implying that it does, this most influential writer put—or seemed to put—the stamp of his approval upon Gaunilo's worst mistake, his failure to see that unless one can disprove the deducibility of 'imperfect' from 'contingent', [and hence (*modus tollens*) of 'noncontingent' from 'perfect'], he has not dealt the Proof any mortal blow.

An important feature of Thomas's attitude, which distinguishes him to advantage from Kant, is that he does not go to the unwise extreme of denying outright that God is immanent in our thought of Him. For, as he says, all creatures tend toward their good, and God is the Good of all goods. So all creatures are directly related to God and may even, if sentient, be said directly to grasp or experience God. Only, thinks Thomas, this is not a clear or cognitive grasp, as (in the case of the lower animals at least) seems obvious. Hence, runs the reasoning, we cannot use this immanence of deity in our experience as basis of a proof. We have to turn to features of created things, such as change or degrees of value. But if we cannot elevate our direct sense of the supreme Good into a premise for a theistic proof, what reason is there for thinking we can do better with other aspects of experience as means toward so exalted an objective? By scorning the nonsensory awareness of deity in favor of mere sense perception, Thomas is preparing the way for the débacle which theistic proof-making met at the hands of Hume and Kant. He is the greatest single preparer of this misfortune, and Anselm is the man who (properly read) could have prevented it.

Thomas goes part way with Anselm in admitting that of course 'the nonexistence of God', adequately understood, is contradictory. By means of other proofs we know that God exists in such a way that there is in Him no separability between essence and existence. So we do know this much about the essence of God, that 'existence pertains to it' (Spinoza), but we know this not immediately and directly (through faith) as Anselm seems to imply, but in a slightly roundabout way via knowledge of the creatures. Is this really so wise as many have held? Science has been probing ever more deeply into the creatures, and in some ways they seem more mysterious than ever. And if it be said that for a theistic argument we need only understand the creatures as such, the bare idea of a creature, then that almost comes around to the Anselmian position, that one goes a priori from an idea to the divine existence. For what does it add to say, 'the idea of a creature known to exist'? Would a merely possible creature, or the concept of creature, be independent of deity? The creator is necessary if creatures are to be so much as possible! Why should not the self-understanding of faith be at least as reliable and pertinent here as our ability to see into the meaning of 'change', for instance? If change does, in principle, involve deity, then to understand change as such (existent or not) is to understand deity to that extent.

There is, however, another way of interpreting Thomas's attitude. Perhaps what he obscurely felt was that Anselm had no right to presume that he did understand his faith. And here, I believe, Thomas would have been correct, for no classical theist as such can understand himself, since his identification of God with the absolute, or with 'pure actuality' and self-sufficiency, is a confusion. But if this is Thomas's ground for rejection, then he is himself in the same fix as Anselm. For he too was a classical theist, guilty of the confusion in question.

In the light of the foregoing, the Thomistic objection that we do not know the essence of God, and hence cannot make use of its oneness with His existence, is both relevant and not relevant. It is relevant in that Anselm (like Thomas) was committed by implication to a notion of the divine essence (the total absence in it of relativity or becoming) which could not be right. The objection, however, is not relevant, in that Anselm's definition, when its ambiguities are left open rather than resolved classically, is merely the religious truism that it must be impossible for God to have a conceivable superior. It is here faith which defines the religious question; and this question turns out to be self-answering. To tell us to turn away from faith to the mere existence of the world is to forbid us to take as our problem the rational testing of faith. It is to allow unfaith to set the question. But in metaphysics he who sets the question largely determines what answers can be given.

[Refutation of *Proslogium* II]

It seems that . . . as soon as the significance of the name God is understood, it is at once seen that God exists. For by this name is signified that thing than which nothing greater can be conceived. But that which exists actually and mentally is greater than that which exists only mentally . . . Therefore the proposition *God exists* is self-evident.

On the contrary, no one can mentally admit the opposite of what is self-evident. . . . But the opposite of the proposition *God is* can be mentally admitted: The fool said in his heart, There is no God. . . .

I answer that a thing can be self-evident in either of two ways: on the one hand, self-evident in itself, though not to us; on the other, self-evident in itself and to us. . . . Therefore I say that this proposition, *God exists*, of itself is self-evident, for the predicate is the same as the subject, because God is His own existence, as will be hereafter shown. Now because we do not know the essence of God, the proposition is not self-evident to us, but needs to be demonstrated by things that are more known to us . . . namely, by His effects . . .

Perhaps not everyone who hears this name God understands it to signify something than which nothing greater can be conceived. Yet, granted that everyone understands this name . . . nevertheless, it does not therefore follow that he understands that what the name signifies exists actually, but only that it exists mentally. Nor can it be argued that it actually exists, unless it be admitted that there actually exists something than which nothing greater can be thought; and this precisely is not admitted by those who hold that God does not exist.[13]

That what the fool says in his heart cannot be self-evidently wrong is correct only if 'self-evident to us' means, self-evident to any human being able to say the words with a feeling of understanding them. But this is a rather crude view; Anselm's discussion of the point in the *Reply* is subtler. A mere feeling of understanding what we say is not a guarantee that we do understand. Logical relations need not be obvious at first glance to everyone. I fail to see that Anselm had anything to learn from Thomas in this respect. Similarly crude is the disjunction, knowing the essence of God (which in classical theism meant knowing all that God is) and knowing nothing at all about His essential nature, not even that it excludes a conceivable superior. No more is needed for the proof!

The last two of the quoted sentences obviously have relevance at most to the nonmodal form of ontological proof. Even in that reference we seem to be given little but a dogmatic denial that the proof is valid.

A writer who admits that the Thomistic distinction between the two ways of being self-evident does not furnish a good premise for refuting Anselm offers a different passage as turning the trick:

No difficulty befalls anyone who posits that God does not exist. For that, for any given thing, either in reality or in the understanding, something greater can be conceived, is a difficulty only to him who concedes

---

13 *Summa Theologica*, Qu. 2, Art. 1, trans. Fathers of the English Dominican Province. Second and revised edition. (London: Oates & Washburn, 1920), Part I, p. 20.

that there is in reality something than which a greater cannot be conceived. (*Summa contra gentiles.* I. 11.) [14]

The significance of this is explained as follows: atheism may be put in a disjunction: either (a) there is nothing than which a greater cannot be conceived, or (b) there is such a thing, but 'in the understanding only'. Even if we grant to Anselm that (b) is contradictory, still—it is urged—(a) is certainly free from contradiction. But let us see. (a) may be offered (a^1) as a contingent, or (a^2) as a necessary truth. If contingent, there must be no logical impossibility in the existence of a not conceivably surpassable being. But since, according to (a), there is in fact no such being, its nonexistence is also taken as possible. It would follow that the not impossible existence of an unsurpassable being could only be contingent existence. But, as we have seen, a contingent being could not be unsurpassable. Thus (a^1) is contradictory. Atheism is no contingent truth. There remains (a^2). A necessity that, given any being, a greater can be conceived implies the logical impossibility of an unsurpassable being. This, however, is the positivistic not the atheistic tenet. Moreover, if a concept is logically impossible, this can be no mere truth of fact. Modal statements themselves, as Aristotle saw, have the mode of necessity, not of contingency. We conclude that atheism (the merely factual denial of God's existence) is not saved from contradiction by Thomas. Neither the divine existence nor the divine nonexistence could be a mere fact, i.e., a contingent truth. The question is conceptual not observational. Anselm correctly located the theistic

---

[14] G. B. Matthews, "Aquinas on Saying that God Doesn't Exist," *The Monist,* 47 (1963), pp. 472-477.

issue in the logical landscape. Did Aquinas? If indeed the tenability (or at least initial plausibility) of positivism was his objection, this never becomes very clear in his discussion. (And Gaunilo had already made the point quite as definitely.)

In Thomist circles one often encounters some such formulation as the following:

The idea of God, the infinitely perfect being, does include existence, but only ideal, not real, existence. Therefore, it would be a contradiction if I were to think the infinitely perfect being without thinking it as existent, because I would be affirming and denying existence in the same order *(Ordnung);* however, a contradiction is not present if I attribute ideal existence to the most perfect being, while leaving the question open whether it exists in ontological reality. (Lehmen, *Lehrbuch der Philosophie,* Freiburg, 1901, B.II, p. 547, quoted in Esser—see Bibliography.)

This way of talking makes me wonder how stupid I perhaps am, for I can make no clear sense at all out of what is said. What is 'ideal existence'? Merely that something is thought to exist? (For a legitimate distinction between conceptual and real existence in terms of the contrast between the *that* and the *how* of actualization, see Part One, Sec. 18.) But then a necessity to think infinite perfection as (ideally) existing is the necessity to think that it is thought to be thought to exist—and so on. And besides, the defect with which Anselm's second Argument (against which Esser quotes the above passage) shows that Greatness cannot be combined is the conceivability of failing to have real existence. A being whose not really existing is conceivable is inferior to one whose not really existing is inconceivable. Therefore it is precisely real existence which must be taken as inseparable from Greatness. What special merit would there be in ideally existing necessarily while really existing contingently? And if one can only think divinity as really existing then atheism is not thinkable, and only a positivist can reject the conclusion of the Argument. Is that what Lehmen and Esser are trying to say? Then let them for pity's sake say it. For it is painful to be unable to find sense in what must seem sensible to the many who write in this way.

When it is suggested, as by Esser (p. 36), that while we must think God as existent, still we may also think that he perhaps does not exist 'in the real order', I derive from such formulations only this: we *must* think divinity as existent, but we may also think the proposition, 'divinity may not exist'. Once more my intelligence fails to arrive at a coherent meaning. Is it our old friend, 'God exists necessarily if he exists at all'? This seems implied by Esser (p. 35). As I have argued in various places, this expression also means nothing clear and consistent. If it only means, God either fails to exist or else exists eternally and without dependence upon any other existent, then I think (a) it misuses 'necessarily', and (b) it implies a radically unintelligibile form of contingency, i.e., that something is but might not have been, yet no cause enabled it to be or furnished its real possibility. To be able not to exist yet to owe one's existence to no actual condition is a combination of ideas that gives me for one 'logical seasickness'. In addition I have given many reasons for denying that the 'nonexistence' of something is conceivable unless the something is competitive, partly exclusive, in its essential nature, so that another thing could exist in its place. But there is no 'place' of God which another thing could occupy instead of Him. I deny that an argument can be refuted by formulations so full of paradoxes as those just considered.

On the whole, Thomism sheds not much light and some darkness on our topic.

5. *Descartes, Gassendi, and Hobbes*

According to Gilson, it is not provable that Descartes had read Anselm. He may have taken the Argument from Thomas, which would explain why he put it in the weaker form of *Prosl.* II until, under Gassendi's prodding, he came to his own version of the second and stronger argument. In any case, there can be no doubt that he knew some of the usual objections —this being the least that everyone has known who ever discussed the subject! On the whole, Descartes did not reach Anselm's level in this matter. He did, however, furnish an interesting reason for taking the idea of God to be logically admissible. If we doubt, and hence realize our cognitive imperfection, it must mean something to talk about a degree of clarity and distinctness which excludes all doubt, that is, the divine clarity, infallible or omniscient awareness. But Descartes weakened his argument here by claiming—or seeming to claim—absolute clarity and distinctness for us human beings in certain cases.

[Echo of *Prosl.* II]

Being accustomed in all other things to distinguish between existence and essence, I readily believe that existence can also be disjoined from the essence of God, and that God can therefore be conceived as not actually existing. But on closer study, it becomes manifest to me that it is no more possible to separate existence from the essence of God than . . . the idea of a mountain from that of a valley. . . .

Nor may it be objected that though it is indeed necessary to grant that God exists, provided the supposition has antecedently been made that God possesses all perfections and that existence is itself one of these perfections, the supposition is not . . . itself necessary . . . It is not indeed necessary that I should at any time be dwelling on the idea of God. None the less, as often as I may be concerned to entertain the thought of first and sovereign being, . . . I must necessarily attribute all perfections to Him . . . And as soon as I take notice that existence is a perfection, I am thereby constrained to conclude that this sovereign being truly exists . . .[15]

[Echo of *Prosl.* III?]

In the idea or concept of a thing existence is contained, because we are unable to conceive anything except under the form of an existent; that is, possible or contingent existence is contained in the concept of a limited thing, but necessary and perfect existence in the concept of a supremely perfect thing . . . Necessary existence is contained in the nature or concept of God.

Hence it is true to say of God that necessary existence is in Him, or that God exists.[16]

Descartes's critic, Pierre Gassendi, in the following 'objection', gives a lucid anticipation of Kant's principle that existence is not a predicate (or, as Gassendi puts it, a 'perfection').

[Refutation of *Prosl.* II]

You (Descartes) place existence among the Divine perfections, without, however, putting it among the perfections of a triangle or of a mountain, though in exactly similar fashion, and in its own way, it may be said to be a perfection of each. But, sooth to say, existence is a perfection neither in God nor in anything else; it is rather that in the absence of which there is no perfection.

---

[15] *Descartes's Philosophical Writings,* selected and translated by N. K. Smith (London: Macmillan & Co., 1952), pp. 243, 244. [The stronger form of Cartesian ontological argument is omitted from this edition.]

[16] From *Second Replies to Objections,* trans. T. V. Smith and Marjorie Grene. In *From Descartes to Kant* (Chicago: The University of Chicago Press, 1933), pp. 161-62.

. . . that which does not exist has neither perfection nor imperfection, and that which exists and has various perfections, does not have its existence as one of the number of its perfections, but as that by means of which the thing itself equally with its perfections is in existence . . . Hence neither is existence held to exist in a thing in the way that perfections do, nor if the thing lacks existence is it said to be imperfect (or deprived of a perfection), so much as to be nothing.[17]

Here we have one more refutation of the 'First Ontological Argument' (to speak with Malcolm). Nonexistence may be no defect in a thing (for there is no thing in the case). However, Anselm had argued, contingency in an existing thing is certainly a defect; and where it could not be, neither could contingent nonexistence, but only sheer impossibility or necessity of existence.

Descartes in his *Replies* brings this out, though not so fully as Anselm had done:

Nay, necessary existence in the case of God is a true property in the strictest sense of the word, because it belongs to Him and forms part of His essence alone. Hence the existence of a triangle cannot be compared with the existence of God, because existence manifestly has a different relation to essence in the case of God and in the case of a triangle.[18]

Did Kant know this exchange between Gassendi and Descartes? It certainly would have been relevant. That existence

---

[17] *Philosophical Works of Descartes,* trans. E. S. Haldane and G. R. T. Ross (New York: Dover Publications, 1955), 1, 186. My colleague Douglas Morgan has pointed out to me that Aristotle had explicitly denied that 'existence' is a predicate. Thus it is as clear that Aristotle would have rejected Anselm's first argument as it is that he could scarcely have rejected the second. See *Metaphysics* 1003 b 26ff.

[18] *Op. cit.,* p. 228. [The Everyman edition of 1922 also contains this stronger or "second" version of the Proof.]

is not, in ordinary or contingent cases, a (deducible) property is without prejudice to the status of necessary existence, which is different in kind and inapplicable except to God.

The only advantage Descartes has over Anselm is in the *phrases,* 'necessary' and 'possible [i.e., contingent] existence'. The ideas are certainly Anselmian. And, as we saw in Part One, Sec. 23 (1), Anselm's language has its merits.

Not only did Descartes encounter a lucid anticipation of Kant's chief criticism (and rebut it), he also dealt with a clear formulation of the favorite twentieth-century (Wittgensteinian) contention that rational necessity derives from language, and asserts nothing about extralinguistic reality. In other words, modality is purely *de dictu* and not *de re*!

Consider the following:

Hobbes: "Reason gives us no conclusions about the nature of things, but only about the terms which designate them, whether, indeed, or not there is a convention (arbitrarily made about their meanings) according to which we join names together."

Descartes: ". . . in reasoning we unite not names but things signified by names; and I marvel that the opposite can occur to anyone . . . For, if he [Hobbes] admits that words signify anything, why will he not allow our reasoning to refer to this something that is signified, rather than to words?"[19]

It is true that the ontological proof was not the topic which Hobbes had introduced here; but it is clear, I think, what Descartes would have said had that been the topic. I submit

---

[19] *Op. cit.,* Vol. II, pp. 64f. For this reference I am indebted to Dr. Bowman Clarke.

that it is time for historians to tell us the facts in this case, which
are that, down to Wittgenstein, the Anselmian problem had
been left nearly where it was in Descartes's time. Real novelty
came with Barth, Koyré, Hartshorne, Findlay, and Malcolm.
Most of the others have been treading old trails, often with
the airs of pathfinders.

If I overstate, please remember that the contrary overstate-
ments are in a thousand textbooks and works of reference!

What Hobbes actually said (in his Fifth and Seventh
Objections) about Descartes's proof for God, without specifying
whether it was the ontological or the proof from the axiom
that there must be a cause for the content of every idea, was
that in fact we have no idea of God. In short his view on the
issue was the positivistic one—an intelligent position.

The logical possibility and consistency of 'infinite perfection' follows—Descartes argues—from the fact that he has a
clear and distinct idea of it. In short, he has an absolute intuition at this point. Leibniz rightly rejected this claim, as
Hobbes had done. And indeed, since Descartes holds to the
sheer unity of the divine reality, an absolute intuition of the
divine nature should endow us with omniscience at one blow.
Moreover, even if, with neoclassical theism, one admits real
distinctions between elements and aspects of the divine life,
one still is not entitled to put absolute trust in our intuitive
grasp of even the most abstract aspect of deity. One cannot
oscillate between the appeal to logical inference as against intuition and the appeal to intuition as against inference, in this
arbitrary way. The possibility of inferring inconsistency must
remain open, and so must that of having a genuine though not
infallible intuition of consistency. Leibniz is more penetrating
on this issue, though as we shall see, not much more.

Descartes, however, also argues (condescending to his opponents' lack of intuition) that perfection is the positive idea, and imperfection derivative from it by negation. One cannot, he thinks, impugn the positive case and leave meaning for the negative. True, he must then defend himself against the observation that 'infinite' is negative, and so derivative from the positive idea of finitude or limitation. He reacts by denying the trustworthiness of the linguistic indication in this particular case. By the divine infinity we do not intend a numerical or quantitative *un*limitedness, but a reality wholly positive, lacking nothing. There is some plausibility in this, but yet the reasoning is unsound. Limitation implies a negative element; but it is no mere negation. For, since there are mutually incompatible yet positive values, as we shall see more particularly in discussing Leibniz, to reject all limitation (being this and not that, or that and not this) is to lose all concrete definiteness and become indistinguishable from mere indeterminate potentiality for positive value. The linguistic indication which Descartes spurns here might have led him to a great discovery, had he taken it seriously. 'Perfect' can be given a wholly positive meaning, but this proves it to be irreducible to sheer infinity. These terms are not synonyms. Perfect in the appropriate religious meaning implies the impossibility of being surpassed by another. This is, insofar, negative. But one can equivalently say it implies the necessity that the X defined as perfect should surpass any being other than itself. Or: In any possible state of reality, X surpasses y, whatever y may be. Sheer infinity is not deducible from this definition. For such a deduction one must assume that a wholly infinite being could also be all-surpassing in richness of actual value, and against this is the argument that to be wholly infinite is to be wholly indefinite or indeterminate (as Thomas put it, a wholly 'indeterminate sea of being'); and it is just not self-evident that this can be distinguished from the totality of the logically possible, in entire abstraction from any actualization. One may verbally stipulate that it is wholly actual, but then one has two absolute infinities, pure possibility as such and 'pure actuality' as such. (For some such reason David of Dinant and still others argued that God and prime matter were indistinguishable.) If this is not a paradox, what would be? Self-evident consistency cannot be claimed for any such idea.

Descartes's weakness, as user of the Argument, was his uncritical acceptance of Classical or Neoplatonic theism. In this he was like countless others, Anselm included.

Descartes, like Bonaventura, Spinoza, Malebranche, and Leibniz, indeed probably all the defenders of the Argument, assigned a different origin to the idea of God than to ideas of sensory things. This nonsensory origin was the point of 'innate ideas'. Locke's criticisms, as Peirce said, implied a meaning for the phrase which 'nobody' had intended. (It may also be fair to say that the intended meaning was not as clear as it ought to have been.) It was of course primarily his sensory theory of knowledge which barred the way to Thomas's acceptance of Anselm's proposal. According to all the Ontologists, the idea of God comes from God, not merely from creatures to us as creatures, but direct from God to us as His creatures. We do not exclusively infer God, we experience Him spiritually and intellectually. Inferences in this field are, in part at least, *reductio ad absurdum* arguments against the denial that we know or have God all along, and cannot simply not know or have Him. Bonaventura and Malebranche even emphasize the direct awareness of God to such an extent that the Argument is no longer an inference at all, but merely the recognition of the divine givenness as self-existent. (On this point, Jalabert is very illuminating—see Bibliography.) The error consists in not seeing the value of the intellectual experiment by which we *test* the assertion that God is given with this character of necessary existence. Human intuitions are not so clear, or so easy to put into words without danger of confusion, that we can rest content with their mere assertion. We must also investigate logical relations among our other nonsensory ideas. It turns out that to deny the givenness of God is to deny His existence (for, being conceived as universally immanent, He could not be conceived as nevertheless not given), and that this in turn is to deny even His logical possibility. The positivist is willing to make this denial. But this question, too, is further arguable, and there are *reductio ad absurdum* arguments concerning it.

What, however, does 'nonsensory' amount to? One way to put it would be this. To understand arithmetic or logic one needs no *special* sense organs, or *special* physical environment perceived through such organs. One may, if one is not God, require *some* sense organs or other and *some* external environment capable of supporting one as a thinking animal. But it makes no difference what the organs or the environment are like, provided thinking (presumably with something like language) can develop freely on a sufficiently conscious level. Given this, arithmetic and logic can arise and be understood. So can the idea and knowledge of God! But the ideas of 'oxygen' or of 'vertebrate', with the meanings that these terms actually have, are in a different class. Certain special perceptions are required. The geometrical shape of a backbone is not enough to fulfill the requirements of 'vertebrate', and it is impossible to put all the requirements into an a priori definition. For we mean something historical by the term, as also by 'oxygen', something which has actually arisen in our cosmos in our cosmic epoch, something whose nature is permanently more or less hidden from us, and must be referred to by denotation, by pointing, not by pure description. On the contrary, to grasp what number is, or what God (in His purely necessary aspect) is, one needs no special historical reference or special perceptual experience whatsoever, but only the intelligence to grasp the most universal aspects of absolutely *any* kind of experience or history. If this is what 'innate' (or not sensorily produced) means, then I hold that Locke was mistaken: there are such ideas, and very important they are. No one ever held that we are always conscious of them, or even that all men can be infallibly led to the consciousness of them by any course of argument or instruction. Some men resist arithmetic, or have scarcely had need to consider it beyond the uttermost extreme of simple cases, and there are strong forces opposing the careful consideration of God. But it remains true that no special sensory (including emotional) experiences are *logically* required, any more for the idea of God than for the ideas of arithmetic.

True, one must have some emotion or other, because the idea of value is involved. God is unsurpasssably great, and great here means having or being 'whatever it is better to have or be than not to have or be'. But the purely *general* idea of value, or of better, is all that is required, and it is absurd to suppose that anyone would bother to think if nothing seemed better to him than anything else. Indeed the notion of a value-free experiencing or thinking is nonsensical or contradictory. To have some emotion or other, and some sensory experience or other, is presupposed by any thinking at all (in spite of so-called thinking machines). Even God, in Neoclassical Theism, has something analogous to sensation. An innate idea is not one which could arise with no sensations or feelings, but one which logically could arise *no matter what* the sensations or feelings, provided they favored conscious thinking, including thinking about thinking, on sufficiently complex levels, and with sufficient freedom from inhibitions.

How far this is what the rationalists meant I shall not further inquire. It is, I suggest, at least as close to what they meant as anything which Locke set up to attack.

6. *Spinoza*

Spinoza seems to have been the first, though he was not the last, to employ the Proof in support of another doctrine than classical theism; in his case, a more rigorously formulated version of classical pantheism or Stoicism. In one sense this was logical. If God is a superconcrete yet wholly necessary being, then all concreteness must be within Him—otherwise He is but an abstraction from the total reality—and since, on classical assumptions, nothing contingent can be in Him, all things must be necessary. But then the distinctive meaning of 'necessary' is lost!

About the Proof itself Spinoza had no misgivings, and he is well beyond the mere notion that existence is better than nonexistence. His proof of Proposition VII rests on the idea (which had been indicated by Anselm, and developed by Scotus and Thomas Bradwardinus) that what cannot be caused by another cannot exist contingently, which is a version

of the true Anselmian Principle. Also the first auxiliary proof
for Proposition XI is a way of stating still another version,
apparently not clearly seen by the magnificent doctor, that
contingent existence is competitive, the things which exist
preventing ('annulling') the existence of many otherwise
possible things. Here Spinoza seems to have made a genuine
advance. However, he could not do justice to this approach,
since if all things are necessary, 'otherwise possible things'
has no clear meaning.

Spinoza blithely assumes as a matter of faith (he says,
'intuitive knowledge') the logical possibility of divinity as
he defines it, not noticing how paradoxical it is that he has
ostensibly deduced the 'necessity' of the entire concrete
totality of things from an abstract definition. The inconsistency
in the notion of a necessary yet *concrete* reality is left out of
the reckoning.

[Echoes of *Proslogium* III?]

Prop. VII. *It pertains to the nature of substance to exist.*

Demonst. There is nothing by which substance can be produced
(Corol. Prop. 6). It will therefore be the cause of itself, that is to say
(Def. 1), its essence necessarily involves existence, or in other words
it pertains to its nature to exist.

Prop. XI. *God, or substance consisting of infinite attributes, each
one of which expresses eternal and infinite essence, necessarily exists.*

Demonst. If this be denied, conceive, if it be possible, that God does
not exist. Then it follows (Ax.7) that His essence does not involve
existence. But this (Prop. 7) is absurd. Therefore God necessarily
exists.

Another proof. For the existence or nonexistence of everything
there must be a reason or cause. . . . and if it does not exist, there
must be a reason or cause which hinders its existence. . . . If, therefore,

there be no reason nor cause which hinders God from existing, or which negates His existence, we must conclude absolutely that He necessarily exists. But if there be such a reason or cause, it must be either in the nature itself of God or must lie outside it, that is to say, in another substance or another nature. For if the reason lay in a substance of the same nature, the existence of God would be by this very fact admitted. But substance possessing another nature could have nothing in common with God (Prop. 2), and, therefore, could not give Him existence nor negate it. Since, therefore, the reason or cause which could negate the divine existence cannot be outside the divine nature, it will necessarily, supposing that the divine nature does not exist, be in His Nature itself, which would therefore involve a contradiction. But to affirm this of the Being absolutely infinite and consummately perfect is absurd. Therefore, neither in God nor outside God is there any reason or cause which can negate His existence, and therefore God necessarily exists.

Another proof. Inability to exist is impotence, and, on the other hand, ability to exist is power, as is self-evident. If, therefore, there is nothing which necessarily exists excepting things finite, it follows that things finite are more powerful than the absolutely infinite Being, and this (as is self-evident) is absurd. . . .[20]

Spinoza's view is that all things, granted their causes, are necessary; though in ordinary things, the causes are outside their own natures. But then there is no contrasting term to necessity, no true contingency. The totality of things is as necessary as God. To retain the contrast upon which the meaning of 'necessary' depends, we need to admit that things other than God are ultimately contingent. And God transcends their contingency only by taking it wholly into Himself so that it becomes the infinite tolerance of the divine life for alternative states. To this divinely flexible alternativeness there can, therefore, be no alternative. The absolute 'patience' of

---

[20] *Ethic Demonstrated in Geometrical Order,* trans. W. H. White (London: Trübner & Co., 1883), Pt. I.

God for the variety of existence constitutes His immunity to nonexistence.

However, Spinoza is right in saying that a thing can only fail to exist if something 'prevents' it from existing; in other words, all facts are partly positive. But he misconstrues this to mean that effects are necessitated by their causes. They are necessarily prevented from existing if the causes are sufficiently unfavorable, but even favorable causes cannot reduce to zero the creativity—involving contingency—which is becoming itself. One must also take temporal aspects into account in considering how one thing may prevent another from existing. Granted that creativity could, at a certain point, have taken another course than it has, the course actually taken henceforth excludes this other possibility. It was, but no longer is, an 'open possibility'. But no possibility is closed unless the realization of some incompatible possibility has closed it. Only the future is still an open possibility, and an eternal being, which can never be merely future, can never be an open possibility. Whatever made its nonexistence a fact would also make its existence impossible.

God's absolute "power to exist" is His ability to assimilate any and every causal condition, to *make* it 'favorable' to some appropriate responsive state of His own awareness. This is the opposite of being influenced by nothing other than Himself. Nothing can be merely other or alien to God; all have something 'in common' with Him. This neoclassical view is about equally far from that of Spinoza and that of Anselm.

7. *Ralph Cudworth*

Here is one of the few writers who have arrived at a good

understanding of the essentially modal structure of the Argument. What is still more rare, he has apparently done this without deriving his understanding from *Prosl.* III and the *Reply.* His source seems to have been Descartes (or perhaps Henry More, whose ideas were similar), but Cudworth makes the modal considerations more explicit than Descartes did. He sees that something which could not exist contingently also could not contingently fail to exist; so that to deny its existence is to assert its impossibility.

If God, or a perfect Being, in whose essence is contained necessary existence, be possible or in no way impossible to have been, then He is: . . . for if God were possible, and yet He be not, then is He not necessary but contingent Being, which is contrary to the hypothesis.[21]

[This necessity of God's existence] must not be taken hypothetically only . . . that if there be anything absolutely perfect, then its existence was and will be necessary; but also absolutely, that though contradictious things cannot possibly be, and though imperfect things may possibly either be or not be; yet a perfect Being cannot but be; or it is impossible that it should not be.[22]

How melancholy to reflect that so clear and firm a grasp of the subject (buried, alas, in the third volume of a diffuse and rather formless work dealing with many topics, some of little present-day interest) was published a century before Kant's *Critique,* and that now, nearly three centuries later, so much of the philosophical world is still (as Barth puts it) "stuck in the dialectic of *Prosl.* II," that is, in the nonmodal or false version of the Proof.

---

[21] *The True Intellectual System* (London, 1895), vol. iii, p. 49. [This edition contains long notes by J. L. Mosheim, which seem to exhibit most of the misunderstandings to which an ontological argument is open.]

[22] *Op. cit.,* p. 40.

Of course Cudworth lacks any realization of the abstract-concrete paradox, and he asserts rather than explicates the incompatibility of perfection with contingency. On this second point, Anselm is more helpful.

8. *Leibniz*

No more than with Descartes, Spinoza, Cudworth, or most of those we shall have to deal with is there evidence that Leibniz knew the contents of the *Proslogium* (after the by themselves scarcely intelligible first two chapters). My guess is that he did not. He was, however, too much a metaphysician to be wholly victimized by the Gaunilo tradition. Like Scotus, but first among the moderns, he sees the need of establishing the logical possibility of the theistic concept, and he attempts to meet this need, partly by connecting the problem of logical possibility with the principles which he believes underlie logic generally, an intelligent procedure, if it can be carried through successfully. Like Thomas (and all the great theists) he is clear that if we know anything at all about God we know that He could not exist contingently. Unlike Thomas, but like all the Ontologists, he disbelieves in the sensory origin of the most universal conceptions. God is a direct datum of the soul, always given but not always attended to.

One of the best-known passages of Leibniz concerning the Argument betrays the persistent influence of Anselm's initial blunder (see Part One, Secs. 6, 19, 20).

To exist is something more than not to exist, or rather, existence adds a degree to grandeur and perfection, and as Descartes states it, existence is itself a perfection. Therefore this degree of grandeur and perfection . . . which consists in existence, is in this supreme all-great, all-perfect Being. . . . The Scholastics, not excepting even their Doctor Angelicus, have misunderstood this argument. . . . It is not a paralogism, but it is an imperfect demonstration, which assumes something that must be proved . . . that is, it is tacitly assumed that this idea of the all-great or all-perfect being is possible, and implies no contradiction. And it is already something . . . [to have] proved that, assuming that God is possible, He exists, which is the privilege of divinity alone. We have the right to presume the possiblity of every being, and especially that of God, until someone proves the contrary. So that this argument gives a morally demonstrative conclusion, which declares that, according to the present state of our knowledge, we must judge that God exists.[23]

In the opening sentences Leibniz seems to be repeating the *Prosl.* II confusion between saying that the fact of not existing would be a defect in deity and saying that even the bare possibility of not existing would be a defect. Of course the fact entails the possibility, hence whatever excludes the latter excludes the former; but this complex relationship, not the direct and simple exclusion of nonexistence, is the point of the Argument. Only necessary existence can enter into the notion of a kind or essence. In another passage Leibniz does somewhat better.

En disant seulement que Dieu est un être de soi ou primitif, *ens a se* c'est-à-dire qui existe par son essence, il est aisé de conclure de cette définition qu'un tel être, s'il est possible, existe; ou plutôt cette conclusion est un corollaire que se tire immédiatement de la définition et n'en diffère presque point. Car l'essence de la chose n'étant que ce qui fait

[23] *New Essays Concerning Human Understanding,* trans. A. G. Langley (New York, 1896), pp. 502f. Reprinted, LaSalle, Illinois: Open Court Publishing Co., 1949.

sa possibilité, il est bien manifeste qu'exister par son essence, c'est exister par so possibilité. Et si l'être de soi était défini en termes encore plus approchants, en disant que c'est l'être qui doit exister, parce qu'il est possible, il est manifeste que tout ce qu'on pourra dire contre l'existence d'un tel être serait de nier sa possibilité.[24]

Here we have something a little like *Prosl.* III. Essential or self-existence is the unique existence of deity. But Anselm retains the advantage of having made it clear that one does not 'define' God as the necessarily existing being (which leads to the objection that one must then show what necessary existence has to do with divinity), but rather, having defined deity as the worshipful, hence Unsurpassable, one then from this definition derives the trait of necessary existence. Thus it is the Unsurpassable which necessarily exists, not merely the necessarily existent which necessarily exists. Surely the former procedure is superior!

That Leibniz is not very sensitive to the difference between mere existence and necessity of existence as a 'perfection' is partly due to certain features of his theory of existence which are well elucidated by Jalabert (see Bibliography). Every essence 'tends toward' existence, and insofar includes existence in its concept; but ordinary essences are partly in conflict; they compete with one another for existence, and only Sufficient Reason, or the divine affirmation of the Best compossible set of essences, resolves the conflict. The divine essence, however, is not in competition with the others,

---

[24] Untitled essay on Father Lami's proof for the existence of God. *Die philosophische Schriften von Gottfried Wilhelm Leibniz,* ed. Gerhardt (Berlin: 1887), vol. 4, pp. 405-406. [In this and the following quotation I have followed the spelling and punctuation given by Jalabert (p. 82— see Bibliography).]

being quite independent of them. And its tendency to exist is infinite, and hence could not fail to be fulfilled. 'Tending to' means, 'will if nothing prevents'. With the divine essence, and only with it, nothing could prevent. Hence, a priori, God exists.

This is a much subtler theory than Spinoza's. Indeed it is the supreme effort of a classical metaphysician to employ the Argument. To say that an essence exists if no competing one does is to say that no fact can be merely negative, that the nonexistence of X is the existence of a world incompatible with X. This, I hold, is quite correct. Spinoza, too, takes nonexistence to imply that the thing is 'prevented' from existing; but he spoils this by also saying that all possible things exist, hence there are no such things as competing possibilities. Leibniz wants to preserve the contrasts (with the collapse of which the Argument loses all point) between: that which is necessarily existent, that which is possible but not existent, and that which is possible and also (contingently) existent. Any theist who does not recognize these distinctions is cutting off the limb upon which he would perch.

Had Leibniz been willing to qualify Sufficient Reason, so that truly *arbitrary* decisions, both divine and otherwise, could be admitted, and to follow through by admitting contingent divine decisions as real qualities of deity, that is to say, had he been willing to break with two thousand years of ada-mantine resistance to the idea of divine accidents (contingent predicates in God), the distinction between competing world possibilities and the noncompetitive essence of deity might have enabled him to solve the Findlay paradox and legitimately employ the Argument. But what monstrous proposals he would have thought these! Nevertheless, the question remains, can he meet the conditions of the Argument on his own more traditional foundations?

Does it really have a coherent meaning to say: (a) there is no impossibility in any of the various incompossible essences, taken one by one, and they are therefore severally really possible; (b) no essence could exist without a divine decree favoring it; (c) only one decree is compatible with the divine wisdom and goodness; (d) that God and His wisdom and goodness exist is logically necessary? Russell holds that this adds up to a miserable self-contradiction or quibble; I think it is a magnificent attempt to find a difference where no room has been left for one. Leibniz is clear that a possible world is correlative to a possible divine decree favoring it; but in what sense is a decree 'possible' to a being whose character strictly forbids his making it? If the divine character as eternally necessary uniquely designates one world as best, and therefore alone worthy of existence, is not God by His very essence in competition with the remaining possible worlds? But clearly, in such a competition with absolute necessity, a possibility is simply no possibility! Thus I hold with Russell, and in spite of Jalabert's skillful pleading on Leibniz's behalf, that the great attempt is a flat failure. It was, however, a truly great attempt. Consider the problem: there are unrealized possibilities, not all *could* be realized together, yet severally all are genuinely possible, so that there is no 'metaphysical' necessity in the world's detailed character; however, there must be adequate reason for that character; how can this be? A happy thought: suppose one possibility is supreme over all others. God would then—and only then—have a reason for its selection. And God, at least, could not act irrationally or without adequate reason!

The grandeur of Spinoza was that he made no pretences about saving contingency, but sternly stuck to his denial of it. This, however, was moral even more than intellectual grandeur. For the untenability of such a one-sided modal theory is only too manifest. Leibniz saw that one must at least do better than that. But, alas, Leibniz was not the man to pay the immense price of challenging tradition as rudely as Spinoza had done, though in another and more appropriate place, in its denial of contingent divine properties. Nor was he the man to be so out of tune with the confident science of his age as to resist the attraction of the Phantom of Sufficient Reason of which Spinoza also, in his own way, was a victim. Some things may perhaps be contingent, but this *must* not mean that they are without ultimate reason. Yet is not that what 'contingency' does mean, if anything?

An ultimate reason for the entire world, just as it is, must be exactly as definite and complex as the world. It cannot be the mere abstract notion, 'best of all'. By a stroke of genius, the dilemma seems to yield to solution: as possible this world is just as definite and complex as the same world as actual; it also, in this definite complexity, surpasses every other possible world. Hence, by what appears almost as magic, a definite world in all its details does deduce itself, so to speak, from the mere abstraction 'better than any other possible world'. The feat that Spinoza could not quite manage appears to have been accomplished. Spinoza had had to admit that his 'modes' do not follow directly from God's essence but rather from antecedent modes; only the totality of modes follows from the essence. But how? What connects the concrete particulars with the bare abstraction, 'absolutely infinite substance'? Only the verbal bridge: 'absolutely infinite reality must consist of all possibilities exhaustively actualized, hence there can be no unrealized possibilities'. But how empty or circular this proof is. If it shows anything it is only this: the intelligibility of Spinoza's definition of deity (suspiciously like that of other Classical Theists) stands or falls with the intelligibility of 'all things are necessary', or 'what is possible also is'. However, what reason does Spinoza have for assuring us that both stand, rather than both fall? Only his alleged intuitive understanding, which is his secret, or at most that of Classical Metaphysicians generally. Thus the doctrine is a rather transparent though unconscious bluff. In Leibniz the bluff is harder to see through. But is it anything beyond a more complicated bluff?

To allow the theory to pass is to agree not to attack the logical admissibility of 'one among possible worlds is best'. Yet why should it be any more admissible to suppose this than that one number is greatest, or one possible velocity the swiftest—formulae which, as Leibniz rightly points out repeatedly, one may employ with a feeling of understanding, though when examined they turn out to be logical absurdities. He will not allow Descartes to assume the internal coherence of his definition of God, but asks that this be proved. He makes the same demand of Spinoza. But 'best possible world', this he will not undertake to prove consistent (if so, where?) but rather he wants us not to notice the problem of consistency at this point. And how does he know that the demand for an ultimate reason for the nonnecessary is anything more than the demand that the supposedly nonnecessary should be shown necessary after all?

Leibniz argues that if we renounce Sufficient Reason we give up all hope of proofs for God, or indeed of rational knowledge.

However, he here overlooks some important distinctions. On the one hand, if there is genuine contingency there cannot be an ultimate reason specifying which possibles are actualized. Actualization is brute fact, capricious, undeducible. It is not a concealed syllogism of any kind. On the other hand, for possibilities themselves there must be a reason. Possibilities are not capricious or arbitrary, but rational. Deductive reason is concerned with the rationale of possibilities, not of actualities. We must, however, distinguish between 'pure' or eternal possibilities, and spatio-temporally localized possibilities: what is possible in a given time and place. The pure possibilities are *wholly* rational, and there is no caprice in them. If something is eternally possible, then this is a necessary not a contingent truth. No choice, decision, or selection is presupposed. But what is possible here and now depends upon what has previously happened, including the arbitrary decisions previously made. We can always ask, what events, what brute facts, put the world in a situation in which what could happen had to fall within such and such limits? Real spatio-temporally localized possibilities are narrowly limited, as compared to the realm of pure possibility; this difference, these limitations, constitute causality and make science possible. But the entire difference between pure and real possibility is *ultimately* arbitrary, brute fact and nothing else. Not that a chaos of innumerable arbitrary decisions could miraculously add up to a world-order. This would indeed be unintelligible, and Leibniz would be right to reject this. What saves the world from being such a chaos, however, is not that there is an ultimate reason for the particular limits of real possibility, i.e., for the particular causal laws, but rather, first there is indeed an ultimate reason and necessity that there should be orderly limits or laws of some kind, and, second, the preeminence of certain arbitrary decisions, those of God (called in the Bible 'fiats'), means that all other decisions are swayed and kept within appropriate limits by the influence of these supreme decisions. Like traffic laws, 'natural laws' have arbitrary features; but it is not arbitrary that there are laws, and that there is a power to make them. For this, the Reason is indeed sufficient. Mere chaos is not among the possible worlds. Nor is any possible world a godless world, which would be an unordered order, and nonsense. (This is the form the 'argument from design' ought to take, but the subject transcends the scope of this book.) So I think there is no need to admit that the principle of rationality which connects the world to God must be the ultrarationalistic one implicitly destructive of contingency itself. And certainly the ontological argument depends upon no such ultrarationalism; quite the contrary, it cannot be well defended without abandoning that doctrine.

Before asking whether the supreme axiom of rational understanding, taken to be that of Sufficient Reason, is absolutely true, or must be renounced or weakened, we should ask the prior question, Is Sufficient Reason itself a sufficiently reasonable formulation of the supreme axiom of rational understanding? I hold that it is a quite unreasonable one. By requiring the principle of rational derivability to apply to everything in every aspect, one prevents it from applying distinctively or effectively to anything. This is the usual penalty for one-sided simplifications in metaphysics. (The contrary one-sidedness of Humian empiricism, which is still very much with us, has its penalties also. It just happens that our age is not so sensitive to them.)

We may be grateful to Leibniz for having put his superb in-

tellect into the effort to do the impossible, to justify the unjus-
tifiable. For this helps us in our search for the truly justifiable.
By making clear the *best* that could be said for ultrarationalism, Leibniz put us in an excellent position to evaluate
that way of thinking. The verdict seems clear enough; the
doctrine is mistaken.

The sane principle of sufficient reason implies as corollary that pure possibility consists only of possible kinds and
degrees of causal order: a causeless chaos is eternally impossible. Hence, when it was said above that the entire difference
between pure and real possibility is arbitrary, this was not
in conflict with what was subsequently said about the element
of rationality in the form of divinely-imposed laws. For God
could not fail to exist, nor could He fail to impose some
order. He does not arbitrarily decide that there shall be
order, but only what order. This last, however, is, from an
ultimate point of view, simply arbitrary. It has to be so,
for the notion of an ulterior reason leads to an idle regress,
or to the denial of contingency and therewith any intelligible
necessity also. 'From an ultimate point of view' means this:
in a given situation only certain kinds of decision would be
appropriate, and for rejecting inappropriate kinds, there is a
sufficient reason. But the situation itself grew out of prior
decisions (not those of God alone) and to ask, 'What is
the reason for the entire series of decisions?' is to ask a nonsensical question. The design argument so put is, I hold, fallacious.
No wonder Hume and Kant could make little or nothing out
of it. To imagine God before *all* creation deciding upon the
whole once for all is to slide into the eternalistic dream in which
nothing really makes sense. Creation is not a one-step process.
Merely possible worlds set no soluble problem, even to the

All-wise; for where no conditions are fixed, there is no definite problem to solve. Only a world already in being gives God anything to decide about. Not that the world was there before He decided anything, but that His prior decisions and their results were there before any *given* decision of His, or of anyone else's. The old doctrine, which Leibniz professes, that God's initial creation and His preservation of the world are but a single act, is a confused one, and it assumes the dubious idea of a beginning of the creative process itself. But all beginnings presuppose the process, not the other way. There is then no one act of creation and no one act of preservation; creation consists of definite steps *one after another.* Just so did the Myth present the matter. Theologians (with some exceptions) thought themselves wiser. But in truth they had their own intellectualized myth, worse not better than the popular one in not a few respects. Leibniz is the last great philosopher who was really confident about the intellectual myth in question. Our mandate is to do better, by looking in another direction.

Leibniz's procedure was clearly not to survey the possible worlds and see that one was best. How could he do this? He had a notion of what makes one world better than another, namely that it integrates more diversity. But 'best' would then have to imply an unsurpassable diversity unsurpassably well unified. And what can be meant by unsurpassable diversity, whether or not ideally unified? A greatest possible number of kinds of thing? But since Leibniz himself denies a greatest number, number must be left out of it. If quantity cannot be maximized, then it must be totally abstracted from in conceiving the best world. Also, since there are incompossibles, not all possible diversity could be integrated. It seems safe to conclude that the notion of 'best possible' was not independently established, but was deduced from another notion whose consistency was held beyond challenge. This was, of course, Sufficient Reason. Unless one possibility is best, actuality cannot have a reason. But this is hardly a proof that one possibility is best. Since the Principle of Sufficient Reason, applied to the contingent, leads to the reduction of Leibniz's optimism to the paradox of Spinoza's necessitarianism, Leibniz has no right to assume the Principle and thence deduce the intelligibility of his theory that one possibility is best. If the latter is to be questioned, the former certainly cannot be secure, and both are dubious, if not clearly false.

Our search for explanations rightly rests upon a hope of finding them, but explaining things by deriving them from premises or conditions is not the absolute end or principle of existence, which is rather happiness (inclusively the divine happiness). Deriving happiness from causes or reasons is something else again. Doing so may increase happiness, but is not its whole content. The interest of logicians in derivations, and of scientists in causal predictions and postdictions, is legitimate; but there are other values, and the simple absolutizing of this one interest (or cluster of interests) in an alleged principle having unlimited right of way is at best a huge risk, and at worst a vast folly. It is not a harmless axiom to be put beyond question.

There is another notion that one must agree not to challenge if Leibniz's bluff is to remain uncalled. One must admit that a possible world is as definite and complex as the corresponding actual one. This, I hold, reduces the distinction between possible and actual to nullity. Value is in definiteness, and definiteness is 'the soul of actuality'. Were possibility equally definite it would be redundant to actualize it. There is no definite set of sets of 'possible things', and therefore it cannot be asked which set of possible things is best. Only properties, not particulars or instances, are possibilities (see below, Sec. 21). Moreover, only the most abstract properties are eternally distinct possibilities among which God might eternally choose. And even then, it is not really a question of choice, since all abstractly possible world forms have a claim to be realized, 'each in its due season'. But the infinity of these possibilities is such that no actual world process could ever exhaust them. In addition it is a dubious assumption indeed that God can simply choose a world order without leaving anything open for the lesser creative powers of the creatures to further determine.

It is time to turn to Leibniz's admitted problem of establishing the consistency of his idea of deity.

He has two devices. One is to refer to his Universal Characteristic as showing that simple notions or their objects, 'simple perfections', cannot conflict. But this Characteristic never quite came into being, and so far as I know it has not been found possible to construct anything like it on the required basis of simples. The idea of 'simple perfections' can only refer to empty abstractions like 'knowing everything in all its aspects', or 'loving all things for all they are worth'. These indeed are mutually compatible, but what about knowing the various possible kinds of worlds (not possible worlds, for there are none) *as actual?* Here one confronts the exclusive or: this and then not that, or that and then not this. Not all possible sorts of worlds can be actual, hence not all can be known as actual.

The other device is the following:

Si l'être nécessaire était impossible, tous les êtres contingents le seraient aussi, et ainsi il n'y aurait rien de possible. Car les êtres contingents n'ayant point en eux la raison suffisante de leur existence, il faut recourir a l'Être nécessaire qui est *ultima ratio rerum,* la dernière raison des choses.[25]

Suppose we grant that there must be something existing necessarily, it does not follow that this something is consistently conceivable as Classical Theists (and Leibniz) conceived God. Therefore, the right of theists of this kind to employ the Argument is not established. I hold that they have no such right. And I think the sole advance Leibniz has made here is to have pointed his finger over and over again at the weakest point in the Anselmian reasoning, the failure to establish the logical possibility of the religious idea as defined. But it never occurred to Leibniz that the price of making good this failure might be to start over again with an untraditional way of defining God, or an untraditional way of construing the traditional definition of God as uniquely perfect.

That the Findlay paradox was not apparent to this philosopher is no cause for surprise. The rationalistic dream of Sufficient Reason implies, so far as it has a clear meaning at all, that there is no paradox, that the eternal and necessary is really completely concrete, and that abstractness is only a human illusion. But if abstractness is an illusion, so is concreteness; for, like necessity and contingency, these concepts stand or fall together. There is a paradox, but unqualified rationalism makes it insoluble. (So does unqualified empiricism.)

---

[25] Letter to Jaquelot, Nov. 20, 1702. *Ibid.,* p. 44.

To have the right to employ the Argument, one must make sun-clear that one is not playing fast and loose with the contrast between necessary and contingent. The necessity of God is distinctively and uniquely His, which means that nothing else (except the widest class of individuals as such) has any ultimate necessity, whether one calls it metaphysical, logical, or moral necessity. The existence of God, alone among individual existences, is an eternal or a priori truth, which means that other truths of individual existence (and specific kinds of existence) are not eternal and not a priori. But we find Leibniz holding that for God (who sees things as they are, *nota bene*) *all* truth is eternal and a priori. Therewith the game is up, the initial standpoint abandoned, and all clarity lost. To favor the distinctively a priori truth of theism is precisely *not* to favor the a priori truth of things in general. It is to insist upon the general absence of such truth. Spinoza and Leibniz both quite missed the point here. And of course Anselm had preceded them in the error, since he too believed that in God all truth is timelessly contained in the a priori self-vision of the divine essence.

I feel I must emphasize and insist upon this, since even Boyce Gibson, generally sympathetic as he is to neoclassical theism, seems to feel that the Argument belongs with an eternalistic point of view.[26] I say, just the contrary, it belongs with the view that only the bare essence and existence of God, taken as an extreme empty abstraction, is 'timeless' or a priori. All else is empirical and in some fashion temporal—even for God,

---

[26] Gibson, A. Boyce, "The Two Strands in Natural Theology." *The Monist,* 47 (1963), pp. 335-364. [In this excellent introduction to what I call neoclassical theism the ontological argument is rejected, though without discussion.]

indeed *especially for God,* who does not share the illusions of ultrarationalists! God is not concerned to give ultimate 'reasons', whether to us or Himself, for His decisions. He makes decisions such that no other could be better, that is, such that the decisions are unsurpassable for the given situation (concerning all situations at once there is no decision, but only an eternal abstract ideal). But that there is just one best possible decision is a groundless, confused notion. Possible entities, including decisions, are not so definite as to be relatable in any such fashion. Only actual decisions are fully definite. All that is required for divine reasonableness is the negative, it would not have been possible to do better. (This does not mean that a better state of the world at that point in its development was impossible; for the creatures' decisions also enter into the result, and there is no metaphysical necessity that *they* should always obey the maxim, never do less well than possible. For their goodness or rationality is not to be defined as perfect.)

Only a concretely temporalistic theology can rightfully employ the Argument. The others will always compromise the uniqueness of the divine eternity and necessity, and the genuineness of its contrast with all else. It is only creative, self-enriching process which can unite harmoniously within itself an abstract, necessary eternal aspect with concrete, contingent, ever partly-new actual states. The contrast with the contingent which is essential to necessity must be within the divine life, not merely between it and something else. Everything must be within that life, without prejudice to the vast and genuine contrasts involved.

Here we may revert to the problem, common to Descartes, Spinoza, and Leibniz, of the 'simplicity' and wholly 'positive' character of the divine perfection. Descartes argues that the religious idea cannot be self-inconsistent, since it is simple and without negative elements. Spinoza, pointing out that determination is always (partly) negative, seems to think that, nevertheless, although God must include all the complexity of things, somehow this need not mean that He is limited by any negations. Leibniz has his way of trying to turn the same trick. But since God knows all things, the complexity of the content of His knowledge can only be the greatest complexity there is; moreover, since kinds of worlds are possible which are not actual (if 'possible', 'actual', 'necessary'—any of our basic categories—have meaning) and since obviously God knows as actual only the world which is actual, and does *not* know as actual any of the kinds of world which are merely possible, determination and negation must be admitted as constitutive elements in His reality.

Apart from the ultra-optimism of the Best Possible World, what most discredited Leibniz's system for his contemporaries and successors was surely his denial of interaction between monads. Even this, I submit, is incongruent with the proper understanding of the Argument. For it put Leibniz in the following position. God's existence is that upon which all monads utterly, and by strict logical necessity, depend in their every aspect; this absolute dependence, however, is not the supreme example of a principle generally operative in the system; it is rather the sole example. A sole example is not a supreme example. How often this is forgotten! We do not exalt God by giving Him a unique category, like creative power, for His very own. For if *A* is simply incomparable to *B*, then it is not inferior or superior to *B* but simply—incomparable. This is the real objection to a *'deus ex machina'*, where no general principle of the system can mediate the comparison between God and other things. The unsurpassable power of God should be the supreme form of 'power' in the general sense, exhibited elsewhere in inferior degrees or 'resemblances'. But Leibniz wants to say, not that there is a weak dependence of one monad upon another and a strong dependence upon God but that there is a zero dependence of one monad upon another (in the logical sense of dependence, and that is what is in question), but infinite dependence of all upon God. True enough, the whole issue is subtly befogged by the doctrine of 'ideal' influence via the divine choice of the most harmonious and richly varied whole. But this is like the befogging of the contingency issue by the distinction between direct logical necessity and indirect logical necessity via the necessary goodness of God and its logically predesignated result in the best possible world. These are not solutions but subtle and brilliant evasions. Thus it is still true that one jumps from monads absolutely independent logically among themselves (or, if you want to insist upon the interdependence, via the divine goodness, monads absolutely interdependent to monads absolutely dependent upon God. There is either no difference or no real comparability at all. How is all this related to the Argument? I hold that the independence or necessity (it is the same) of the bare divine existence (not actuality) from the creatures, its sheer neutrality as between one world and another, implies a supreme dependence of the creatures upon the divine existence (for mutual independence here would be purely absurd) and that this in turn implies nonsupreme forms of dependence, which could only obtain between one creature and another. So Leibniz's 'denial of windows' was really antitheistic (like every other metaphysical mistake!).

It is notable that our principle, the supreme must not be the sole form of a category, is implicitly Leibnizian. In some ways he adhered to it better than any man before him. Thus he treated the divine freedom as the supreme form of something found also in every creature, namely being moved by the apparent good. Determination by the apparent good is his theory of the will, and it applies even to God. (Of course, with God the apparent good is simply *the* good, but then even with us there is more or less conformity between appearance and reality.) And Leibniz, to his lasting glory, will not have any weak dualistic compromise, according to which some creatures are moved by the apparent good, and others, mere bits of matter, are not. For though resemblance to God can have all degrees, and the total gamut of these degrees is the same as the range of possible diversity among creatures, the zero degree coincides with nonentity, since being a creature at all means having some positive relation to deity. Here I salute Leibniz for being the first great philosopher (some minor figures in the Renaissance had said it, but not with power) to have really grasped a basic metaphysical truth. There is no room for caprice in considering the mere possibility of creatures; if to be a creature means (speaking loosely) to express something of the nature of God (and what else?), then anything supreme in God's essence may be as near to zero, to total absence, in a creature as you please, but present in some positive degree it must be.

What spoiled the picture was that Leibniz denied to both God and creatures any genuine creativity. Giving the nod to the completely defined possible world which most of all 'requires' actualization is not creation and is not freedom. God puts the penny in the right slot, and the right thing comes out. Rather, possible worlds are vague directions for further determination, and the process (to which each creature contributes) of determining the antecedently indeterminate but determinable can never end, since each new creature opens up new real possibilities for advance, and in this way the potentialities are inexhaustible. God has the supreme form of creativity, creatures have lesser forms. One cannot ascend to the divine form of a category one simply lacks. Leibniz (he was in good company here) managed never to intuit creativity at all. His appetition or force which made the monad a 'spiritual automaton' is the exact denial of creativity. The dream of explaining and justifying particular things by some ultimate reason or necessity, a superstition if ever there was one, condemned Leibniz to this blindness.

The denial of 'windows', though unique to Leibniz, is connected with another implicitly antitheistic tendency of Rationalism, and indeed of most modern philosophy, until recently at least, which is the calamitous notion that an experience can have simply itself as datum. The monads experience —what? Their own ideas and sentiments, that is, their own mental states, plus—God. God is actually given, not merely an idea of Him, but God Himself. And this must be said, for otherwise the whole system falls to pieces. Something besides one's own experiences must be experienced, or solipsism is not only irrefutable, it is unintelligible how it could even be an issue. And if God is that upon which all absolutely depend, if He is constitutive of the very possibility of things, not to experience God would be to experience nothing at all. But if God is our sole datum, in that sense in which a datum is not the experience itself but the thing it is the experience 'of', then once more we have a 'supreme' which is also 'sole'. There is but one genuine datum, God. But then nothing mundane can mediate the transition from no datum to the supreme datum. Leibniz would doubtless say, one's experience of oneself is the mundane datum. But this, in the system, is something absolutely different. For Leibniz, a monad is a single subject of predicates and its self-relations are then identities. But the relation to God is no identity. Here there are two subjects. There is still no mediation.

Like other Classical Theists Leibniz must hold that God's awareness of the creatures is sheer self-awareness. He intuits His own essence, which includes His choice of the best possible world. But either-or: God could have refrained from selecting that world, so that His selection itself is a contingent reality (meaning, its nonbeing was possible), or He could not have refrained, and then we have Spinozism: all is strictly necessary. If the selection is contingent (and otherwise the world is not contingent) then God must know something contingent in Himself, and this cannot be His mere necessary essence. So God must know something other than Himself taken as necessary, and yet something literally in Himself (can an act of selection be outside the acting agent?). It appears that the divine knowledge and will are far indeed from the reach of this type of Rationalism. Had the abstract-concrete paradox inherent in the recognition of the divine necessity been attended to, the need for a very different approach might have become apparent.

And after all, it is not even enough that God should know what world He selects. He must also know the actualization resulting from the selection. For actuality, we are told, is more than mere possibility. Can what is added be a mere additional essence of actuality as such? Surely not. This is just the wrong way to take actuality as a predicate. For 'possible actuality' will then already include any essence that might be meant. No, God must know the resulting actual world, not just the possible one, including His selection of it. God, the ancient myth says, beheld the world he had made and 'saw that it was good'. He did not merely look at it as possible and see that it *would* be good. Classical Theists have to claim a superior wisdom to Scripture at this point. I should have no objection, if I could see the superiority. But in this case I cannot, and I think I have read a reasonable number of explanations of the doctrine.

Yet the great rationalists had their deep insights. They were perfectly sound in their conviction (and the present age is deluded in going to the contrary extreme) that not all knowledge of existence can be empirical, and that, above all, the bare knowledge that God exists must be of a logically different type from genuinely empirical knowledge. They were correct in holding that there is a proper idea of God which implies a certain simplicity and absence of negation or possible contradiction. They only overlooked the little qualification: what the simple, purely positive idea refers to is not God in all His reality, but only—to use their term but not in their meaning—the divine essence, i.e., what God essentially is, an expression which implies, by contrast, what God is inessentially or accidentally. ('Accidentally' does not at all—and here many have been misled—imply not really or genuinely. The next time a harshly painful accident occurs to the reader, let him ask himself if it makes sense to say, "This accident has not really happened to me, since it is inessential to my nature." Reality is one thing, the essential or necessary, another, and the latter is but an abstract aspect of the former.) The mere essence of God is simple and wholly positive in certain senses. It has no definite parts and contains nothing of the actual complexity of the world, nor does it even know that complexity. God knows the complexity, but in His accidental not His essential aspect. (Not that He might have failed to know what existed, but that what existed to be known and hence the knowing, might have been indefinitely other than it is.) The divine essence, qualified by necessary existence, as God in His full reality is not, is wholly positive in just the sense that it is strictly noncompetitive, its mere being somehow actualized not contradicting the actualization of *any* positive possibility you please. Nor is God required by His essence to combine incompossible things, for the essence does not say that He creates or knows all possible things, each actualized, but only that He infallibly knows all actual things (and they at least must be compossible) and that He could and would know any set of compossible things, should it be actualized. In this way the rationalists' groping search for an idea of perfection which could not be contradictory may, it seems to me, come to its goal. For consistency seems built into the idea, so constructed, just as inconsistency seemed (and I believe was) built into it constructed in the classical way.

Is there not also a good case for Leibniz's suggestion that the burden of proof is primarily upon those who deny the logical possibility of deity? But Leibniz fails to note that the logical paradoxes in the classical idea of God were clearly pointed to as far back as Carneades, and never genuinely disposed of. Arnauld mentioned one to Leibniz, who virtually admitted that it was not to be evaded.[27] However, our present situation is that we have an alternative form of theism which also, and with better right, can employ the ontological argument. So I incline to the view that the next move is up to the skeptics.

9. *Hume*

Hume makes a remarkable concession concerning the possible importance of the ontological argument: he grants that its validity would dispose of the argument against theism based on the evils in the world. And of course, no empirical facts can testify against a logical necessity. Indeed, the argument from evil itself rests on the supposed analytic truth that Greatness *must* result in a world without evil. This, in turn, means that Greatness in God implies an absolute absence of independence or initiative of action in the creatures. For, if they have any such independence, evil may be their doing, for all we could know, not God's. ('They' here means creatures generally, not just human beings!) And to say that God should, and as Great logically would, grant no freedom in this sense is to say that a being who can and must deny all genuine independence of action to others is better than one who could and would foster suitable degrees of independence in them. So far from finding this analytically true, some of us find it analytically false. Perhaps 'omnipotence', in the sense of a *monopoly* of power, an infinitely stingy denial of real power to others, is even a mere absurdity. In any case, it

---

[27] Leibniz, *Discourse on Metaphysics and Correspondence with Arnauld* (LaSalle, Illinois. Open Court Publishing Co., 1924), pp. 96-114 (letters vi, viii).

has not been validly deduced from Greatness. 'Greatness' means having whatever properties it is better to have than not to have, as compared to other conceivable individuals. Perhaps monopolizing freedom is not such a property—is not at all a good thing. One of the beauties of Anselm's formula is that it frees us (far more than he realized!) from automatic commitment to traditional views about God. It may very well not be 'best' to be 'omnipotent', in the sense which generates the problem of evil in its classic form.

Hume found this problem crucially important, not so much because of his 'empiricism' as because of his quite unempirical espousal of determinism. From the presumed, not observed, perfect regularity of nature he inferred the absolute control of all things by the hypothetical regulator. If God does anything, He must do everything, since the laws leave no indeterminacy. The problem in this form springs from a false a priori, incompatible with the theistic a priori.

The following is Hume's conception of the ontological proof:

Nothing is demonstrable, unless the contrary implies a contradiction. . . . Whatever we conceive as existent we can also conceive as nonexistent. There is no being, therefore, whose nonexistence implies a contradiction.

It is pretended that the Deity is a necessarily existent being; . . . and that if we knew His whole essence or nature, we should perceive it to be as impossible for Him not to exist as for twice two not to be four. But it is evident that this can never happen, while our faculties remain the same as at present. It will still be possible for us, at any time, to conceive the nonexistence of what we formerly conceived to exist; nor can the mind lie under a necessity of supposing any object to remain always in being; . . .

But further, why may not the material universe be the necessarily existent Being, according to this pretended explication of necessity. . . . 'Any particle of matter,' it is said, 'may be con-

ceived to be annihilated; and any form may be *conceived* to be altered' . . . But it seems a great partiality not to perceive that the same argument extends equally to the Deity. . . . It must be some unknown, inconceivable qualities which can make His nonexistence appear impossible, or His attributes unalterable: And no reason can be assigned, why these qualities may not belong to matter. As they are altogether unknown and inconceivable, they can never be proved incompatible with it.[28]

Here is a blunt challenge. We shall meet it. As Anselm knew, the fool can 'think' that God is not, but he cannot genuinely conceive it, understanding what he is saying. Just so Hume. He is here not genuinely asking, in a more than verbal sense, what it is to 'conceive something to exist', or not to exist. Is it, perhaps, to imagine experiencing its presence or absence? But how does one experience an absence? As Popper says, by experiencing something positive incompatible with its presence. It has been shown above (Part One, Sec. 15) to be a contradiction that anything positive could contradict the existence and ubiquity of deity. Hence there is no way genuinely to conceive the nonexistence of God. Hume is only showing that we can say in words, "God (perhaps) doesn't exist." This disposes of the first two paragraphs of the quotation. They are mere question-begging dogmas.

The 'quality' which makes deity necessarily existent is Greatness. The notion of a 'material universe' which is Greatest has no clear meaning unless it be supposed equivalent to God, endowed with all the attributes which follow from Greatness, for instance, infinite flexibility in relating itself to possible worlds, while yet remaining genetically identical as an

---

[28] *Dialogues Concerning Natural Religion,* Part IX. *Philosophical Works* (London, 1827), vol. ii, p. 496.

individual. If the material universe is conceived in such fashion it is simply being conceived as God, and 'material' loses all its sting.

That the properties of matter can be conceived to alter is not what makes matter contingent; for the very necessity of deity (according to the neoclassical resolution of the 'none-greater' ambiguity) consists precisely in unique alterability, not in unique fixity. The trouble with 'matter', however, is that its identity through alterations has no positive meaning. Abstract from all particular forms, and 'matter' is but a word; abstract from all particular forms, and mind as Great is still the infinitely flexible correlate of all possible forms, yet able to recognize itself as genetically identical in knowing them, regardless of which ones are actual.

Put in another way: unless mind is the sole ultimate determinable, we have two such determinables, only verbally distinguishable: mind and matter. But one of these must be superfluous; which shall we keep? That we have experience, that we love and know, cannot be denied; the notion of necessary being we need, therefore, is that of Greatness as infinite spiritual capacity for knowing and feeling diverse things. Only because Greatness takes account of particular forms do they have any importance in final perspective; whereas, matter as such, as other than mind, could appreciate or register no value. The necessary being is the ultimate determinable without which determinates would determine nothing. And religious experience tells us how to conceive it. Physics as such cannot do so, and never—"so long as our faculties remain the same as at present"—can it do so.

It scarcely needs saying that Hume shows no sign of having read Anselm—after all, who does?

Hume makes one positive though unintended contribution to the Anselmian problem. His analysis of the self, often regarded as wholly destructive, is a somewhat crude version of the Buddhist-Whiteheadian view which, as we have seen (Part One, Sec. 11), is of assistance in escaping the abstract-concrete paradox in the employment of the argument. And here, Hume's empiricism is methodologically in the right. For, in contrast to God, man is a merely empirical reality. His 'soul' is nothing but a contingent entity, and the attribution to it of transcendent properties, like absolute self-identity throughout its history (or even indestructibility and eternity!) belongs in neither a sound rationalism nor a sound empiricism. Only Greatness enjoys *perfect* genetic self-identity, and the attribution of this perfection to man was one of the sources of the notion that God's identity must be simply nongenetic, must be sheer immutability. Either there is no perfect case, or anything like it, of genetic identity, or else God is the sole unqualifiedly genidentical being. And if He does not necessarily exist, then perfect genidentity is not even logically possible. To the realization of this point in neoclassicism Hume unknowingly made a valuable contribution by his honest adherence to the empirical method where it was entirely appropriate.

We must be careful, however. Man, as having the idea of God, contains a transcendent element. But this element, as transcendent, has nothing peculiarly human about it. Purified of all contingent and anthropomorphic eccentricities, it coincides with something in God's knowledge of Himself. There is here nothing to support the soul-substance which Hume rejects.

Looking over Hume's procedure as a whole, from the

Anselmian point of view, we see the following. (1) Anselm showed that Greatness is inconceivable except as necessarily existing; from which it was a corollary that to deny the conceivability of 'necessarily existent' is to affirm, 'God is inconceivable'. Hence the universal contingency of existence, affirmed by Hume as beyond all exception, is the downright denial even of the thinkability of deity. The stark contradiction between such absolute empiricism and theism does not necessarily refute theism; perhaps it rather refutes absolute empiricism! Moreover, the unqualified validity of empiricism cannot itself be an empirical truth. So Hume is simply appealing to his own a priori, against the religious a priori. It is his say so against that of (theistically) religious mankind.

It can easily be shown that Hume makes such a dogmatic antitheistic decision in more than one additional respect. (2) He posits as an a priori truth that "what is distinguishable is separable," i.e., there are no internal relationships of any kind among existing things. Yet, among the implications of Greatness is this: at least one sort of internal relationship between existing things must obtain, the relation of dependence of all other existents upon Greatness. Relation to God must be intrinsic to things. Therefore, since to deny Greatness is to declare it absolutely impossible, Hume's doctrine of universal separability cannot be empirical; for no fact can show something to be absolutely impossible. So here again he is appealing, not to experience but (if anything) to a priori self-evidence; he is again attempting to show, in effect, that theism is logically impossible. Finally, when (3) Hume asserts the truth of absolute determinism, he is contradicting another implication of theism, that free creativity (not simply free in the sense of voluntary and without impediment, but rather of determining the otherwise indeterminate, or of *adding* to the antecedent or presupposed definiteness of reality) is the universal principle of actuality. For, if supreme reality consists in supreme creativity (and the abstract-concrete paradox cannot, I hold, otherwise be resolved), then lesser realities must be lesser—but not zero—forms of such creativity. The step from great to Greatest, inherent in the logic of Anselm's definition, cannot be from nothing to something; it must be from something to the supreme something. Hence all creatures must have some creative power. Unqualified determinism, therefore, is contradictory of Greatness. If so, then, in this third way too, Hume assumes the logical invalidity of theism (not its simple falsity, for there can be no such thing).

Is it then surprising that the outcome of the *Dialogues,* resting as the whole discussion does on this triply dogmatic mechanistic and pluralistic positivism, should be 'skeptical'? The result is built into the method. Absolute empiricism, absolute pluralism, absolute determinism, contradict the existential necessity, the unifying function, and the actual freedom, bountifully overflowing into lesser forms of freedom, which are the very meaning of 'God'. One must choose, and Hume's arguments for his choice merely reiterate the choice as already unwittingly made.

On such an argument in a circle so much modern antimetaphysical and skeptical philosophy is founded! The reckoning with Anselm lies in the future: it has not taken place in the past. Has Hume refuted Anselm? Or has Anselm (not as classical theist, but as theist) refuted Hume? This question has not even been discussed. How could it be, when Anselm was virtually unknown? So a little error in scholarship, collectively compounded through centuries, becomes a great error, not of mere detail, but of methodological principle. The central philosophical question, that is, the rationally accessible content, if any, of the central religious question, is not an empirical matter, and empiricism, persisted in to the end, merely makes the muddling of this question the guaranteed outcome of all our philosophical efforts.

Will the great Kant cure the muddle, where the brilliantly lucid Hume could not? Or will he complicate and compound it by adding an alleged class of problems which are neither empirical nor a priori, and concern neither the intelligibly necessary nor the intelligibly contingent, but "something we know not what," the *noumenon*? Will he return to the Anselmian problem on at least the level of profundity to which Anselm penetrated, or will he deal with it only in the loose pseudo-Anselmian form current in modern rationalism? The reader perhaps foresees the answers.

10. *Kant*

Apparently Kant knew nothing of the *Proslogium*. Even the Cartesian argument he probably thought of chiefly in the forms given to it by Leibniz and, above all, Baumgarten. These forms were, at best, no improvement upon the Anselmian original. Moreover, they employed definitions of God which were less rich in possibilities than Anselm's own, being more hopelessly committed to 'platonism'. And indeed Kant, after more than seven centuries, was no freer than Anselm had been to investigate the possibility that the Greek way of construing the idea of God as an absolute and immutable maximum of reality or perfection might be a mistranslation of the religious idea, and that a better translation might remove some of the difficulties which philosophy had encountered in dealing with this idea or in attempting to find evidence of its truth. Kant is the last really great representative of classical theism, differing essentially from his predecessors not in his theoretical idea of God, but in his restricting of the grounds for faith to the argument from ethics.

One has only to read the relevant passages in Baumgarten's *Metaphysics* (see the Bibliography) to realize that from him, as from Leibniz or Wolff, Kant could only learn what I have argued is the wrong version of the Anselmian proof. God's existence is held to be necessary simply because all His properties or qualifications are necessary. He must have or be everything possible, except such things as—since they connote imperfection—He could not possibly have or be. Thus His entire reality is wholly 'determined' by the requirements of His eternal essence. This, I submit, is precisely *not* the principle of the divine necessity. On the contrary, it is necessary that God be capable of contingent qualifications, and that His capacity for such qualifications be unsurpassable. (For *all* contingent things are contingent items of the divine knowledge.) The divine existence indeed cannot be contingent, but not because existence in general is a property and God can have no contingent properties, rather, because even the capacity for existing contingently, or for contingently failing to exist, is a defect and only the unique kind of existence, eternal, inevitable, self-existence, is compatible with divinity. The modal distinction between kinds of existence, which *Prosl.* III brought into the literature, is the only proper basis for the Anselmian proof.

Baumgarten simply follows Leibniz in his proof of the consistency of Classical Theism: all perfections or admirable qualities are as such purely positive, and hence no contradiction can arise from attributing them all in maximal degree to God. As Kant saw, this is invalid. To take an example which he did not—but I am tempted to say should have—suggested: God can know a universe of which proposition p is true, or he can know one of which p is false; God cannot do both. Yet either is a possible positive qualification of God. (The negative character of 'p false' is not significant here. Suppose 'p' stands for 'there is an oak tree just here'. Then there might have been something else, say an ash tree, just here. Call the assertion that this latter possibility is realized 'q'. Then God might have known that p, or he might have known that q, but he could not have known that p and also have known that q. Yet, knowing that p and knowing that q are both possible positive qualifications of God. Kant's own example of incompatible positives was that of velocities in diverse directions. We shall presently consider an objection he might have had to our example.)

Kant saw that Baumgarten's case cannot be made out; he did not see that the opposed case can be made out, and that Neoclassical Theism may well be the residuary legatee of the inquiry if carried through without fear or favor.

The Argument of *Prosl.* III and subsequent passages was not what Kant refuted; he relied upon authors who had no knowledge of this argument. The Anselm of *Prosl.* III, also the Descartes of the *Replies,* as well as Spinoza, are refuted by Kant only in the sense that, as he showed, they had failed to establish a consistent meaning for their view of God. They did not fail, however, because their proof must stand or fall with the predicate-status of existence in general. Existential modality (necessity versus contingency) is the predicate required. And that this is not a predicate not only Kant, but the entire philosophical world, has yet to show.

In spite of his negative attitude toward theoretical theism, Kant, in the essay *Der Einzig-Mögliche Beweisgrund des Daseins Gottes,* makes a contribution to theism which should never again be lost and which is not invalidated by anything he himself later said. This is the proposition that there is no point in adducing the facts of worldly existence in arguing to a necessary Being. Since the necessary must furnish the ground of the very possibility of things, it is irrelevant to inquire which possibilities are actualized, or whether any are. For the point is that without God as ground of possibility (and this ground the necessary cannot fail to be) not only would no world be actual, but none would even be possible. This being inconceivable, God as at least potential creator is required, whether or not there are creatures. All theists should feel indebted for this clarification. It was near the surface in the neglected work of Anselm. It was Thomas, as much as anyone, it seems to me, who, with his sensory empiricism, covered up the insight so deeply that only a great disturbance like Kantianism could bring us back to it, in spite of Kant's later 'critical' views.

In his early essay *Nova Dilucidatio* (1755), Kant proposed a quasi-ontological proof, which he later—in the essay above referred to—revised, and still later, in the *Critique,* quietly abandoned. Throughout this development, Kant adhered essentially to the same idea of God, though his confidence in our ability to justify it theoretically suffered a complete reversal. God, as absolutely perfect, must be free from all negation of being, He must have all predicates so far as positive or expressive of reality. Thus in the *Critique* we read:

All negative concepts are . . . derivative, and it is the realities which contain the data and, so to speak, the material, of the transcendental content, by which a complete determination of all things becomes possible.

If, therefore, our reason postulates a transcendental substratum for all determinations . . . such a substratum is nothing but the idea of the sum total of reality (*omnitudo realitatis*).

. . . the concept of an *ens realissimum* is the concept of an individual being, because of all possible opposite predicates, one, namely, that which absolutely belongs to being, is found in its determination. It is therefore a transcendental *ideal* which forms the foundations of the complete determination which is necessary for all that exists, and which constitutes at the same time the highest and complete condition of its possibility, to which all thought of objects, with regard to their contents, must be traced back. It is at the same time the only true ideal of which human reason is capable, because it is in this case alone that a concept of a thing, which in itself is general, is completely determined by itself, and recognized as the representation of an individual.[29]

What a wonderful account—of certain assumptions of classical theology! All that anything can positively be (all that 'absolutely belongs to being') God must be actually and without restriction. This apparently (a) guarantees that He deserves to be worshiped as without flaw; (b) makes Him conform by definition or a priori to the law of excluded middle as the criterion of an individual or wholly determinate reality; (c) makes it possible to argue (in the next paragraph) that "the complete determination of everything [else] depends

---

[29] *Critique of Pure Reason*, trans. Max Müller (New York and London: The Macmillan Company, 1920), pp. 465-66. This and subsequent citations from this work are by permission of the publisher.

on the limitation of this total of reality, of which some part is ascribed to the thing, while the rest is excluded from it"; hence (d) shows that the content of the idea of God is the presupposition of possibility as such, so that if it were not real, nothing would be so much as possible. And so, Kant at first thought, he can infer that God exists as the necessary being. For the nonbeing of the ground of all possibility cannot itself be a possibility.

Compared to the usual *Prosl.* II version of Anselm or Descartes, this proof is not unimpressive. Yet, compared to *Prosl.* III, it has no decisive superiority, though it is valuable for the way in which it focuses on some aspects of the problem; and it does have certain defects, above all because it argues, not from the Unsurpassability of deity, which in some sense inheres in the very idea of worship (See Part One, Secs. 4-5), but from a nonreligious and philosophically dubious notion of absolutely complete reality or a priori determinateness. Kant never explicitly repudiates just this proof, but clearly he found it wanting in the end.

What was wrong? According to Kant, a number of things. (1) The needs of our thinking are not legislative for reality: *we* may need the idea of God, but only as regulative, not as constitutive of nature or supernature. (2) We cannot know that the sum of all predicates as positive is really possible. Positive predicates, as Kant argued in his *Versuch den Begriff der negativen Grössen in die Welt-Weisheit einzuführen,* may be "really repugnant" to one another. (3) We cannot know that an unlimited being is the only sort that could exist by absolute necessity. True, we could not deduce such necessity from the concept of a limited being; but then Kant denies that we can really do this from that of the unlimited being. We cannot validly deduce anything from so problematic a concept as that of unlimited being, and since a limited being cannot even be defined a priori, as an individual, its necessity can certainly not be deduced. However, neither—he argues—can its contingency. Kant is really saying little more, in all this, than that such contrasts as necessary-contingent, limited-unlimited, transcend our experience and therefore our knowledge. Essentially his attack on the Argument is on positivistic grounds (in the agnostic form: for all we know, 'God' has no genuinely possible content).

In seeing that negative concepts presuppose positive ones Kant was close to discovering the competitiveness of contingent existence. For just as one cannot know that x is not white without knowing white, and indeed, without knowing that x has some positive character exclusive of white, so one cannot know that such and such is nonexistent except by knowing that there is something else whose existence excludes the such and such. But then, if an idea is such that its being actualized is omnitolerant of all other forms of positive actualization, its object could not significantly be said to exist unless necessarily.

There is an ambiguity in the assumption, characteristic of classical metaphysics, that to be determinate a thing must relate itself positively or negatively to every possible predicate. Sophocles was non-Shakespearean, but does this mean that the entire quality of Shakespeare must have been available for Sophocles to negate? If qualities can be *created,* as neoclassical views hold, then so can negative relations to those qualities. Sophocles did not need, for his own definiteness, any relation to the emergent qualities which subsequently appeared in Shakespeare. It is Shakespeare who had to define himself relative to Sophocles, not vice versa. This is the asymmetry of time, according to creationist metaphysics. Kant seems not to have had any such idea. But he was right, on this ground too, in his suspicion of the reasoning which led to his 'transcendental ideal'.

Moreover, the insight that positive qualities can conflict implies more than that we cannot know the possibility of God as an absolute maximum of reality. It implies the impossibility of such a maximum. God could not possibly know as actual all possible worlds, for they are not mutually compatible. Yet the knowledge of an actual world as such is surely something positive. Hence some values must be possible for God but not actual. In addition, if all God's properties were fixed as actual by a priori necessity, He would have no freedom whatever. And freedom too is positive.

Kant would have interposed here: God does not really 'know' or 'act freely' in any sense which we could understand. Just as Anselm had said that in God there is not really 'compassion', but only its appropriate effects in us, so the redoubtable Königsberger argues (in the *Prolegomena,* for instance) that God is not really an intelligence—this he says would be anthropomorphism. However, the world is to be viewed *as if* made by an intelligent cause. What God may be 'in Himself' we can have no idea whatever. Thus, like his medieval predecessors, Kant has his doctrine of theological 'analogy'.

Certainly knowledge in God is, in its concrete quality, very different from anything we can clearly conceive. But it does not follow and, as we argued in Sections 16 and 17 of Part One, it is not tenable that there are no abstract principles or rules of meaning which apply to all thought, and hence to thought about God. Among such rules are these: that actuality differs from possibility by its arbitrary determinateness and that possibilities for concrete values are competitive. Also, that what a thing is in itself, independently of relations, is an abstraction from the full concreteness of the reality containing the thing and its relations. (Thus God merely 'in Himself' would be *less* than God relative to us.) Like other classical theists, Kant appears to reject the evidence we have concerning the most universal aspects of 'value' and 'existence', and to suppose that the Object of Faith must violate or transcend every rule of concept-formation which experience illustrates. This overlooks the truth that the most general or abstract principles cannot be unknowable, for they are somehow embodied in any concrete thing. One has only to abstract from the specific restrictions; the universal is what remains.

Of course, *if* we can in principle know nothing about possibility, actuality, incompatibility, abstractness, and concreteness, then we can know nothing about what God is or might be. The indecisive result here is built into the method. The trouble, however, is not with the Argument, as such, rather, with certain features of Kant's subjectivistic philosophy, together with that traditional (and idolatrous?) identification of God with the absolute or the infinite which Anselm, Descartes, and Leibniz sought to support by the Argument.

Surely Kant did well to drop the search for a proof which would be valid when so used. But had he been a freer mind, he might have drastically reconsidered the question: have we properly conceived God, or is there a better way? Instead he dismissed rational (theoretical) evidence, and fell back upon moral and religious faith alone.

Suppose, however, he had reconsidered his problem: to

define an individual a priori, as essential to the possibility of all other things. One way, the only one he saw, is to posit an absolute maximum of actuality. This failed. What is left? Obviously, to posit an absolute maximum not of actuality but of potentiality. God, simply as necessary, can have neither limited nor unlimited actuality (for no actuality, no particular *how* of concretization, can be necessary) but only unlimited potentiality. Divine potentiality—thus conceived—is as free from arbitrary limitation as you please, indeed it is absolutely free. Moreover, it is more plausible to relate all possible particular determinations to an infinite potentiality than to an infinite actuality (which indeed, as Kant suspected, is an absurdity). The particular is a determinate under a determinable; the ultimate determinable is the divine creativity. A possible creature is a possible state of the creator-as-having-creatures. But the mere existence of the creator in *some* state *or other* is wholly without arbitrary, competitive restriction. It is the disjunction of all restrictions, itself unrestricted. If the necessary is defined in this way, there is no Findlay paradox; for the ultimate determinable, as such, has no arbitrary determinations, and its assertion is logically weak to an infinite degree. Like all necessary statements it is factually 'empty', cuts off no genuine possibility.

But how, Kant might have asked at this point, could the ultimate determinable, the least determinate thing, define an individual? In the first place, even an ordinary individual need not and should not be defined as wholly determinate, unless all freedom and chance are to be denied. An individual's life is of course determined retrospectively, but then there is a new individual (as determinate) each moment.

The Buddhists alone, before Whitehead, seem to have adequately—or almost adequately—realized this.

Taking this *schema* of individuality seriously (a course precluded to be sure by Kant's phenomenalistic theory of time), we can still define *one* individual a priori. To do this we must distinguish between its individual essence and its mere accidents. Only the essence needs to be defined; for its existence merely means that the essence is actualized somehow, in some suitable accidents—any you please so long as they embody the essence. And here the essence is *unlimited capacity*, e.g., cognitive capacity. Only one individual can have such capacity. In this way we escape the difficulty by which Kant was rightly appalled, the difficulty that positive predicates may conflict. God's uniqueness is not that He exhaustively actualizes possible value (this is impossible), but that there is no consistent set of possible values He could not enjoy.

Unfortunately, no such view was conceivable for Kant, since he thought as a platonist—with the difference that he is full of skepticism, without a glimmering of hope that the view could either be justified or improved upon theoretically. On the contrary, with his usual eagerness to claim finality, he solemnly pronounces the platonic concept to be 'the only true ideal' that human reason can attain to. But there is an ideal he dreamt not of, that of the self-surpassable, otherwise unsurpassable Creativity.

Though Kant's 'critical' objections to the Argument take no account of the reasoning of *Prosl.* III, and though some of them are irrelevant to that reasoning, yet others might be used against it. Thus, e.g., Kant argues: if the reality of God can be inferred from our idea, God must be identical with the idea. By this reasoning, as no one seems to have noticed, Kant proves rather too much. For, by its principle, if God can be inferred at all, He must be simply identical with that from which He is inferred; but then not only is no non-question-begging proof for God possible, more than that, either God must be identical with the creatures, or else they cannot logically require His existence as cause of their own! Accordingly, it is theism itself which Kant has refuted here, if anything at all! He is really saying that God can in no fashion be 'immanent' in the creatures. For if He can be, then He can be in our idea, as a creature! And if in it, then knowable from it.

In addition, if our neoclassical analysis is right, the mere necessary existence of God (His being actualized somehow, no matter how) is not the concrete actuality which realizes this existence, but is an extreme abstraction, such as might well be within our conceptual grasp. And in any case, a universally immanent being cannot but be somehow constitutive of everything, including every thought. So of course God is somehow in our thought of Him, and also in the animal which cannot think Him. According to Wolfson, a central point of the ontological argument is precisely that God is immediately given.[30] Moreover, it is deducible from the idea of God that this must be so. Hence, if God is not given, He does not exist, and if He does not exist, then He is either logically impossible or logically contingent—which are here the same since, as Anselm discovered, 'contingent perfection' is contradictory.

---

[30] Wolfson, H. A., *The Philosophy of Spinoza* (Cambridge: Harvard University Press, 1948), vol. i, pp. 170ff.

In the same paragraph Kant asks, is the judgment of the divine existence analytic or synthetic? And if the former, does it not beg the question? This is in part a merely technical question. What "follows from the rules of our language" depends upon how we set up those rules. What Anselm discovered was that rules allowing one to treat a proposition as contingent *merely because it asserts existence* are rules which decide a priori against even the logical possibility of God's existence! Is this a legitimate decision to leave to linguistic rules? Only if such rules have decisive advantages other than that of invalidating the ontological argument—and what other advantages do the rules have? If there are none, it is their adoption, and not the argument, which "begs the question." Our analysis has suggested that the rules in question have, in truth, grave disadvantages, since they make not only deity but also contingency unintelligible and require us to admit merely negative facts, for example, and other monstrosities.

Like Hume, Kant has put his skeptical results into his initial assumptions. He knows all along that God must either be given as a sensorily perceivable object or be inaccessible. And he knows that God cannot be given as such an object, ergo. . . . No elaborate reasoning is required to draw the conclusion. But the definition of God tells us that this disjunction is invalid. God can neither be given in the obvious fashion of a sense-object, since He is in *all* such objects and therefore is not peculiarly given in any one of them, nor can He be simply inaccessible, for then He would not be the universal ubiquitous ground of things. And this ground, Anselm would say, "it is better to be than not to be." Hence God can only be conceived as having such a status. In saying that we could not in any fashion know or experience God, Kant is saying that God could not exist.

The great but, even so, calamitously overestimated German philosopher holds that if there be a concept which implies the existence of its object, still that concept is "accepted voluntarily only, and always under the condition that I accept the object of it as given."[31] If Kant were here confessedly representing positivism, not atheism or agnosticism, he would be in the right in the first three words of the quotation: the concept need not be accepted as 'well formed' or 'cognitive'. But the atheist does not reject, he uses, the concept, and if it does imply the necessary existence of its object, then the atheist contradicts himself. He is saying, "God or Greatness, whose appropriate definition (and Anselm's argument for its appropriateness has not been refuted) implies that He cannot be conceived not to exist, I yet do conceive as (perhaps) not existing." If this is allowed, what can be forbidden?

Kant thus fails to define the ground of his negations sharply as between atheism and positivism. Anselm proved that only the latter has a case. Here is another example. Kant says: "In introducing into the concept of a thing, which you wish to think in its possibility only, the concept of its existence, . . . you have been guilty of a contradiction . . . you have achieved nothing, but have only committed a tautology."[32] However, it is simply false that Anselm, Descartes, or Spinoza wished to think God 'in His possibility only'. They wished to think God in whatever way is compatible with the suitable definition of this term. The definition says it cannot be as

---

[31] Kant, *op. cit.*, p. 479.
[32] *Ibid.*, p. 481.

'possible only'; so how can it be? Either as necessarily existent, or not at all, i.e., existence must be affirmed, or the concept dropped as not genuine and consistent. If this last was Kant's point, why did he not say so more clearly? Am I deluded or was Kant? If it is I, then forty years have gone by, and I have not been able to see that he was right, though I have made many attempts. Will someone, out of the many who with Kant are so much wiser than I, not help me?

But might not what was neither contingent nor logically impossible yet be *really* impossible? This seems to be the purport of some of Kant's remarks. However, real possibility or impossibility can only mean, on such and such existing conditions. If, then, the conditions required for a thing are themselves logically possible—and if not, neither is the thing itself—yet are really impossible, we have a vicious regress of conditions of the conditions. To avoid this, we must give up the alleged distinction between real and logical possibility, as applied to our problem. The distinction is quite valid with respect to localized items of reality; for what is logically possible *somewhere* may lack the required conditions just here, or here. But a nonlocalized reality such as deity cannot be treated in this way. It can have no special conditions whatsoever. If it were not really possible everywhere and always, it would be impossible absolutely and in its very meaning. All *possible* conditions must be compatible with its existence, and then either real and logical possibility coalesce, or else the idea is not possible at all, whether logically or really.

Let us now consider an extended passage.

Being is evidently not a real predicate, or a concept of something that can be added to the concept of a thing. It is merely the admission of a thing, and of certain determinations in it.

Logically, it is merely the copula of a judgment. The proposition, *God is almighty,* contains two concepts, each having its object, namely, God and almightiness. The small word *is,* is not an additional predicate, but only serves to put the predicate *in relation* to the subject. If, then, I take the subject (God) with all its predicates (including that of almightiness), and say, *God is,* or there is a God, I do not put a new predicate to the concept of God, but I only put the subject by itself, with all its predicates, in relation to my concept, as its object. Both must contain exactly the same kind of thing, and nothing can have been added to the concept, which expresses possibility only, by my thinking its object as simply given, and saying, it is. And thus the real does not contain more than the possible. A hundred real dollars do not contain a penny more than a hundred possible dollars. For as the latter signify the concept, the former the object and its position by itself, it is clear that, in case the former contained more than the latter, my concept would not express that whole object, and would not therefore be its adequate concept. In my financial position no doubt there exists more by one hundred real dollars, than by their concept only (that is their possibility), because in reality the object is not only contained analytically in my concept, but is added to my concept (which is a determination of my state), synthetically; but the conceived hundred dollars are not in the least increased through the existence which is outside my concept.

By whatever and by however many predicates I may think a thing (even in completely determining it), nothing is really added to it, if I add that the thing exists. Otherwise, it would not be the same that exists, but something more than was contained in the concept, and I could not say that the exact object of my concept existed. Nay, even if I were to think in a thing all reality, except one, that one missing reality would not be supplied by my saying that so defective a thing exists, but it would exist with the same defect with which I thought it; or what exists would be different from what I thought. If, then, I try to conceive a being, as the highest reality (without any defect), the question still remains, whether it exists or not. For though in my concept there may be wanting nothing of the possible real content of a thing in general, something is wanting in its relations to my whole state of knowledge, namely, that the knowledge of that object should be possible *a posteriori* also. And here we perceive the cause of our difficulty. If we were concerned with an object of our senses, I could not mistake the existence of a thing for the mere concept of it; for by the concept the object is thought only as in harmony with the general conditions of a possible empirical knowledge, while by its existence it is thought as contained in the whole content of experience. Through this connection with the content of the whole experience, the concept of an object is not in the least increased; our thought has only received through it one more possible perception. If, however, we are thinking existence through the pure category alone, we need not wonder that we cannot find any characteristic to distinguish it from mere possibility.

Whatever, therefore, our concept of an object may contain, we must always step outside it, in order to attribute to it existence. With objects of the senses, this takes place through their connection with any one of my perceptions, according to empirical laws; with objects of pure thought, however, there is no means of knowing their existence, because it would have to be known entirely *a priori*, while our consciousness of every kind of existence, whether immediately by perception, or by conclusions which connect something with perception, belongs entirely to the unity of experience, and any existence outside that field, though it cannot be declared to be absolutely impossible, is a presupposition that cannot be justified by anything.

The concept of a supreme Being is, in many respects, a very useful idea, but, being an idea only, it is quite incapable of increasing, by itself alone, our knowledge with regard to what exists. . . . The analytical characteristic of possibility, which consists in the absence of contradiction in mere positions (realities), cannot be denied to it; but the connection of all real properties in one and the same thing is a synthesis the possibility of which we cannot judge *a priori* because these realities are not given to us as such, and because, even if this were so, no judgment whatever takes place, it being necessary to look for the characteristic of the possibility of synthetical knowledge in experience only, to which the object of an idea can never belong. Thus we see that the celebrated Leibniz is far from having achieved what he thought he had, namely, to understand *a priori* the possibility of so sublime an ideal Being.

Time and labor therefore are lost on the famous ontological (Cartesian) proof of the existence of a Supreme Being from mere concepts.[33]

In these famous passages Kant seems scarcely aware that from the standpoint of the second Anselmian or Cartesian Proof the question is not whether ordinary or contingent existence could ever be derivable from the mere concept of a kind of thing, but only whether a uniquely excellent kind of existence, necessary existence, can be derived from a unique concept, that of divine perfection or Greatness.

Insofar as the Critical Kant was aware of the relevant question, his view was apparently similar to that of Hume before him: necessary existence, taken as a quality or excellence, is without intelligible content, so that the idea of it could amount to no more than this: the necessarily existent (supposing the phrase means anything) necessarily exists. No other quality, in short, is logically connected with this alleged quality. We still should not know *what* necessarily exists.[34] Yet Anselm had tried to exhibit some two-way logical bridges between necessary, essential existence, or self-existence, on the one hand, and eternal existence, existence without parts, dependency, or defect, and thus existence as that of the Unsurpassable or Greatest, on the other. And we have seen

---

[33] *Ibid.*, pp. 483-86.

[34] Henrich (see Bibliography I) reaches approximately this conclusion in his study of Kant's criticism of the Proof.

in Part One that still other and stronger bridges can be constructed or found. Neither Kant nor Hume is adequately aware of the classical literature of this subject, much less of the unexplored possibilities which neoclassicism discloses for accomplishing the end more convincingly.

By remarking that existence is not a predicate, did Kant state clearly the abstract-concrete paradox involved in the Anselmian use of the Proof? It seems not. Existence in the necessary case, for all Kant shows, might be a predicate; but it could not, as necessary, be concrete, or identical with God as concretely actual. There must then in God be a real distinction between His necessary existence and His total reality. Where does Kant even touch on such an idea? Yet the logic of the problem leads us straight to it, unless we have made up our minds not to go in that direction.

Furthermore, Kant overstates his case in denying that 'existence' is, in any way, a predicate, or that the existing is in any sense more than the merely possible. There must be some sense in which it is more. And when Kant says, if real dollars contained anything [a penny] more than possible dollars, "my concept would not express the whole object, and would not therefore be its adequate concept," he gives himself away. For by what right does he assume the possibility of such a thing as an 'adequate concept' in this sense? Of course, there are only one hundred pennies in a real, as in a possible, dollar, but neither a dollar nor a penny can be fully expressed in a concept. Only sheer intuition could do this. The conceptual description of a kind of thing may at most account for so much of its quality or value as is expressible in merely abstract terms. But the full quality is not thus expressible. The actual *in its unity* has quality or value, and this is no 'predicate' or bundle of predicates to which reference can, in a particular case, be made, save by pointing to the concrete and speaking of 'its' value. To treat this value as a universal, or a 'possibility', is merely verbal, as Bergson (also Dewey) has pointed out; for there is no way to separate it from its actuality. We are only setting up a verbal duplicate of the actuality, and assigning it to another date, in speaking of it as an 'antecedent' possibility, if we really mean the unitary quality of the actuality. Thus Anselm and Descartes were not wrong in saying that the actual is greater than the unactualized yet possible. The former has a uniqueness, a concrete definiteness, which mere possibility lacks. And in this unique definiteness is all the richness and beauty of the real world, beside which 'possible worlds' are pale shadows. If it were not so, possibility might just as well be left unactualized, and God did nothing when He created the real world.

Yet the foregoing sense in which existence is a predicate is irrelevant to the ontological argument. For, manifestly, that in actuality which is 'more' than what is conceptually or abstractly expressible *for that very reason* cannot follow from any concept or definition; hence it cannot be used to establish the necessity of God. And yet *Prosl.* II and the parallel passages in Descartes give the impression of trying to use it in this way.

Kant seems to feel that it is absurd to suppose that we could know an individual without empirically perceiving it. Yet note that "Such that nothing greater is conceivable" refers to no empirical or contingent fact; Greatness is defined with reference to what could be, not with reference to what is. It is a concept wholly a priori. By contrast, 'dollar' cannot be defined without some empirical reference. Moreover, whereas a particular dollar exists at or for a certain time—and all dating is empirical—'God exists on August 26th, 1963' says nothing more than that He exists, and that there is such a date as the one mentioned. For God's existence (not His actuality) is regardless of dates.

True, since God is necessarily somehow actualized, our experience (and all things else) must be in relation to this actuality, and so it may well follow that in some sense, not necessarily conscious, we must intuit, experience, or feel it. And how does Kant know that we do not do this? A lack of distinct awareness of something is not a distinct awareness that it is not given. It is merely an absence of conscious perception of the thing as in experience, not a conscious perception of its absolute absence from experience. (Such an absolute absence could only be perceived by a mind with unrestricted cognitive power.) Moreover, it follows from the idea of God that either the idea is illogical, or God exists necessarily and ubiquitously, and from the latter it follows that all experience *must* have Him as datum, however inaccessible the datum may be to easy and clear conscious detection.

To the query, how do we distinguish God from a mere possibility, we reply, simply by the contradictoriness of 'mere possibility of Greatness'. Nothing can make Greatness possible, or self-consistent, but its own necessary reality as inevitably somehow actualized. We do not 'add' existence to the 'bare possibility of God', we deny that this latter phrase has a consistent meaning. Nor do we 'add to our concept' of God in affirming His existence; for the only proper concept of God is *as* existent. He can have no other status.

From a recent article (see Bibliography, Engel) I quote the following:

Kant . . . goes on to conclude . . . that when I, . . . think a Being as the highest reality, without any defect, the question still remains whether it exists or not—that is, whether (as he goes on to explain) it exists as some *part* of this (whole) world of my experience. Now the obvious answer . . . is that of course God does not exist in *that* way. . . . But this simply means that God lacks *contingent* existence . . . this is hardly a defect, for if he had contingent existence he would not be God, or what we ordinarily understand by that term.

The author adds in a footnote: "if the ontological argument fails to prove what it sets out to prove, the reasons for its failure must be other than those given by Kant." This article is at least a bit of evidence that the almost hypnotic spell of Kant's 'refutation' has now been broken. For this we need, no doubt, to thank Norman Malcolm more than anyone else.

We have already dealt, early in this section, with the Kantian contention that we do not know that 'all realities' could be combined in one reality, the Supreme Being. In any case, this is the positivistic, not the atheistic, objection to Anselm, and it leaves his refutation of atheism intact, so that he still would have proved something and something important, i.e., that God could not be an unrealized possibility. Moreover, the Proof need not, and in neoclassical use does not, take God to be the actual union of all possible realities, the *ens realissimum*, but only the actual union of all actual realities, and the potential union of all possible ones *so far as mutually compossible.*

If Kant were to insist that only experience could tell us— but yet it does not and cannot tell us—that perfection, thus defined, is possible—or impossible—we should ask him, who then could know the truth here? Or is it unknowable absolutely? Obviously God could not know His own impossibility! We too, it seems, cannot know it. What meaning, then, has the term 'impossible' in this case? And if it has none, what is the dispute about? Certainly God could know—if He could do anything—His own possibility and (the same thing) His own (necessary) existence. Also, it cannot be simply impossible even for us to know it, since by definition the divine existence would be the necessary ground of ours, in its every aspect. Hence, *whatever* we know must somehow imply the existence of God, and so exclude His impossibility. How then could this be wholly unknowable?

The strongest objection of Kant's is much like one of Thomas's. How can we deduce existence—or anything else—from a divine nature of which we do not initially have a clear conception? Anselm's answer was that his definition does not claim to tell us anything about God beyond the mere impossibility of something superior to Him. Another answer might be that 'nature' is here profoundly ambiguous. If it means, the most abstract, necessary, or merely eternal aspect of God's reality, then to know this is nothing hopelessly difficult, since we have only to abstract sufficiently from more concrete conceptions, in all of which the most abstract nature must be immanent. Concreteness, not abstractness, is the most baffling thing. (In view of mathematics and formal logic—compared, say, to psychology—this should be commonplace.) If, in contrast, 'nature' means the concrete quality of God as God of this world, and of all created worlds in the near and remote past of the cosmic process, then this nature indeed we cannot know; but it is contingent, and not in question in the argument. There is no more tremendous difference than that between these two aspects of deity.

(If it seems to some remarkable, to the point of absurdity, that one being can unite such contrasting features, the appropriate comment is simple: it is not one whit more remarkable than all the other implications of Greatness. Omniscience must somehow unite all things whatsoever. We are back at the positivistic objection, which must always have some plausibility: can God's existence be conceived at all? There is no obvious reason why it should be wholly easy, nor yet simply impossible.)

Kant's entire philosophy rests heavily upon the assumption that theism must mean classical theism. It follows that space and time cannot in any way describe the highest form of reality, for deity is classically viewed as strictly immaterial and immutable. Kant is assuming that Greatness excludes every conceivable kind of becoming as inferior; but this assumption is never really argued, it is never shown that it is better to be so complete that change is irrelevant than to be capable of enrichment of content. Nay, Kant himself holds that we cannot know completeness in this sense to be possible. But if not possible, it is also not better; for there is no virtue in sheer impossibility. Hence Kant does not know that divine Greatness implies immutability, he merely assumes it. Had he gone back to Anselm's proposal, he might more easily have seen that he was begging a most important question.

Again, take Kant's view that *noumena* could be known only by a wholly active mode of intuition or perception. This is classical theism again, for it assumes that to be wholly without receptivity or passivity is a merit. But on what ground? Are men less receptive than atoms, or incomparably more? The latter seems obvious. Then are men inferior to atoms? Kant was here repeating Anselm in his weakest aspect, his mistaken deduction of the negative theology from Greatness. Greatness is indeed defined negatively, but what it negates is not properties in God, but only the possibility of better properties in another individual. This allows God to have any positive property which is wholly good. And receptivity, sensitivity to the realities making up the universe, is indeed wholly good. The more of it a being has, the higher it stands. The absolutely insensitive is the absolutely dead, not the supremely alive. The Platonists (perhaps not Plato) are blind to this truth.

Suppose Kant had seen this. He might then also have seen that true knowledge requires conforming the subject to its objects, not sheer making of these objects. (The latter would mean that the known was merely one's own thinking, one's own thoughts or feelings.) Kant's whole epistemology could have been very different—and less subjective—had he realized the arbitrary character of his presupposed idea of God. And the study of Anselm, if 'critical' enough, could have taught him this.

Kant repeats, for the phenomenal world, Hume's determinism, and he does not effectively or ontologically overcome even Hume's radical pluralism, in that he makes, not things or events, but only our experience of things or events, an interconnected whole. Thus he, like Hume, is playing against theism with loaded dice. One of the penalities of accepting the Newtonian conception of absolute causal regularity is that the way was thus barred to an objective or ontological view of modality. (Most logicians are still resolute Newtonians even today in their insistence upon the strict independence of denotation and truth from time.) Only if there is a real contrast between the determinate past and the determinable future can we have a basis for the concept of real possibility, of which real necessity is the most general or abstract aspect. Here is the crux of the modal problem. So of course Kant disclaims any ontological knowledge of modality. But it follows immediately that he must disclaim any knowledge of God as necessarily existing, hence any knowledge of God, who only so could exist. Kant's dictum that all our conceptions must find their clue in the temporal structure of experience is correct; however, (a) determinism obscures that structure, and (b) Kant's phenomenalistic restriction upon the scope of time makes the dictum entail a general agnosticism. According to the idea of divine unsurpassability as entailing divine self-surpassing there must even be an eminent or divine kind of time! So here too Kant has decided against theism before even taking up the subject.

Other features of Kantianism come under the same heading. Thus Kant falls behind Hume in his account of the self by admitting a transcendent timeless soul or noumenal absolute personal identity other (it seems) than that of deity, and at least morally certifiable. And he makes still other concessions to the classical theory of 'substance'. Kant also is farther than Hume was from seeing that classical theism is not the only form theism can take. (Hume's Cleanthes makes an energetic, though not successful, effort to formulate what would have been neoclassical theism had he succeeded.)

When our valiant Königsberger took it upon himself to declare as "labor lost" all future efforts to discover a valid point in the Argument, was he not "barring the path of inquiry"— alas, only too effectively?

Yet Kant did make a contribution to the Anselmian problem. This was in his contention that the supposedly empirical arguments for God's existence conceal an a priori. If it were in principle impossible to 'argue from idea to existence' in respect to God, there could be no theistic argument at all. Kant thus supports Anselm's intuition that it is wrong to turn over the stones of fact to see if perchance God's existence—or His non-existence—can be found lurking under them. If anything can indicate God, everything must do so, including particularly the bare idea of God itself. What Kant refuted was not the ontological a priori proof of God—he never clearly stated that (in any form equivalent to *Prosl.* III). What he refuted was the claim to avoid the a priori in the religious sphere. And indeed, to say that we cannot infer God from the logical possibility of His idea, though we can infer Him from cats, mountains, or our own existence, seems downright frivolous. Either the idea of God is a creature, or it is God's self-knowledge (simply that, or as participated in by a creature); there is within theism no third thing it could be. Either way, its reality entails that of God, if anything whatever can do so. For delivering us from the notion that there is a special order of entity, such as the existing world, or our sense perceptions of this world, with which we must start in order to reach God, we can thank chiefly two men, Anselm and Kant. We can start anywhere, and with anything whatever; the question only is, can we understand it well enough to see the reality of God which, unless theism is absurd rather than false, must be there?

11. *Hegel*

Hegel's defense of the Proof did it little good, first, because he never properly stated it and second, because his system was too unclear to appeal permanently. Anselm had a lucid mind; he generally used words with a nice exactitude. He meant by God the absolute actualization of all that is desirable and good. This complete actualization did not include that of the world, which was, strictly speaking, superfluous. God might not even have been 'supreme', since He might have been solus. Deity is absolute self-sufficiency. This at least is clear. Spinoza also was clear enough: God is indeed absolute self-sufficiency, absolute actualization, but because His essence includes the world and because the world is all possibility exhaustively actualized. There is a third view: God is not in every sense self-sufficient, for although He exists independently, He depends for His particular actuality, or *how* He exists, upon what other things exist. Necessary or absolute in His bare essence and existence as divine, or simply as God, He is yet, in His concrete actuality, contingent, relative, and forever incomplete, because forever in process of further enrichment, value possibilities being inexhaustible. This, roughly stated, is neoclassical theism.

What is Hegel's position? Perhaps he is a neoclassical theist? On the whole, I think he is a man who is and wants to be in a perpetual systematic muddle between classical theism, classical pantheism, and something like neoclassical theism, with a dose of humanistic atheism, or the self-deification of man, thrown in for good measure.

In his astute but cloudy way, Hegel accepts the Proof as integral to his system. He rightly points out that we should expect the infinite to obey partly different laws from the finite. For Hegel, the infinite, or God, is the absolute unity of subject and object, or thought and reality. Hence the notion of God as mere idea is absurd. As usual in Hegel, there is sense in this but sense entangled in ambiguities. Divinity, for one thing, is not simply identical with infinity; as Hegel himself knew, the merely infinite without the finite is an empty abstraction. But just how the concrete finiteness and the abstract infinity are together in the divine reality—has anyone ever been able to learn this from Hegel? Most of us have had to look elsewhere for any clear light on the topic. That 'every step toward concreteness is contingent' is either denied by Hegel or at best admitted in most grudging and unclear fashion. I think it needs to be accepted outright, and without cavil. That the ultimate abstraction is *somehow* concretized may be necessary, but all else must be contingent. Only so can we avoid "deducing" the logically stronger from the weaker.

(It is only fair to say that the work from which the following is quoted was assembled from notes, partly by students.)

As is well known, the first genuinely metaphysical proof of the existence of God took the turn, that God as the idea of the being which unites in itself all reality must also possess the reality of existence. . . . 'For if it is merely an object of thought' it is not the highest thing; 'it can therefore be assumed that it exists: this is greater' than something merely thought. . . . This is quite right; however, the transition is not exhibited, the subjective understanding is not shown to transcend [*aufheben*] itself.

. . . for the true proof it is requisite that the procedure should not be according to the [abstract] understanding; but that thought should, of its own nature, be shown to negate itself, and . . . to determine itself to existence. And conversely, it must be shown of existence that it is its own dialectic to transcend itself and posit itself as the universal, as thought.[35]

There is in Hegel's pages on Anselm not a hint of the content of the vital passages which come after *Prosl.* II, mostly in the *Reply.* Thus Hegel essentially re-echoed the Gaunilo tradition, adding the peculiarities of his own dialectic of universal

---

[35] Translated from the text of Georg Wilhelm Friedrich Hegel, *Sämtliche Werke* (Stuttgart: Fr. Frohmanns Verlag, 1959), vol. xix, *Vorlesungen über die Geschichte der Philosophie*, bd. iii, pp. 165, 167. [Hegel did a better job on the Cartesian ontological argument, giving some idea of the second or stronger version. See *op. cit.*, p. 347.]

and concrete or particular, thought and reality. Obviously he is dealing in his own way with the abstract-concrete paradox, but is he making a clear advance toward its resolution? Or is he showing a muddled awareness of problems which are left for someone else to subject to lucid analysis?

12. *Ludwig Feuerbach*

Because it is arguable that Hegel's greatest influence has been through the Marxists, it is worth noting that his acceptance of the Gaunilo legend was in a sense echoed in that main source of Marxist atheism, Feuerbach's *Essence of Christianity*. There, after quoting the Latin of Anselm's definition of divine Greatness, the author tells us that the Proof runs: nonexistence is a defect (*Nichtsein ist ein Mangel*), therefore. . . .[36] This of course is *Prosl.* II, for the hundredth time posing as the heart of the matter. One need add only two syllables to get an approximation to the proper form of the major premise: *Nichtseinkönnen ist ein Mangel,* the possibility of nonexistence is a defect. But to be wise enough to make and understand this addition, one might perhaps need to read what Anselm wrote on the subject. And this, it seems, one does not do, no matter to what school of philosophy one belongs.

Notable also is Feuerbach's assumption that the real existence of God, or of anything else, must be 'particular' or 'empirical'. Much of Feuerbach's brilliant attack upon theism reads like a diffuse exploitation of the abstract-concrete or Findlay paradox, that God both must and must not be an

---

[36] *The Essence of Christianity*, trans. George Eliot (New York: Harper's, 1957, p. 198 (ch. 20). German edition (Leipzig, 1904), p. 300 (ch. 21).

empty abstraction, devoid yet not devoid of concreteness or particularity. I find in this writer no notion of the neoclassical solution of the paradox, that it is the actuality, not the existence, of God which must be particular or empirical, and that the existence is merely the being-somehow-particularized, not the how of particularization. Only the latter need be empirical. It is precisely the extreme abstractness of the divine essence which makes necessary its being somehow actualized or particularized. The essence of the human mind, which Feuerbach would substitute for divinity, is by no means so abstract. As Barth points out, man dies, his actions are pervasively tinged with evil, and he exists not as a single universal individual but as each one of us in our distinct individualities.[37] These and many more restrictions upon the pure essence of understanding, love, or will are required to transform these concepts, with which divinity is identified by Feuerbach, into that of humanity. Such restrictions cannot be necessary. Thus Feuerbach, like his 'bourgeois' teachers, Kant and Hegel, failed to deal clearly and logically with the Anselmian challenge at its center.

13. Robert Flint

This author belongs with Cudworth as having come closer to Anselm than any of the other moderns considered so far in Part Two. Yet even he could not prevent the Gaunilo tradition from warping his presentation somewhat. Thus, he begins by stating the thought of *Prosl.* II as though it were the entire

---

[37] See the conclusion of Barth's preface to *The Essence of Christianity* (1957).

technical argument, and only then begins to show that he really knows better.

It is heartening to note his awareness that Descartes had two forms of ontological proof (the second coming close to *Prosl.* III), and he may possibly be the first modern thinker to take clear note of this fact. Is it not permissible to salute this tough Scotchman's insistence upon doing his own reading and thinking, instead of letting a dozen other persons do it for him?

This reasoning [he has summarized *Prosl.* II] . . . has commended itself completely to few. Yet it may fairly be doubted whether it has been conclusively refuted, and some of the objections most frequently urged against it are certainly inadmissible. . . . There is . . . no force, as Anselm showed, in the objection of Gaunilo, that the existence of God can no more be inferred from the idea of a perfect being, than the existence of a perfect island is to be inferred from the idea of such an island. There neither is nor can be an idea of an island which is greater and better than any other that can ever be conceived. Anselm could safely promise that he would make Gaunilo a present of such an island when he had really imagined it. Only one being—an infinite, independent, necessary being —can be perfect in the sense of being greater and better than every other conceivable being. The objection that the ideal can never logically yield the real—that the transition from thought to fact must be in every instance illegitimate—is merely an assertion that the argument is fallacious. It is an assertion which cannot fairly be made until the argument has been exposed and refuted. The argument is that a certain thought of God is found necessarily to imply His existence. The objection that existence is not a predicate, and that the idea of a God who exists is not more complete and perfect than the idea of a God who does not exist, is, perhaps, not incapable of being satisfactorily repelled. Mere existence is not a predicate, but specifications or determinations of existence are predicable. Now the argument nowhere implies that existence is a predicate; it implies only that reality, necessity, and independence of existence are predicates of existence; and it implies this on the ground that existence *in re* can be distinguished from existence *in conceptu,* necessary from contingent existence, self-existence from derived existence. Specific distinctions must surely admit of being predicated. That the exclusion of existence—which here means real and necessary existence—from the idea of God does not leave us with an incomplete idea of God, is not a position, I think, which can be maintained . . . the idea becomes either the idea of a nonentity or the idea of an idea, and not the idea of a perfect being at all. Thus, the argument of Anselm is unwarrantably represented as an argument of four terms instead of three. . . .

The second form of the Cartesian argument is, that God cannot be thought of as a perfect Being unless He be also thought of as a necessarily existent Being; and that, therefore, the thought of God implies the existence of God. . . . It is futile to meet this by saying that existence ought not to be included in any mere conception, for it is not existence but necessary existence which is included in the conception reasoned from, and that God can be thought of otherwise than as necessarily existent requires to be proved, not assumed. To affirm that existence cannot be given or reached through thought, but only through sense and sensuous experience can prove nothing except the narrowness of the philosophy on which such a thesis is based.[38]

Flint overlooks the abstract-concrete paradox, and the consequent need to transcend classical theism. But it was fifty years after his writing the above words, at least, before more than a minute fraction of the philosophical world had anything like so definite and accurate a grasp of what either Anselm or Descartes had meant. It is probably still a small fraction.

14. *W. E. Hocking, Josiah Royce, and George Santayana*

Anselm's Proof has seldom played a positive role in Ameri-

---

[38] *Theism* (Edinburgh and London, 1877), pp. 278-80, 282-84 [Since Flint refers to Cudworth, the latter's rare understanding of the Argument was not quite lost in his vast volumes, after all.]

can philosophy. Two of our philosophers, however, Hocking and Royce, early in this century called an argument of theirs 'ontological', and one of these said, some fifty years ago, that it was in principle the 'only' argument for God. The rather pathetic facts, however, are that neither writer has given a tolerably accurate account of the original Argument and that one of them gives an exceedingly inaccurate account.[39] (Since the writer of this commentary is deeply indebted to Professor Hocking as a former teacher, he wishes it were otherwise.) Hocking intended to improve upon Anselm. But alas, his Anselm never existed. In one short paragraph, four incorrect notions concerning the Saint's procedures are expressed, as anyone who compares the account with the relevant *Proslogium* pages may ascertain for himself. Nor is there any suspicion of the central principle: that, the nonexistence of which is inconceivable, is greater than that the nonexistence of which is conceivable.

This is how Anselm has been treated—even by many of those with the least motive for misrepresenting him.

In a more constructive and characteristically ingenious passage, Hocking briefly presents his own so-called ontological argument,

The ontological argument is the answer to the question, May the idea of God be 'merely subjective?' That answer is, In forming the essence 'merely subjective,' you have at the same time formed the essence 'not merely subjective' as in contrast thereto; and God as essence belongs to the 'not merely subjective.' Whatever artificiality there is in the argument hails entirely from the

---

[39] "The Ontological Argument in Royce and Others," *Contemporary Idealism in America,* ed. C. Barrett (New York: The Macmillan Company, 1932), p. 49.

artificiality of the question. The natural situation may be stated thus: the essence of God must be real, because it is an essence inseparable from my continuous consciousness or experience of reality.[40]

The second sentence by itself looks like the very argument of *Prosl.* II which Hocking has rejected. However, taking into account the last sentence, and the setting of the quotation in Hocking's general position, what we have is not an ontological argument at all, but a Berkeleyesque version of what I call the epistemic or idealistic argument. This version runs: we experience nature, this amounts to experiencing God, since nature is only something in or 'between' minds, not a possible thing in itself, and since our perception of nature is not our own doing and can only be God 'creating us', at least to that extent. Berkeley had said much of this in his own way: nature is ideas, but not essentially our ideas; hence God's, which He causes us to share (or approximate to), and thus a 'language' whereby God speaks to us. Calling such an argument 'ontological' seems to be twisting words to little purpose. The original Argument proceeded directly from the logical possibility or conceivability of God to His necessary existence. Nothing about our human situation relative to nature needed to be invoked. The conceivability of God is not the fact that human beings conceive Him; no failure to conceive can nullify a logical possibility. If we understand that God is conceivable, we also understand, for it is the same, that He necessarily exists. For in this unique case, nonnecessity is equivalent to nonpossibility. The point is related to what nature might be only insofar as all metaphysics is one. There may be a valid form of epistemic argument, but it is not the argument Anselm

---

[40] *Op. cit.*, p. 65.

invented (and Descartes used) in either its weak or its strong form. It needs another name.

In the same essay—based in part on students' notes of some of Royce's lectures—Hocking deals with the Roycean so-called ontological argument. It does not appear that Hocking's teacher came any closer to Anselm than Hocking himself. Nor is this surprising. "Our American Plato" (as Peirce called him) based his views mainly on German philosophy which, almost throughout its history, has been unaware of the real Anselm. And for another reason also, Royce was not in a good position to appreciate the Argument. (He did much better with the epistemic argument.) For Royce, though less clearly and candidly, took the view of the Stoics and Spinoza (and Leibniz by implication) that the eternal essence of God implicated the entire detail of existence. Thus everything is as necessary as God. To use the Proof for this view, with its glaring paradoxes, is to misuse it in one way as Anselm had in another. Classical theism and classical pantheism are the two horns of the classical dilemma. But of the two, it is the Spinozistic doctrine which more obviously must in effect "deduce the concrete from the abstract." And, just as Hume's absolute denial of internal relatedness makes nonsense out of theism, so does Royce's absolute denial of external relatedness and hence of contingency. This is an example of the power of Anselm's discovery; it forces us to regard either theism, or else both extreme monism and extreme pluralism, as self-inconsistent.

That Royce, as a classical pantheist naturally would do, distorted the Proof by attenuating to the vanishing point the distinctiveness of necessary existence compared to existence in general is made quite clear in Hocking's account. Royce wants to generalize the ontological principle that 'essence entails existence' by making experience entail the entire universe. Otherwise, he thinks, we cannot escape solipsism. Now, that experience cannot be of nothing, and that it must somehow exhibit the experienced, may indeed be a valid metaphysical axiom. But the inference from our experience to the particular world experienced is one from brute fact to brute fact, from particular to particular. This is almost as far as one can get from the original ontological argument. Royce conceals this from himself by identifying 'essence' with whatever is experienced or in the mind. However, Anselm starts from an abstract definition, not a concrete experience or anything concrete, and deduces that no matter what else there may be, God as defined must really exist. This is the total independence or self-sufficiency of God's existence, its absolute neutrality with respect to all other individual existences. This notion—essential to the Proof—is swept away in Royce's version (as in Spinoza's).

Yet Royce is groping toward a metaphysical truth (so subtle is this problem, and so inclusive of all the metaphysical problems). The ontological principle may indeed be applied to more than just God. What it cannot do is apply to individuals other than God; rather, it applies to all abstractions or determinables on the highest level of generality. God in His merely necessary reality is an abstraction, though a perfectly individual abstraction for all that! But God as such and world as such are correlative, and equally abstract; both must be somehow concretized. However, this our *actual* world—which was Royce's theme—is the absolute opposite of the uttermost abstraction or determinable, since it is the uttermost determinate. To lump together these two problems without clear notification of what is going on is confusion indeed. We are being entangled in the pantheistic version of the Findlay paradox inherent in all classical thought, without the admission of how paradoxical it is. The Perfect individual can be necessary only because its individuality is totally noncommittal as between particular alternatives of actualization. So far from the entire actual universe following from or being presupposed by its existence, nothing follows, and nothing is presupposed, save that some divine and some worldly actualization there must be. (That world as such is equally noncommittal does not make it a rival necessary being. For world as such is simply the content of the divine knowledge so far as more than mere self-knowledge. It designates, not an individual in the primary sense, but the completely indefinite generalized collection of nondivine individuals.)

As Hocking shows, Royce defined his ideas about the Argument partly by reaction to those held by his brilliant colleague George Santayana. In the first chapter of the latter's *Realm of Truth,* we find the following characteristically luminous discussion.

The most real of beings, said St. Anselm, necessarily exists: for evidently if it did not exist, far from being most real, it would not be real at all. Is then reality, we may ask, the same as existence? And can existence have degrees? St. Anselm explains . . . a nonexistent essence would woefully lack moral greatness, perfection, or dignity: it would be a contemptible ghost, a miserable nothing. Undoubtedly for a careladen mind seeking salvation—unless it sought salvation from existence—power, which certainly involves existence, must be the first mark of reality and value. . . .

At the other pole of reflection, on the contrary, as among the Indians or the Eleatics, the most real of things might seem to be pure Being, or the realm of essence, excluding change and existence altogether: because in change and existence there is essential privation. . . .

I do not mention this paradox in order to laugh at St. Anselm or at his many disciples . . . their argument was fallacious and even ridiculous, if by 'necessary existence' we understand a necessity attaching to events or to facts, that is, to contingencies. Yet the same argument breathes a fervent intuition and a final judgment of the spirit, if it intends rather to deny final validity to an existential order which, by definition, is arbitrary, treacherous, and self-destructive: a realm of being over which inessential relations are compulsory and essential relations are powerless.

. . . we may come to see how the maximum of reality might logically involve infinity, impassiveness, and eternity: all of which are contrary to the limitation, flux, and craving inherent in existence. No essence, not even this essence of existence, has any power to actualize itself in a fact; nor does such actualization bring to any essence an increment in its logical being. . . .

The existence of God is therefore not a necessary truth: for if the proposition is necessary, its terms can only be essences; and the word God itself would then designate a definable idea and would not be a proper name indicating an actual power. If, on the contrary, the word is such a proper name, and God is a psychological moral being energizing in space and time, then His existence can be proved only by the evidence of these natural manifestations, not by dialectical reasoning upon the meanings of terms.[41]

Our Americanized Spaniard's brilliance has not saved him from missing much of the import of Anselm's reasoning.

First, the proof which he attributes to the Saint is but a loose paraphrase of *Prosl.* II. In spite of his claim that when he began his studies at Harvard the scholastic proofs for God's existence were "warm in his mind," the evidence before us strongly suggests that he either had not read, or when he wrote the quoted passage had forgotten, *Prosl.* III and *Reply* I, V, IX.

---

[41] *The Realm of Truth* (New York: Scribner's, 1938), pp. 7-10.

Second, it is assumed, not proved, that all essences have the same relation to existence—of course, the very point at issue. Actualization, it is urged, involves arbitrary limitation, negation, or exclusion of other essences from actualization. Essences being thus competitors for actualization, their existence is always contingent. But what Anselm, in effect, proved is that there is one noncompetitive yet individual essence, wholly independent, in its mere existence, of what else does or does not exist. A dogmatic statement that all essence is competitive is worthless against this explicit argument for an exception to the rule.

To say that "no essence, not even this essence of existence, has any power to actualize itself" prompts the rejoinder, does any essence have power even to 'subsist' totally out of relation to existence? We confront the old Aristotelian question. Santayana cannot refute Anselm merely by voting, against Aristotle, for the complete "separability of forms." (See Part One, Sec. 13.)

That no actualization can "bring to any essence an increment in its logical being" is correct; but it may for all that be true that the *denial* of actualization to so abstract or noncommittal an essence as existence as such, or God the universal existent, is contradictory of its logical being. In spite of Kant, it is illicit to substitute, Can you add existence to an essence and get a greater essence? for the only relevant question, which is, Can you without contradiction subtract existence from, or deny it to, a certain supreme (and noncompetitive) essence and have the essence at all? Such an impossibility of subtraction does not imply the possibility of a prior addition, rather the contrary! Kant's point here was an *ignoratio elenchi.* No Anselmian who remembers *Prosl.* III wants to "add" existence to the divine nature. He wants to show that there is no room for such an addition, since existence is inherently there. The alternative to 'God existent' is not 'God nonexistent and therefore inferior'—it is contradiction or nonsense.

So what we have is: lack of acquaintance with Anselm, inconclusive and in part irrelevant objections and dogmatic platonism. Here is no secure hiding-place from the Anselmian challenge.

Santayana also begs the question, not only by his extreme platonism, but by his extreme Humianism, or pluralism. Each momentary state of experience ('spirit') is independent logically of its predecessors. Mind has no power, only matter. But then of course there is no sense to the idea of God!

True enough, the "actual power" influencing our world transcends any essence; but all that the Proof tries to show, neoclassically interpreted, is that *some* divine actuality, genidentical with any other, is influencing it.

Santayana and Royce are interesting opposites to one another. Whereas Royce held, in effect, that all genuine essences must be actualized, since the world, in every detail, is the best or only 'really possible' choice that the Absolute Wisdom could make among apparent or 'merely ideal' possibilities, Santayana had said that any actualization, and even no actualization, is as possible, as thinkable, as the reality which in fact exists. Here, as always, a critical Anselmian takes the moderate position: the divine essence, and all equally general or abstract essences, cannot conceivably be unactualized, but the more particular essences may or may not acquire actualization. Again, whereas Royce held that all details are providential, a theist who has given heed to the abstract-concrete paradox will not say this; but neither will he, with Santayana, see the world as bald fact influenced by no universal ideal or directive.

So penetrating and various are the implications of Anselm's discovery. The world has evidently felt a deep need to evade these implications; and meeting this need is a job which has been almost incredibly well done. The chief methodological rule for doing it has been simple: do not study or reflect upon Anselm's text for yourself, rely upon another. Read only with another's eyes, reflect only with another's mind. Scholarly thoroughness, self-reliance, one or both, have nearly always been in scanty supply in this context.

There is a third quality insufficiently manifested in the Anselm debate: intellectual curiosity, the desire to explore ideas as a mathematician explores them with a view to learning what could coherently be thought, regardless of whether it has been thought or not, regardless of what one wishes to believe or disbelieve. How *could* one formulate the idea of a worshipful being? Is something like the Philonian-Thomistic approach the only possibility—apart from Spinozism, Leibnizianism, Hegelianism, Kantian agnosticism, or a Comtean rejection of the very idea of God? (The inexhaustiveness of the disjunction should be clear.) Like Anselm himself, Santayana did not seriously put this question, and neither did Royce, who dealt only with the issue between agnosticism (or pure mysticism) and some approach to an Hegelianized Leibnizianism.

Thanks to the influence of William James, Hocking did put the question just referred to. He is essentially a neoclassical theist (to the great profit of at least one of his former students), but with a post-Kantian and Roycean background somewhat unfavorable to lucid analysis. We need a larger dose of 'Latin clarity', such as characterizes the thought of Anselm.

15. R. G. Collingwood

This author gives us an admirable short account of the historical background of the Proof. One may doubt if the special role of faith is properly estimated in this account. But on the other hand, one could hardly have a clearer realization than the passage expresses of the enormous systematic philosophical issues which are entwined in this one.

An ingenious argument, not included in the quotation below, is given to show that logic and ethics, like metaphysics, must assert existence as involved in essence. Thus—for instance— in talking about propositions we create propositions, and hence their existence cannot be denied. This seems rather different from the necessity that God should exist; but possibly the consideration is relevant. In any case, if *all* existence is contingent, metaphysics is a will-o'-the-wisp, and so is much of what has been regarded as philosophy.

Of the three phrases quoted below from Boëthius, the last and most significant is in the *Consolations of Philosophy,* Book III, X. It is indeed close to Anselm: "nothing better than God can be thought of." Boëthius uses the formula to prove that God must have perfect goodness, since otherwise, inasmuch as "perfect things were before the imperfect," there would be something better than He. Still, this is not Anselm. For the procedure requires us to prove independently that perfect goodness exists, whereas all that is needed is that it be conceivable, since then that which is thought of as not admitting even the thought of a greater must be thought of as perfectly good. Similarly it must be thought of as existing necessarily—again assuming only that necessary existence is conceivable and would be superior to contingency. There is another bit of evidence that Boëthius did not have any very penetrating grasp of his own formula: in the very sentence in which he in effect defines God as such that nothing better can be thought, he goes on: "who doubteth but that that is good than which nothing is better?" (*id quo melius nihil est*), thus relapsing from the modal to the merely existential level. Nevertheless, Collingwood is probably right in assigning this passage the honor of most nearly approximating Anselm's definition. Very likely, however, it was Augustine, if anyone, who led the Magnificent Doctor to his formula. Thus in *De Libero Arbitrio* (Vi, 14) we find God referred to as *quo nullus est superior,* or again *quo nihil superior est constiterit.* Also in *De Doctrina Christiana,* L. I, C. VII, we read: *ut aliquid quo nihil melius sit atque sublimius illa cogitatio conetur attingere.* (For these citations I am indebted to F. H. Ginascol.) None of these quite say that God is such that nothing greater can be thought, but only that nothing greater exists, or can be demonstrated, or that thought about God tries to arrive at a being to which nothing would be (*sit*) superior. Perhaps the difference is hairsplitting? If I am right that the modal structure of Anselm's argument is decisive, nothing is more essential to it than the explicit, unmistakable reference to conceivability. And this we find in Boëthius, not quite in Augustine. But whether this passage of Boëthius actually influenced Anselm is, of course, another question.

Plato had long ago laid it down that to be, and to be knowable are the same (Rep. 476 E); and, in greater detail, that a thought cannot be a mere thought, but must be a thought of something, and of something real (ὀντος, Parm. 132 B). The neo-Platonists had worked out the conception of God in the metaphysical sense of the word—a being of whom we can say *est id quod est,* a unity of existence and essence, a perfect being (pulcherrimum fortissimumque) such that *nihil deo melius* excogitari queat (the phrases [except the last] are from Boëthius, *De Trinitate*). Anselm, putting these two thoughts together, the original Platonic principle that when we really think (but when do we really think, if ever?) we must be thinking of a real object, and the neo-Platonic idea of a perfect being (something which we cannot help conceiving in our minds; but does that guarantee it more than a mere idea?), or rather, pondering on the latter thought until he rediscovered the former as latent within it, realized that to think of this perfect being at all was already to think of him, or it, as existing.

. . . Anselm . . . was careful to explain that his argument applied, not to thought in general, but only to the thought of one unique object . . . the slightest acquaintance with writers like Boëthius and Augustine is enough to show that he was deliberately referring to the absolute of neo-Platonic metaphysics; and in effect his argument amounts to this, that in the special case of metaphysical thinking the distinction between conceiving something and thinking it to exist is a distinction without a difference.

. . . Of all the legacy of medieval thought, no part was more firmly seized upon than the Ontological Proof by those who laid the foundations of modern thought . . . and it remained the foundation-stone of every successive philosophy until Kant, whose attempt to refute it—perhaps the only occasion on which anyone has rejected it who really understood what it meant—was rightly regarded by his successors as a symptom of that false subjectivism and consequent skepticism from which, in spite of heroic efforts, he never wholly freed himself.

. . . the Proof is not to be dismissed as a quibble . . . what it does prove is that essence involves existence, not always, but in one special case, the case of God in the metaphysical sense: the *Deus sive natura* of Spinoza, the Good of Plato, the Being of Aristotle: the object of metaphysical thought. But this means the object of philosophical thought in general; for metaphysics, even if it is regarded as only one among the philosophical sciences, is not unique in its objective reference . . . all philosophical thought . . . partakes of the nature of metaphysics, which is not a separate philosophical science but a special study of the existential aspect of that same subject-matter whose aspect as truth is studied by logic, and its aspect as goodness by ethics.

Reflection on the history of the Ontological Proof thus offers us a view of philosophy as a form of thought in which essence and existence . . . are conceived as inseparable . . . unlike mathematics or empirical science, philosophy stands committed to maintaining that its subject-matter is no mere hypothesis, but something actually existing.[42]

Let it be noted well that, even in this exceptionally sympathetic account, there is no distinct echo of the logic of *Prosl.* III. As a result the formulation, like so many others, is less cogent than Anselm's own, when that is taken as he wrote it, without truncation or mutilation. After all, the questions are, *why* does *this* essence involve existence? And how do we *know* that it does? Anselm saw more deeply into these questions than most of those who came before or after him.

The assertion that Kant understood the Proof is of doubtful value in the absence of any evidence that Collingwood had in mind the actual course of the Proof in the ten essential Anselmian pages to which we have repeatedly referred.

16. *Hans Reichenbach*

Here is our last example of a philosopher refuting an Anselm who never existed, an Anselm whose only wisdom was that existence is one of the predicates which a thing may be conceived to have. Anselm was a man who thought this, but he was not a man who had no other thoughts relevant to the Proof. And only that fictitiously unresourceful man is refuted in the following.

---

[42] *Philosophical Method* (Oxford, 1933), pp. 124-27.

[Refuting *Prosl.* II]

[Anselm's] demonstration begins with the definition of God as an infinitely perfect Being; since such a being must have all essential properties, it must also have the property of existence. Therefore, so goes the conclusion, God exists. The premise, in fact, is analytic, because every definition is. Since the statement of God's existence is synthetic, the inference represents a trick by which a synthetic conclusion is derived from an analytic premise.

. . . If it is permissible to derive existence from a definition, we could demonstrate the existence of a cat with three tails by defining such an animal as a cat which has three tails and which exists. Logically speaking, the fallacy consists in a confusion of universals with particulars. From the definition we can only infer the universal statement that if something is a cat with three tails it exists, which is a true statement. . . . Similarly, we can infer from Anselm's definition only the statement that if something is an infinitely perfect being it exists, but not that there is such a being.[43]

Whether, or in what sense, 'God exists' is synthetic is of course the very question at issue. In *Prosl.* III it was shown that 'Greatest Conceivable' is not conceivable unless as necessarily existent; hence, since a statement which is conceivable but only as true is in the broad sense analytic, either 'God exists' is true and analytic, (true *ex vi terminorum*) or it is not conceivable, is not a genuine proposition. It certainly is not synthetic in any but a narrow and merely technical sense.

The *reductio ad absurdum* from the definition of an 'existent three-tailed cat' is invalid against the above argument; for a definition which includes existence in the a priori specifications of a thing makes sense only if the form of existence involved

---

[43] *The Rise of Scientific Philosophy* (Berkeley: University of California Press, 1951), p. 39.

is necessary existence. But then, since '*necessarily*-existing cat', like 'perfect island', is an absurdity, the *reductio* is therefore invalid (since anything can be deduced from an absurd concept, taken not to be absurd).

Concerning particular and universal statements: 'God exists' is not 'particular' in the same sense as 'cats exist' is so. As we saw in Part One, 'Greatness exists' is, in a relevant sense, as nonparticular as 'some individuals exist', which Reichenbach in his logic allows to be an assumption of logic itself.

I think we can dismiss this refutation, along with so many others like it, as missing the mark.

17. *J. N. Findlay*

The most important contribution since Kant to the Anselmian controversy, on its skeptical side, has in my judgment been made by this author.

The proofs [for God's existence] based on the necessities of thought are universally regarded as fallacious; it is not thought possible to build bridges between mere abstractions and concrete existence . . . Religious people have . . . come to acquiesce in the total absence of any cogent proofs of the Being they believe in; they even find it positively satisfying . . . And nonreligious people . . . don't so much deny the existence of a God, as the existence of good reasons for believing in Him. We shall, however, maintain that there isn't room, in the case we are examining, for all these attitudes of . . . doubt. For . . . the Divine Existence can only be conceived, in a religiously satisfactory manner, if we also conceive it as something inescapable and necessary, whether for thought or reality. From which it follows that our modern denial of necessity or rational evidence for such an existence amounts to a demonstration that there cannot be a God.

. . . We ask . . . whether it isn't wholly anomalous to worship anything *limited* in any thinkable manner. For all limited superiorities are tainted with an obvious relativity, and can be dwarfed in thought by still mightier superiorities, in which process of being dwarfed they lose their claim upon our worshipful attitudes. And hence we are led on irresistibly to demand that our religious object should have an *unsurpassable* supremacy along all avenues, that it should tower *infinitely* above all other objects. . . . We ask also that it shouldn't stand surrounded by a world of *alien* objects, which owe it no allegiance, or set limits to its influence. The proper object of religious reverence must in some manner be *all-comprehensive:* there mustn't be anything capable of existing, or displaying any virtue without owing all of these absolutely to this single source. . . . But we are led on to a yet more stringent demand: . . . we can't help feeling that the worthy object of our worship can never be a thing that merely *happens* to exist, nor one on which all other objects merely *happen* to depend. The true object of religious reverence must not be one, merely, to which no *actual* independent realities stand opposed; it must be one to which such opposition is *inconceivable.* God mustn't merely cover the territory of the actual, but also, with equal comprehensiveness, the territory of the possible. And not only must the existence of other things be unthinkable without Him, but His own nonexistence must be wholly unthinkable in any circumstances. And so we are led on . . . to the barely intelligible notion of a Being in whom Essence and Existence lose their separateness.

It would be quite unsatisfactory from the religious standpoint, if an object merely *happened* to be wise, good, powerful, and so forth, even to a superlative degree, and if other beings had, *as a mere matter of fact,* derived their excellence from this single source. . . . Wisdom, kindness and other excellences deserve respect wherever they are manifested, but no being can appropriate them as its personal perquisites, even if it does possess them in a superlative degree. And so an adequate object of our worship must possess its various qualities in some necessary manner. These qualities must be intrinsically incapable of belonging to anything except in so far as they belong primarily to the object of our worship. Again we are led on to a queer and barely intelligible Scholastic doctrine, that God isn't merely good, but is in some manner indistinguishable from His own (and anything else's) goodness.

What, however, are the consequences of these requirements . . .? Plainly (for all who share a contemporary outlook), they entail not only that there isn't a God, but that the Divine Existence is either senseless or impossible. . . . Those who believe in necessary truths which aren't merely tautological, think that such truths merely connect the possible instances of various characteristics with each other; they don't expect such truths to tell them whether there *will* be instances of any characteristics. This is the outcome of the whole medieval and Kantian criticism of the Ontological Proof. And, on a yet more modern view of the matter, necessity in propositions merely reflects our use of words, the arbitrary conventions of our language. On such a view the Divine Existence could only be a necessary matter if we had made up our minds to speak theistically *whatever the empirical circumstances might turn out to be.* . . . This wouldn't suffice for the full-blooded worshipper. . . . The religious frame of mind seems, in fact, to be in a quandary; it seems invincibly determined both to eat its cake and have it. It desires the Divine Existence both to have that inescapable character which can, on modern views, only be found where truth reflects an arbitrary convention, and also the character of 'making a real difference' which is only possible where truth doesn't have this merely linguistic basis. We may accordingly deny that modern approaches allow us to remain agnostically poised in regard to God; they force us to come down on the atheistic side. . . . Modern views make it self-evidently absurd (if they don't make it ungrammatical) to speak of such a Being and attribute existence to Him. It was indeed an ill day for Anselm when he hit upon his famous proof. For on that day he not only laid bare something that is of the essence of an adequate religious object, but also something that entails its necessary nonexistence.[44]

This is the only refutation of Anselm known to me, at least of those published before 1958, which shows an awareness of

---

[44] "Can God's Existence be Disproved?," *Mind,* 57 (1948). Reprinted in Findlay's *Language, Mind, and Value.* [See Bibliography for a relevant quotation from this book.]

what Anselm's Proof in its essential steps actually was. And it puts the matter in a different and clearer light than other refutations. Anselm declared that God could not exist contingently, from which by modal axioms it follows that He could not contingently fail to exist. What then? Obviously, either He could and does exist necessarily, or He necessarily fails to exist, i.e., His existence is logically impossible. Anselm, defended recently by Malcolm, rejects impossibility and infers necessary existence; Findlay rejects the logical possibility of necessary existence and infers the impossibility that God should exist at all. Most critics, so far as they have been at all clear about what they were doing, have by implication at least asserted either that God might contingently exist just as He might contingently fail to exist, *or* that He might contingently fail to exist even though, should He exist, it must be necessarily. The second alternative—here Anselm, Descartes (not quite so explicit on the point), Cudworth, Flint, Koyré, Malcolm, Findlay, and I agree—is modal nonsense. And the first—here again we agree—contradicts the meaning of 'God'.

Findlay's 'disproof' then is: 'if the idea of God is logically possible, the axiom of the nondeducibility or contingency of existence cannot be universally applicable; yet considering the manifest impossibility of deducing concrete actuality from mere universals, abstract concepts, or definitions, the axiom *must* be universally applicable. Not even divine actuality can be an exception'. This is a significant and serious paradox, like those of logic without some equivalent of type theory. It is a mistake to brush it aside as a mere sophistry, thereby refusing a chance to learn, as logicians have learned from their paradoxes. It is this brushing aside of serious difficulties which has partly vitiated nearly every contribution to this controversy.

That the concrete cannot be deduced from the abstract is an unshakable truth. Findlay is right to say so, and Malcolm here seems simply to miss the point. Findlay is also right, however, with Anselm and many other great men, when he says that God is the necessary being—or nothing thinkable. He is wrong only in supposing that a deducible or necessary divine existence must be actual or concrete. And this is the solution of the paradox: God's existence is not itself an actuality and is as abstract as the concepts from which it is deduced. It is their irreducible content. Nor need or can it 'make a difference' (except that our awareness of it makes a difference to us). It is the particular actuality of God which makes objective differences, and this is not what the Proof proves, but only that there is some such actuality, making some appropriate difference or other. Classical theism cannot admit this solution, which implies a real distinction in God between abstract existence and concrete actuality, the former necessary, the latter contingent. We have seen that this is just what neoclassical theism not only admits but gladly asserts.

The strength of Findlay's argument can be seen in this way. To refute the Anselmian contention of the incompatibility of perfection with contingency, one must maintain that God could conceivably exist contingently. Accordingly, skeptics who reject Findlay's conclusion are obligated to explain how they conceive an existence as perfect and yet contingent, or how they explain away the appearance of imperfection or essential limitation in the notion of accidental existence. When have they seriously attempted this? They usually do not even see the problem. And when they do, they treat it casually indeed. But it is the heart of the matter, not a detail. Findlay sees this, and strikes a blow at the heart. He grants that an implication of the idea of God is noncontingency; but since the idea also implies concreteness, actuality, and this cannot be necessary, the idea has no consistently conceivable relation to existence. On the one hand, religious thought and feeling require a unique or absolute security and logical priority for the divine existence; on the other, logic apparently rules out any such thing; ergo it rules out religious belief.

Findlay thus shows us a new aspect of the Anselmian problem which the older refutations failed to make explicit; but he still does not freely explore the terrain. He also knows too well the conclusion he must reach about the whole matter. That the Proof might, while disposing of the old conclusion, point the way to a different but equally positive one, he did not (at the time he wrote the quoted passages) for a moment imagine. At least, however, he explored the terrain in *one* rather new direction.

Certainly a theist must be prepared to 'speak theistically' no matter what the empirical facts. For he sees the meaning even of 'possible fact' in theistic terms; how then can it matter, for the mere question of theism as such, which possibilities are actualized? But a theist need not and will not speak about the concrete divine *actuality* regardless of the facts. 'God knows I am innocent' is inappropriate if in fact I am guilty. But be I innocent or guilty, God exists, and knows me as I am, if in fact I exist at all. And if I do not, then He exists knowing that situation as it is. It drives one almost to despair sometimes that such plain distinctions should be thought esoteric or irrelevant.

The most impressive aspect of Findlay's reasoning is not his reliance on 'modern' views—which is at best rather question-begging. It is rather his point, at the outset, about the abstract and the concrete, or—as one may also say—the logically weak and the logically strong. From the former there cannot be a deductive bridge to the latter. This is not modern, it is timeless good sense. But the question remains: is 'somehow actualized' any less abstract than 'perhaps unactualized'? On the assumption that there is a conceivable status of 'unactualized Greatness' and another conceivable status of 'actualized Greatness', then the assertion of the latter must be less abstract, and logically stronger. But this double conceivability in relation to actualization is just what Anselm and Findlay— wiser than he knows—deny. Naturally, one must admit the double conceivability in ordinary contingent cases; the contrast of God with these conceivably nonexistent natures not only harmonizes with their admission but requires it. The admission of ordinary things as conceivably nonexistent (and therefore not divine) is the same point, put from the other end.

Beyond the abstract-concrete paradox, overcome in neo-classical doctrine, what is left of Findlay's 'atheistic' argument (really 'positivistic', in the categorical or dogmatic sense, as I have been using terms)? Does not what was well designed as an attack on traditional theism become a valuable instrument of defence for a less conventional form of religious thought?

18. *Robert S. Hartman*

Apparently inspired partly or chiefly by Barth's fine work, an exciting and imaginative essay on Anselm's argument has recently appeared. It is not wholly clear what its author would do with the Findlay paradox, yet there is some evidence that he may be aware of it. (The promised sequel to the essay should clarify the question.) This article is another of the recent studies which seem to show that to read Anselm carefully is to see that the standard criticisms are far from adequate, and that we are by no means finished with the most famous— and most misunderstood—of all philosophical arguments.

Hartman tries to save *Prosl.* II by arguing that the existent is richer in properties than the merely possible; hence the 'richest possible' thing must be conceived as existent. One can still object that 'richest conceivable' thing means, that which would, if it existed, be richest; how then can the Argument get under way? For *if* the thing existed, it would also have the richness accruing from existence; while if it did not, there would be no 'it' characterized by the greatest richness, and hence no question of 'its' having a character incompatible with that— hence no contradiction. Only inconceivability-of-nonexistence, as a property, can rule out this escape.

Our author's suggestion is also open to the grave objection that an 'absolute maximum of richness' is doubtfully consistent, as we have seen earlier.

Hartman's contention that the Proof is 'not analytic' should be taken in conjunction with his comparison of it with mathematics. The synthetic element is in the application of a pure logical form to an intuitive datum, in this case religious faith. But (a) nothing is taken from faith except the 'name' of God which specifies what the question about His existence is to *mean.* So the Proof is an analysis of the meaning of 'God' for faith, and in this sense is analytic. Furthermore, (b) since the existence of God is, according to faith, the very principle of all actual or possible existence, and truth about it is Truth itself, this existence is no factual matter, in the proper sense of fact, nor, therefore, is its affirmation synthetic in the most usual sense. The Proof shows that the sole way to render faith consistent is to take it as *necessarily* true. This truth is then analytic in the broad sense that its falsity is either nonsense or contradiction.

Hartman's point of view may be in accord with this. But to be wholly clear as to his meanings one must be acquainted with his own original theory of axiological axiomatics, a doctrine whose careful evaluation belongs to the future.

Proslogion 2-4 consists of four pages . . . All the books and essays written about them . . . would fill libraries . . . What is it in these four pages, that makes them so potent a challenge to the best minds of humanity? . . .

I suggest that we have in these pages the first and so far the last—that is, the only—example in the history of thought of an entirely new philosophical method, which is the exact opposite of what has usually, both before and after Kant, been regarded as this method. It is neither categorical nor analytic, but axiomatic and synthetic. It is the method of mathematics itself, . . . the most effective cognitional method, that of science, applied to the most sublime subject. . . .

The reason that the proof has been so puzzling and challenging is that Anselm's argument presupposes a whole new system of thought of which the argument itself is only a part—like a promontory of a vast hinterland shrouded in fog. The passion aroused by the argument is that of exploring the *known unknown*—the passion of discovery, which is aroused by the expectation of finding unheard-of treasures in a realm which is known to be there but whose nature is unknown.

. . . A featureless existence is the exigentia of an essence: it is a Problem. The most powerful method of problem solving is the scientific, in particular, the axiomatic method, which posits a formula originating a system of thought applicable to the reality in question. The most famous example of this procedure is Newton, whose gravitational formula originated a system applicable to the whole universe. So Anselm, according to his own account, found a formula applicable to divine reality. The result was for him a matter of rejoicing, *delectatio*—the same kind of joy a scientist feels on breaking through to the properties—the definition—of what he knew was there but did not know what it was.

Behind the Anselmian proof there is hidden an axiomatic system of which the proof itself is a small part . . . in such a system Anselm's axiom—the name of God: 'that than which nothing greater can be thought'—would appear not as axiom but as . . . theorem of a system. This system—the meta-Anselmian axiomatic—would have its own axiom, from which the Anselmian name of God would be deduced as a theorem; and the whole proof would become an integral part of the system itself . . . .

. . . Barth makes it clear that the proof is not an analytic but a synthetic or axiomatic one. Anselm posits synthetically the name of God, as a formula, and deduces the proof from it . . . *modo geo-metrico.* The proof thus is purely formal: the name, the *significance,* proves itself. Where the name of God has been announced, heard, and understood, God exists in the cognition of the hearer—but . . . a God who only existed in cognition would be in an intolerable contradiction to His own revealed and believed name; He would have the name of God but would not *be* what the name says . . . The proof is really a *reductio ad absurdum.*

Vere est means God is not only in thought but also *over against* thought. But God does not exist for thought as does any object created by Him: . . . *Prosl. 3* . . . proves that God stands over against thinking in the unique manner in which the creator stands over against the thinking of the created creature.

The premise for Anselm is a word . . . but a word of God in the context of His revelation . . . From this . . . it is true, one cannot deduce His existence; but one can deduce the impossibility of His nonexist-ence. The proof does not satisfy Gaunilo because, positivist that he is, he seems to want a proof of God based on some sense experience; and such a proof has nothing to do with the Anselmian *intellectus fidei* and would be incompatible with Anselm's concept of God.

. . . the third chapter of *Proslogion* adds a higher stage to the *maius* and *minus* of the second chapter. . . . A being whose existence is inde-pendent of the dialectic of cognition and object is *maius* and belongs to a higher stage of being than a being which, no matter how truly it exists, how *vere est,* is subject to this dialectic; that is, whose existence can hypothetically be denied by the same thinking which may also affirm it. The former is an absolute being beyond the opposition of the subjective and objective. It not only exists in truth but it exists *as* truth; it is the truth of existence itself. . . .[45]

19. *Jan Berg*

Among the few careful attempts to apply the techniques of modern logic to Anselm's text is the one we are now to consider.[46] The following symbols are used:

'$\exists x(—x—)$' 'there is an x such that —x—'

'$\imath x(—x—)$' 'the unique x such that—x—'

'G' abbreviates 'nihil maius cogitari possit'. Thus 'G(x)' means that 'nothing greater than x can be conceived'.

'$\sim$' 'it is false that'

After several attempts to formulate Anselm's reasoning in *Prosl.* II, attempts which are found to assume what is to be proved (the divine existence), the following formula is said to avoid this assumption:

'$\sim \exists y(y = \imath x(G(x))) \rightarrow (\sim G) (\imath x(G (x)))$'

This formula says: 'If there is not a *y* identical with the unique *x* such that none greater can be conceived, then the unique *x* than which none greater can be conceived has the property of being not such that none greater can be conceived'. To avoid the contradiction in the consequent one must deny the antecedent in the initial formula, by asserting:

---

[45] "Prolegomena to a Meta-Anselmian Axiomatic," *Review of Metaphysics* 14 (1961), 638, 640, 666f.

[46] "An Examination of the Ontological Proof," *Theoria* 27 (1961), 99-106.

'∃y (y = ɿx (G))' 'There is a y identical with the unique x such that none greater can be conceived (God exists)'.

Though formally valid, the argument throws no light upon the justification of the initial premise. This is not a logical truism, but depends entirely upon an assumed peculiarity of the predicate G from which it is to follow that its failure to be instantiated in a unique individual would be contradictory. Here Berg has nothing to offer unless it be the *Prosl.* II notion that the existent is superior to the nonexistent. The difficulties with this principle are notorious and, as we have seen, are not obviated by rejecting, as Berg does, the dictum 'existence cannot be a predicate'. (See above, Sec. 10.)

Berg does not himself affirm the correctness of the formula, nor (I think) is he convinced of its correctness. This is not surprising since he makes no use of the modal principle that the necessarily existent is superior to the contingently existent. His formalization is in extensional, not modal, logic. And he thinks Malcolm's (and my) distinction between the simple and the modal form of the Proof 'mistaken'. But only the modal form gives a clear reason for imputing a contradiction to the hypothesis of noninstantiation.

If the modal argument is *not* distinct, then what is one to make of the assertion in *Prosl.* III that to be necessarily existent is to be superior to what is contingent? If this principle is valid, why can it not be used as premise for a proof? Will Berg argue that the validity of the principle cannot be known unless it is known that something does exist necessarily? But, as Anselm implies, one needs to assume only the *conceivability* of necessary existence and to have an insight into the superiority of the status so conceived. For, granting these two points, it follows that to apply the property G to a contingently existing thing would be contradictory; furthermore, to assert that a property is not instantiated is to imply that its noninstantiation is conceivable, and hence that any possible instance of it would be something existing contingently. Will Berg say that there is no reason to regard necessary existence as superior? But anyone who holds that is so remote from Anselm's point of view that he might do better than try to construe his text.

Nevertheless it is good that the attempt has been made to express Anselm in nonmodal yet formal terms and that a way has been found to construct in these terms a valid Anselmian argument, valid save (no trifling qualification) for the blindness of its initial premise.

20. *Jerome Shaffer*

One of the many recent attempts to improve upon traditional criticisms of the Argument discards the contention that the Argument is invalid simply because existence is not a predicate. We can, if we wish, make it a predicate in a certain case by definition. But then, it is urged, there still remains the question, does anything correspond to the definition?

Until further arguments are offered, it seems reasonable to hold that there is nothing logically improper in so defining the expression, 'God', that 'God exists' is a tautology and 'God does not exist' selfcontradictory. In fact it seems to me that the definition I have given expresses a concept of God (i.e., as necessarily existing) which many people actually accept (just as it is a common conception of Satan that he merely happens to exist). I wish . . . to show that this concept of God can give no support to the religious. I shall argue that no matter what its content, this concept of God is still simply a concept. What must be shown, and what cannot be shown just by an analysis of the concept, is that there actually exists something which answers to the concept. Even if we have here the concept of an object which necessarily exists, a further question remains whether any existent meets the specifications of the concept. The difficulty lies in showing that this further question makes sense, for I have admitted that 'God exists' is a necessary statement, analytically true, and therefore it looks as if there could be no further question. But that is an illusion. It must however be dispelled.

As a first step, I wish to point out that the concept of God is hardly unique in its capacity to generate a tautological existential statement. . . . Suppose we introduce the word, 'particular' to mean 'object which exists', and the word 'nonentity' to mean 'object which does not exist'. Then . . . we might say tautologically, 'Particulars exist and non-entities do not exist'. . . . The following sentences all have tautological uses: 'Existences exist', 'Fictitious objects do not exist', 'Members of extinct species existed once but no longer exist' . . . these sentences . . . may be used tautologically in those circumstances in which we wish to include as a necessary feature, as a defining element, notions of existence or nonexistence.

. . . Take the tautology, 'Fictitious objects do not exist'. One might think that this means the same as 'There are no fictitious objects'. But . . . this is incorrect, for although the former is true the latter is false. There are fictitious objects, many of them—Alice's looking glass, Jack's bean stalk . . . to mention only a few. In general, given a tautology of the form, 'A's exist', we cannot deduce from it, 'There are A's', nor from a tautology of the form, 'A's do not exist' can we deduce 'There are no A's'. And specifically, given the tautology, 'God exists', we cannot deduce from it, 'There is a God'. The statement, 'God necessarily exists, but there is no God', is *not* self-contradictory.

As it stands the situation is most paradoxical. . . .

It is tempting to try to resolve the paradox in accordance with Aristotle's principle that 'there are several senses in which a thing may be said to be'. Then to say that fictitious objects do not exist would be to say that fictitious objects lacked, say, spatio-temporal existence, whereas to say that there are fictitious objects would be to say that they had some other kind of existence—hence no contradiction. . . . But appeals to the systematic ambiguity of 'exists' will not work in all cases. . . . For example, it will be tautologically true that particulars exist in precisely the sense of 'exist', say, temporal existence, that it might be true that there are no particulars.

A more promising line of argument consists in showing that a tautological existential claim is quite different from a non-tautological existential claim. How are we to explain the difference? Suppose we say that a tautological existential assertion consists in attributing to the subject a special property, the property of necessary existence. We could explain this property by saying, á la Malcolm, that a being which has this property is such that it is senseless to speak of its non-existence or of its coming into existence or going out of existence or of the existence of anything else as a condition of its existence (pp. 44-59). Now this account will not do. First, the attempt to explain the necessity of the statement by postulating a special property commits us to an infinite regress of properties, for presumably this special property might not be one which a being just happens to have but one which it necessarily has and which it is senseless to speak of its not having, and thus by similar reasoning we are led to necessary necessary-existence, etc. And it is most unclear what these properties could be or how we could distinguish them. But secondly, it is not clear what this property of necessary existence, is, if this is any more than a way of saying that the existential proposition is necessary. Am I making anything clearer when I say that squares, which are necessarily four-sided, have the special property of *necessary four-sidedness?* A defining property is not a special kind of property. So the tautological character of the existential assertions I have been discussing cannot be explained by postulating a special predicate, necessary existence. Their tautological character arises from nothing but the definition we have stipulated for the subject term. . . .

What lies at the heart of the puzzle about the Ontological Argument is the fact that our concepts have two quite different aspects, marked by the familiar philosophical distinction of intension and extension . . . In making assertions about the extension of a concept there are typical forms of expression which we use: ' . . . exist', 'There are no . . . ' ' . . . are scarce', . . . etc. That such expressions are typically used in assertions about the extension (or lack thereof) of particular concepts is what is correctly brought out in the slogan, ' 'exists' is not a pred-

icate.' But the typical use is not the only use. Since any statement, with
suitable definitions, can be true by virtue of the meanings of the terms,
sentences with existential expressions can be used to express tautological statements. . . . 'Particulars exist', when asserted tautologically, is
used to make a claim about the meaning of the word, 'particulars', and
therefore cannot be used to make a claim about the extension of the
term. Similarly, if someone uses the sentence, 'God exists', tautologically, he tells us only that being an existent is a logical requirement for
being God. If, on the other hand, someone asserts, 'God exists' non-
tautologically, then he claims that the term, 'God', has extension,
applies to some existent. . . . The *prima facie* plausibility of the
Argument comes from the use of a sentence intensionally when the
typical use of that sentence is extensional. In this way it conceals the
illicit move from an intensional to an extensional statement.

. . . Even when we have an existential tautology like 'Particulars
exist', or 'God exists', it still remains an open question whether the
concept of particulars or the concept of God has application, applies to
any existent. What is settled at one level is not settled at another. It
is important to see that we can go on to settle the question at the
other level, too, for we can *make* it *a priori* true that the concept has
application. For example, let the expression, 'the concept of God',
mean, 'a concept which has application and applies to a being such
that . . .'. Then by definition the concept of God has application;
the statement, 'The concept of God has application', is now a tautology,
given the definition. But nothing is gained by such a maneuver.
. . . We have framed a concept, namely the concept of the concept of
God, and this concept makes certain statements tautologically true.
Yet we can still raise the extensional question, Does this concept
refer to any existent? At this level the extensional question would be
whether there actually is a concept of God such that this concept has
extension, and there is such a concept only if actually there is a God
. . . Nothing has been settled except the meaning of a certain expression. . . .

A . . . troublesome threat to the intension-extension distinction
arises when we try to apply the distinction to certain concepts . . .
suppose we ask whether the concept of a number has extension . . .

What makes this case puzzling is that we have no idea what would count as establishing that the concept of a number has extension or that it does not have extension . . . Nothing would count as showing that the concept of numbers had extension over and above its intensional content, and this is to say that numbers are intensional objects.

The same thing must be said for the existence of God. The most that the Ontological Argument establishes is the intensional object, God, even if this intensional object has the attribute of existence as an intensional feature. To establish that the concept of God has extension requires adducing some additional arguments to show that over and above its intensional features, over and above the content of the concept (or the meaning of the word, 'God'), the concept of God has extension as well. This additional argument will of necessity have to be an a posteriori argument to the effect that some actual existent answers to the concept. We are thus led to the result that the Ontological Argument of itself alone cannot show the existence of God, in the sense in which the concept is shown to have extension. And this is just as the religious wish it to be. They do not conceive of God as something whose being expresses itself entirely in the concepts and propositions of a language game. They conceive of Him as something which has effects on the world and can in some way be experienced. Here is a crucial respect in which His status is meant to be different from that of numbers. The concept of God is a concept which *might* have extension. But some further argument is required to show whether it does or not.[47]

Let us begin with the fifth and fourth sentences from the end of this clever argumentation. As we have reiterated, there is no necessity to identify the full actuality of God with His bare existence and good reason not to make this identification. God can have particular effects on the world without His mere existence being the entire cause of these effects. Existing neces-

---

[47] Existence, Predication, and the Ontological Argument," *Mind,* 71 (1962), esp. pp. 318-325.

sarily, He can also make contingent 'decrees' (and He must make some such decrees or other). It is these free decrees which furnish the concrete reality of deity with which religion is trying, in the feeble way open to man, to deal. So we can reject Shaffer's attempt to show that the God proved by the Argument is merely intentional or abstract and not the God of religion. It is the God of religion, but only in His most abstract, necessary aspect, which is presupposed by all more concrete and contingent aspects. The necessity is that the class of the latter aspects be nonempty.

A concept can have extension only if it has intension. But there are three sorts of concepts, those whose intension is *neutral* with respect to whether or not the concept has extension, those which *forbid* such extension (e.g., 'absolutely isolated part of the universe'), and those which *require* some extension or other, on pain of falling into mere absurdity. Suppose the class of 'existents' were empty. The supposition has no clear meaning. No one could possibly know such a 'state of affairs', and it would not in any intelligible sense be a state of affairs. The reason is not in any mere stipulation. The word 'existent' might have been used for something other than the widest class which *must* have members, but then either another word would be used for this class, or language would be left, insofar, incomplete. Our author seems simply to *assume* that there can be no such necessarily nonempty class. But that is part of what is at issue in an ontological argument. And he fails to remind us that many logicians think it a requirement of logic itself that the widest class of entities should be nonempty.

Specifically, the Argument, neoclassically interpreted, shows that the class 'divine states, genidentical with one another', is necessarily nonempty, and is indeed inseparable from the class of 'existents', since it is essential to any existent to be in relation to divine existence. This universality of relationship between divine existence and all else is implicit in any religiously acceptable definition of God. Hence, so is the impossibility of His nonexistence.

The crucial passage in Shaffer's argumentation is that in which he rejects—while pretending or appearing to accept it—the idea of necessary existence as definitive of deity. To suppose that the divine freedom from existential contingency can only be a property of our statements, arising from stipulations, is to deny the very possibility of God's existence. There is then nothing for an a posteriori proof, or search among facts, to furnish. Only an *objective immunity* to existential contingency is compatible with what religion means by God (and philosophy ought to mean). Our human contingency, which shows us not to be divine, is likewise no mere matter of propositions and languages; it is rather the real potentiality of the world for doing without us, or for making our existence impossible. The very notion of a corresponding anti-God potentiality is contradictory. (There could of course be an anti-demon potentiality!) It is clear that the author has only a hazy notion of all this, or of *why* religion, as he mentions, takes Satan as (at most) something that happens to exist, but God as existing necessarily. When he says, "The question remains, does there actually exist something which answers to the concept of the necessarily existent," he either means, 'does there *happen* to exist such a something', and then he is talking contradictorily; or he means, 'is there necessarily such a something?' But in the latter case the question answers itself. Anything which could be necessary is necessary, by the reduction principle of modal logic. Of course, **Professor Shaffer** can reject this principle. But then *that*, and not what he says in this article, is his ground for the rejection of the Argument. And the principle is reasonable.

Three objections to the idea of objective necessity are offered. One is an argument from regress, the necessity of the necessary property, etc. However, the necessity of a necessity, by the reduction principle, is simply the necessity itself, and so is the possibility of the necessity. Similarly, 'it is true that it is true' only says, 'it is true'. As for the contingency of the necessity, the denial of which starts the regress, it is nonsense and needs no denial. The regress seems spurious.

One could, I think, as cogently accuse Shaffer of having a regress on *his* hands. God 'exists necessarily' only means, he says, that we define Him as existing. But then this description of God is either optional or necessary. He will reply, I take it, that it can only be necessary upon some condition or other, such as that one takes the religious tradition seriously at this point. But is the tradition necessary or contingent? Could there be a religion without it, or a rational being without religion? On certain conditions, perhaps there could. But these conditions are either ultimate or they have conditions. In the latter case we have a regress. And in any case, the statement, 'No being exists necessarily', is not made true or false by any mere definition, nor yet by any mere fact. A fact or contingent truth cannot be precondition of an unconditional necessity. (*Any* being can be conditionally necessary; for instance, all past events are necessary for the present's being as it is.) I say the statement is necessarily false, and any language in which the corresponding necessary truth cannot be expressed is defective.

Clearly, religion has never meant by the divine necessity that we define God to exist. It has meant that to the divine existence there is no truly conceivable alternative, that God owes his existence to nothing, certainly not to a lucky accident, any more than to a rational cause, or to our ways of talking. His existence is taken to be the presuppositon of any meaning, any value, any existence or nonexistence whatsoever. To allow this requirement to be logically permissible, and then ask, but in fact, is there a being fulfilling the requirement? is to contradict the requirement one has accepted; it is to subject God existentially to contingency, either to causeless chance or to a cause beyond Himself. It is to grant that if God exists He exists either by mere chance, or as caused. But so He could not exist!

Shaffer's second objection is that it is unclear wherein the objective necessity lies. We have shown that this challenge can be met. It lies in the divine perfection, which involves an absolute correlation between possible and possible-for-God, between 'reality' and 'divinely-known-reality'. Omniscience, universal creativity, self-sufficiency of existence, all the divine attributes, are inseparable from the status of God as pervasive of reality, actual and possible, hence not, in His bare existence, the actualization of this or that particular possibility. The necessary is the universal element in the possible. That element is the functioning of God, not any particular divine functioning, but divine functioning as such.

The third objection is an analogy offered as a *reductio ad absurdum*. Squares are necessarily four-sided, yet it does not help to say that they have the property of necessary four-sidedness. But why is this locution not helpful? One reason is that 'contingent four-sidedness' is not a common expression, whereas 'contingent existence' certainly is (in traditional metaphysics). It is therefore helpful to make the point that no such existence can apply to God, though it does apply to all other individuals. Nor is 'contingent four-sidedness' an inevitably foolish expression, for 'houses' are only contingently four-sided, since they can be five-sided, six-sided, or circular. By the same token, squares cannot have contingent but only necessary four-sidedness. That this is utterly trivial is because 'square' means by definition having four equal sides. But suppose we say instead that four-sided figures necessarily have four angles, or four-angled figures have four sides. This is a truth independent of names and definitions. For whether or no we have a name for the figure between triangle and pentagon in the series of polygons, the possibility of such a thing and hence of such a name is a necessary truth. And also necessary, regardless of names, is the relation between number of angles and number of sides. Just so the relation between 'divinity' and 'necessary existence' is not created by names or formulae. Worship implies such a relation, and worship is not a 'language game'. And here the hypothetical element in the necessity that four-angled figures be four-sided (*if* anything is the one it is the other) drops out. For necessary existence means, there *must* be something of the specified kind. To insist that every idea be capable of fitting the hypothetical mold is nothing but the positivistic assumption posing as harmless truism. 'God' is not an hypothesis which facts may or may not support but a theory of what it means to be a fact— i.e., to have a certain relation to omniscience. If this view is wrong, it is not merely factually but logically wrong. For it purports to explicate 'fact' as such, and to do this without conflicting with the ordinary meaning of the word. If it fails, the result is confusion, not just factual error. Assertions of existential necessity cannot be factual errors, but only logical ones. Theism is confusion unless it is an assertion of necessity. According to positivism it is confusion whether or not it is such an assertion. But this, Anselm showed, is the issue, and not any question of mere fact.

Shaffer admits that one can put 'has application' into the 'concept of the concept' of God. But then, he says, the extensional question becomes, is there such a concept of God? And, he holds, we cannot know this without knowing that there is a God. I reply, there is no concept of the religious object, appropriate to the idea of worship taken with any strictness, which does not imply noncontingency. A concept of the concept of 'God' which denies this aspect is a misuse of words. So we come back to the disjunction: either there is a coherent concept of the religious object—and then the divine existence is a closed question—or there is no coherent concept of God, and then positivism, rather than atheism or theism, is correct. Our author has not shown that atheism is self-consistent. The insufficiency of the Argument (by itself alone) of which he speaks is only that it fails to refute positivism. It does, however, refute atheism. That is quite enough to make it a very important discovery. Moreover, in refuting atheism it refutes empiricism. The most burning question of philosophy, it shows, is to be settled, not by observation of facts, but by examination of ideas, meanings.

The remark 'a defining property is not a special kind of property' is reasonable, but irrelevant. For the necessary existence of God does not consist merely in His being defined to exist, but in His being defined, and *as the One worshiped correctly defined,* to exist in the unique manner of noncontingency. That this is a special way of existing the author seems at times to admit and then roundly to deny. But in denying it he is either asserting positivism, or else failing to understand the religious idea; while in admitting it he is refuting his own argumentation.

The absurdity of the reasoning appears especially clearly if we consider such cases of 'defining things to exist' as the following, 'existing dodos', 'existing dragons', and the like. Here there is no serious paradox. A dodo or dragon would exist, if at all, contingently, and hence there cannot be any logical impossibility in the nonexistence of dodos or dragons. To use a definition to make it appear otherwise is so flagrant a misuse of the defining process as to need no special further analysis. It is just the question at issue whether the religious idea is or is not the idea of a thing which would or could exist contingently. Anselm showed that it is not. Most of this author's discussion is a series of red herrings distracting his and his reader's attention from this central issue. His most relevant remarks are attempts to prove that all existence must, objectively regarded, be contingent. But on that assumption what Anselm showed must have been, as Findlay rightly points out, the impossibility, not the necessity, of the divine reality.

I conclude that the remarkable ingenuity of this author does not save him from missing—or not clearly seeing—the modal structure of the Anselmian discovery.

21. *Heinrich Scholz and Frederic Fitch*

Our last two examples are distinguished formal logicians.

I sometimes think that Heinrich Scholz was the noblest human being that I have ever known (I met him in 1949), a theologian who turned from theological studies to formal logic because—and this is characteristic of the man—he thought that there was no other equally honest and effective way to further the clarification of theological questions. With White-head he is for me the most high-minded and inspiring rational-ist of our century. With angelic steadiness he stuck to his 'Platonic ideal', as he called it, all through the Nazi period in Germany. Had he not been forced to live almost entirely without a stomach (literally) he might have accomplished far more than this disability, not to mention the spiritual and finally material disorder in his country, permitted him to do.

If any man in Germany was equipped to deal objectively and accurately with the logical structure of Anselm's reason-ing, it should have been Scholz. In one of his lectures, written in 1950-51, he does deal with the topic from the standpoint of 'logistic logic',[48] And what happens? He falls completely into the trap set for him by Anselm's blunder in *Prosl.* II, and Gaunilo's (and most modern writers') failure to see beyond this blunder. We are expressly told that only *Prosl.* II is being considered! So we are prepared for all but a few minor details in the result. I shall not reproduce his formulation of the argument, as it simply duplicates Anselm's first or nonmodal one. With great precision Scholz then shows how, in terms of modern exact logic, existence cannot without begging the question be taken as a predicate of an individual subject; for without existence there is no subject for the predicate to inhere in. Anselm confused himself here by talking about things existing in the mind, even if not in any further sense, and this, as Scholz argues, will not do, for an 'in-dividual', x, 'merely in the mind', is not strictly individual

---

[48] *Mathesis Universalis: Abhandlungen zur Philosophie als, strenger Wissenschaft* (Benno Schwabe & Co., Basel, Stuttgart, 1961), pp. 62-74.

at all, but only a property or class seeking instantiation or members. With this I entirely agree. But the modal argument does not attempt to compare two individuals, one existing, the other not. It compares two hypotheses about the existential status of 'unsurpassable individual', and finds one contradictory: the hypothesis, 'there is an unsurpassable individual which exists contingently', and the hypothesis, 'there is an unsurpassable individual which exists necessarily'. Neither hypothesis needs to be taken initially as asserted. For the point is that the first hypothesis is necessarily false, impossible, if the second is even capable of being true. To exist contingently is to be inferior to anything existing necessarily, so that if the latter is possible, the descriptive phrase 'unsurpassable' is in the former case used contradictorily. And if 'necessarily existing' is not possible, then 'unsurpassable' has no definite and coherent meaning. For only that which grounds all possibility, including its own, and the nonexistence of which therefore cannot be a possibility, can be strictly unsurpassable. Hence either the necessary existence or the impossibility, but not the mere nonexistence, of unsurpassability is permissibly assertible.

Scholz does, as one might expect, refute, on Anselm's behalf, the relevance of the perfect-island analogy, on the rather obvious ground that no finite thing such as an island can be the greatest conceivable, so that, whether or not there is a logically admissible idea of greatest conceivable being, there can be none of greatest conceivable island. It is hard to forgive the multitudes who have not allowed their preconvinced minds to hit upon this reply to Gaunilo's suggestion.

Scholz also explains how Bolzmann and Frege had treated existence as a predicate, but a predicate of a property, the predicate of being nonempty or of having an instance. On this basis also the *Prosl.* II argument will not work. (For we do not compare properties and argue that the better properties are the instantiated ones. In that case, in the words of the proverb, "wishes would be horses and beggars might ride.") Yet here we must be careful. For as we saw in Part One, Sec. 18, it is inherent in almost all theistic traditions, and Scholz as former theologian must have known this, that God does not have but *is* His goodness or supreme worth. In other words, the property-individual distinction, symbolized, say by '*Px*', does not in God have the same structure as in other cases. And this is the very point Anselm had discovered, in a special aspect.

Let us look into this. Some properties are instantiated, but contingently so; others are, equally contingently, uninstantiated. All ordinary properties (those of various kinds of surpassable beings) are contingent in this sense, whether or not they be instantiated. It follows that any instance of ordinary predicates exists contingently; for if its whole species or class might not have existed at all, certainly it might not have done so. But there are predicates which could not be contingently instantiated, since they are logically absurd, like 'round and square in the same respect'. Anselm's claim is that 'unsurpassability' is a third sort of predicate, which is neither contingent nor impossible, but is necessarily instantiated. Its existence alone is possible. What has Scholz against this? He does not even put the question, naturally enough, since he is considering only *Prosl.* II. If ordinary predicates connote contingency, and if this ordinariness, i.e., this surpassability, is the very reason for the contingency, then by the converse of the same reason, unsurpassability connotes noncontingency. Moreover, that the imperfection of nondivine things, their noneternity, compositeness, dependence, lack of self-sufficiency, is the very reason for their contingency is plausibly argued in various ways and in various places by Anselm, and by many before him, including Aristotle. But it clearly follows that even the hypothetical negation of imperfection will imply the negation of contingency. Moreover, the second negation cannot be hypothetical only. For modal status as such is necessary.

It is important to note that existence is no proper or intrinsic predicate of ordinary predicates. That two-handedness exists in my hands is not a part of what is meant by 'two-handed'. For two and hand might have been two and hand, just as they are, though I had been born one-handed, or not born at all. It is really I, as individual, who exist as instantiating two-handedness. G. E. Moore is wholly unrefuted in his contention that, 'this thing exists, and might not have' makes entire good sense. However, since there is no a priori or purely conceptual definition of 'this thing', or of me as an individual, this kind of existence as a predicate cannot be deduced a priori, but only found empirically. 'This thing exists', or 'I exist', is in a sense tautological; and yet it is contingent, for neither 'this thing' nor 'I' might have been possible with this meaning. What *is* a proper predicate of predicates (this too Aristotle had seen) is their modal status. Wholly limited, dependent, composite, generated beings *must* also be capable of failing or of having failed to exist; but by exactly the same principle, the Unsurpassable must be incapable of failing or having failed to exist. And here there is no real distinction between Unsurpassable and the Unsurpassable individual; Unsurpassability is its own 'principle of individuation'. We will return to this point presently.

Not a suspicion of the foregoing is in Scholz's essay. I add that, so far as I know, no philosopher in Germany since Kant (except Anselm's monographer Hasse) has gone back to Anselm and discovered there the modal, or proper ontological, argument, and dealt carefully with its logic. Instead, all have relied upon Gaunilo, Kant, Hegel, or the nonmodal versions of Anselm, Descartes, or Thomas Aquinas, to inform them in the matter. In this case 'German thoroughness' quite failed to operate. More's the pity.

Scholz's oversight is especially remarkable in that he refers to Barth, who was not guilty of it. My explanation is that, since Barth (as Scholz notes) rejected the Argument as a philosophical one, insisting it is purely theological, and since Scholz was interested in the philosophical question, he did not bother to read Barth in detail. But this is a guess.

Scholz believed in truths applicable to all possible worlds. He called these truths metaphysical, and he expected logistic to help in their elucidation. I wish I could have put the following to him.

First, logic can admit the notion of existential necessity, at least in the form, $(x) fx \rightarrow (Ex) fx$; properties universally instantiated cannot be uninstantiated, or in other words, logic cannot deal with a simply empty universe. The widest class cannot be empty. The case for this contention, which Scholz himself accepts, seems to me conclusively made by two recent authors, Jonathan Cohen and William Kneale.[49]

Second, necessary nonemptiness or instantiatedness is all that we need for necessary existence, even in the divine form. True enough, if 'instances' are thought of as 'individuals', in the ordinary meaning, then there is trouble in taking any such

---

[49] Jonathan Cohen, *The Diversity of Meanings* (London, 1962), pp. 255-264; Wm. and Martha Kneale, *The Development of Logic* (Oxford, 1962), pp. 706f.

instance as necessary. (Scholz wonders how one could know
a priori that just one greatest individual, God, instantiates
divinity as defined.) It is indeed essential to the distinction of
type between property and instance that the latter be a contingent illustration. But, as we have seen (Scholz probably
did not see it, such was his respect for the theological and
metaphysical tradition, which at the same time he did not
attempt to defend, since he did not know how to do so with
modern instruments of analysis), it is logically possible to
distinguish between divinity and its contingent instances, and
yet to exclude polytheism, even as possibility, and affirm the
necessary existence of a unique divine individual. The key is
a doctrine held by Scholz himself, the doctrine that the most
concrete particular entities are not enduring individuals but
momentary events or states.[50] The existence of an individual is
the actuality of a certain sort of event-sequence. The sequence
can be defined without specifying all the particular events,
for we identify a person without committing ourselves to
all his adventures past and future. Now this schema can
be applied to deity, and I hold must be applied if antinomies are to be avoided. The property of divinity, defined in the
neoclassical version of Anselm's formula, cannot be contingently, but only necessarily, nonempty, and while any of its
instantiating 'states' is contingent, that there are some such
states, and also that any two of them are 'genidentical', i.e., in
personal sequence, with one another, can and must be necessary.
Is there anything in modern logic to forbid this?

You may say that logic finds the notion of necessary instantiation valid at most only with respect to properties that

---

[50] Scholz, *op. cit.*, pp. 405-410.

are universally applicable. True, but divinity is in a definite, though unique, sense strictly universal. Just as any entity is identical with itself, so is any entity, according to the meaning of theism, related to God as its creator and sole adequate knower. Relativity to the divine is as essential to existence as self-identity. To deny this is to deny not simply the existence but the logical possibility of deity. We have argued this so often that we must leave it at that here. The necessary nonemptiness of the class of divine states is related to the necessary nonemptiness of the only seemingly broader class of states in general (concrete particulars as such) in this way, that for any nondivine state there must be a divine state in which the former is known. The correlation creature-creator cannot be broken up, leaving the mere creature, or the mere creator, without making the very idea of either a meaningless or incoherent notion. Thus, if there must be entities, there must be entities divinely created and known; the only alternative being the rejection of the very question of theism as incoherent.

Had Scholz glimpsed these relationships, would he have had to confess, as he did, that while he could defend *metaphysica generalis*, as the theory of all possible worlds, he could find no rational approach to *metaphysica specialis,* or the theory of 'last things', including presumably some sort of answer to the theistic question?[51] A 'possible world' as such is already God, in one of His creative potentialities, and it is and can be neither more nor less than this. True, there are some difficult and important questions concerning the relation of such ideas to the language of pure formal logic. But the locus of the questions at least begins to appear when they are seen from the neo-

---

[51] *Ibid.,* pp. 430-432.

classical standpoint, whereas from the classical there seems to be, as Scholz found, no promising way to connect logical to theological questions. Anselm had already come closer to the heart of the matter than anyone in the Gaunilo tradition could do. Existence is indeed, in a loose sense, an attribute, and, moreover, in ordinary cases of special or exclusive attributes, it is a contingent 'attribute of attributes'. But of universal, all tolerant, or nonspecial attributes, existence is always a necessary attribute, and divinity is in a sense the sum of all nonspecial or strictly universal attributes. The divine knowledge must be able to take on or acquire the form of any object whatever. Hence to assert the existence of this knowledge as such excludes nothing, is not a 'special' topic at all, in the relevant sense, but a, or the, strictly universal one. That some particular entities or other must exist means that some such entities must be known to God, whose infallibility means the logical impossibility of a divorce between being and being divinely known. There is only one metaphysics, general metaphysics, but there are levels of explicitness in its results. If God seems to be left out, this can only mean that something is left obscure.

Whether or not Scholz would have been convinced by all this I am fairly sure that he would not have brushed it aside as irrelevant or unimportant. I believe he would have admitted that these matters deserve further inquiry. And he might have seen that, since the theistic view of 'possible existent' is simply, 'something God might create', it is absurd to treat the divine existence as among the things which might be and also might not be. The supposition already begs the theistic question by assuming that possibility has a meaning independent of deity. The supremacy imputed to deity includes not merely depen-dence of what actually exists upon God, but dependence of everything whatever, whether actuality or possibility, and whether the latter be real or 'merely logical'. The notion that the least item of meaning can be independent of the divine existence is a proclamation of atheism, or rather, of positivism. It is not a neutral basis of argument. Once more, there is here no room for a merely factual question; the issue is one of meaning.

It is a great pleasure to be able to end this survey with the consideration of so refreshingly original an essay as the one which Professor Frederic B. Fitch has recently published on "The Perfection of Perfection."[52] He rejects the idea of possible entities exhibiting various properties; he also rejects the idea of existence as a property of individuals, remarking that, whereas the traditional ontological argument seems first to treat God as a perfect possible entity, and then to object that if this entity lacked the attribute of actuality it would be imperfect, what he proposes to show is rather that the attribute of perfection is logically nonempty, 'existence' being the nonemptiness of some attribute. Fitch then argues, with remarkable independence of the traditional disputes, that the attribute of perfection must itself be taken as supremely perfect, as its own unique instance. But then, since an empty attribute, one which is *merely* an attribute, is insofar deficient or imperfect, and *this* attribute is necessarily perfect, it must also be nonempty. When I first read this, I thought it was more curious than convincing. But further reflection has considerably altered the perspective. At worst, it is wonderful to encounter a writer who has done some thinking of his own on this old topic which

---

[52] *The Monist,* 47, No, 3 (1963), 466-471.

has become so surrounded with what one is (no doubt wrongly) tempted to call parrotry.

Let us grant that there are no 'possible instances' of predicates but only predicates whose instantiation is possible. However, does it follow that existence is really an attribute of (ordinary kinds of) attributes, with nonexistence a corresponding negative attribute of attributes, their being empty? To have an empty stomach is to have a special kind of stomach, in that the emptiness really qualifies the stomach at the time, giving it a different tension and so on. But an 'empty attribute' is not, in any parallel sense, qualified by its emptiness. Here I think (with some diffidence, however) that we confront a characteristic tendency of a formal logician to mistake a feature of our symbolic machinery for a reality beyond that machinery. It is the universe, not green gianthood, which is empty of green giants. All discourse is about the actual, though the reference to actuality may be more or less involved and disguised. Even 'person of normal size' is, in itself, empty of actual people, though the world is full (too full perhaps) of such entities. Of course, taking things purely extensionally, the *class* of green giants is indeed empty (but is there such a class, in a nontechnical normal sense of 'is'?) and that of 'person of normal size' is nonempty; but what holds for classes, in this respect, does not hold for properties. The class attribute never contains the individual instances, no matter how many the class itself contains.

However, it does not appear that this point affects Fitch's argument. For what he wants to show is not merely, as he says, that the attribute of 'perfection is nonempty', but rather that it is *necessarily* nonempty. (This seems quite clear from the structure of his reasoning.) And of course an impossibility of being uninstantiated is a very different thing from merely being (contingently) instantiated. Against taking *contingent* non-emptiness of an attribute as an intrinsic attribute of that attribute is just the contingency itself. A quality must not change in being instantiated, if it can also be uninstantiated; for if it did change then, by an adaptation of one of Kant's arguments, it would not be that very quality but another which was instantiated. However, if the attribute is incapable of being uninstantiated, then, since being instantiated is the only status we have to recognize for it, there can be no problem of how instantiation would alter or enrich the attribute. The point is that the denial of instantiation is here absurd. We still, to be sure, must be able to distinguish the particular instances from the attribute; however, as explained in Sec. 11 of Part One, this does not entail a further distinction between the attribute and its merely being instantiated somehow. Just as the abstract must be somehow embodied in some actuality (Aristotle's contention against platonism), so that we *mean* by 'an abstraction' something somehow housed in the concrete (if only by being thought about) and yet no particular concrete entity or set of entities is required by the abstract entity, similarly a necessarily instantiated attribute could be clearly nonidentical with its instances, and yet in its very being, as an attribute, instantiated somehow.

Fitch apparently holds that it is not a fallacy (some have called it the 'homological fallacy') to take perfection as its own unique instance, but rather, it is obligatory so to take it. Since I have said that Greatness or Unsurpassability (clearer, in my opinion, than Fitch's seemingly rather circular 'highest degree of perfection') is the very individuality of deity, that which makes God God and no one and nothing else, can I object to his saying that the divine essence, attribute, or individuality is the unique case of supreme perfection, i.e., of itself? If the values of the variable X are taken to be individuals, then the unique X which is divinely perfect is just the existing divine perfection itself. This is a form of the Findlay paradox. It would constitute a *reductio ad absurdum,* so far as I can see, were it not for the possibility of taking the values of X to be, not individuals, but states. For here we have a class whose members are contingent, yet through them the class property is necessarily exemplified. That is, the class necessarily has extension (and I have argued, with Cohen, the Kneales, and others, that there must be necessarily nonempty classes, such as the class of concrete entities), and yet the class property could exist with quite other instances. So I am perhaps in agreement, insofar, with Fitch's double contention that perfection is its own unique instance, and therefore not a *mere* attribute, since it must have whatever else it needs to be perfect. He seems correct also in holding that being a mere attribute is an imperfection. Certainly, if to be perfect is to surpass all (except self) a mere attribute does not do this, for it is an abstract entity, and the concrete transcends in richness any and every abstraction, its assertion being logically stronger. Moreover, a mere attribute cannot surpass itself, and the Findlay paradox, we saw, can be resolved only through the idea of self-surpassing.

Thus there is a sense in which the attribute of perfection is not itself perfect, for it is not the 'self-surpassing surpasser of all things'. And now we see that it is not quite correct to identify the divine essence with God as an individual. The divine essence is the individuality of God, but not God as an individual. An individual can surpass itself, but not an individuality. The distinction is between the 'defining characteristic', in Whitehead's careful phrase, of an enduring society or ordered sequence of states or unit events, and the society itself. 'Society' is really more exact than 'sequence' (and Whitehead's language is often more exact than that of those who condescend to him); for the identity of a society is not dependent upon that of its members. A society is not an extensional class of events in a certain order. What identifies it is not its members, but the characteristic shared among them which is taken as definitive of the society. The Wilson Ornithological Society has an identity which we can project far into the future (barring overwhelming catastrophe), but we do not do this by knowing members of it for future generations and centuries. Similarly, a man has, for his acquaintances or himself, an identity in the future though neither they nor he know a single one of the future events which will actualize this identity. They know that these events will share certain characteristics, such as (barring serious disease) ability to recall various events now in the past, exhibiting certain personality traits (including, from the scientific point of view, a certain unknown but rea-sonably-posited gene structure which will persist until death).

On my view God is the supreme form of 'personally-ordered' society. His defining characteristic, the divine perfection, His gene structure, as it were, is precisely His perfection, His neces-sary surpassing of all, including self. Each of His states will be the uniquely adequate summing up of the cosmic actuality correlated with it and of all past states of the divine society. And it will be the only society whose defining characteristic could not fail to be actualized in ever new (and greater) states.

In what sense is this defining characteristic itself 'perfect'? It does not surpass all concrete individuals other than God, for an abstraction—a mere attribute—cannot intelligibly be said to surpass concrete things. But we may compare the divine attribute with other attributes. In this comparison we can say that the divine attribute is at least equal to any essence in universality, for it is omnipresent, inherent in reality as such; but at the same time it surpasses all other essences in individuality, since it is the only pure essence which distinguishes an individual from all others. In it alone are universality and individuality completely harmonized or at one. It is the sole individual universal, or universal individual, in which neither the individuality nor the universality needs to be qualified or diluted. A man, for instance, is a sort of universal, in that his defining characteristic keeps receiving thousands of new exemplifications each day that he is alive; but on the one hand the individual identity of a man is a very relative and fluctuating affair (as a conscious person he seems not to exist at all in dreamless sleep, as a rational person in delirium or far-gone intoxication, and his ability to remember his past and his purposes and what he has been and intends to be is an affair of more or less, mostly less from some points of view) and on the other hand, the universality of the man is also a very restricted affair. It spans only a vanishingly small stretch of time, and at any one time is appreciably relevant to a vanishingly small part of space. Again, one might say that the cosmos is an individual, with a strictly universal defining characteristic. But here we must drastically dilute the significance of individual identity. The cosmos is not *for itself* identical through time. The unity of its sequences of events is not of a high order, even as compared to that of a man. Or, if we wish to say that the cosmos has personal order, we must also say (and I do) that the personally-ordered dominant society of the cosmos is God Himself. But the cosmos is not a well-integrated individual other than and rivalling God. Apart from the dominant society which *is* the divine 'soul', we have but the cosmic body, which is an individual only in something like the sense in which a man's body, abstracting from his consciousness, is so. Rather the body is a nonpersonal society of cells (themselves societies of societies), and the cosmos a nonpersonal society of societies on all sorts of levels.

So the unique intersection of unqualified universality with unqualified individuality is indeed a merit elevating the divine essence among essences generally. One may also say that the divine essence is the only fully self-explanatory one. 'Cosmos' by itself is a riddle; it is an ordered system, but what orders the parts? It either could cease to be, or its cessation is impossible; take it whichever way you please, you will be baffled. But the personal order of the divine life is the one case in which 'self-ordering' and eternal self-maintenance make clear sense. Each new divine state harmonizes itself with its predecessor and with the previous state of the cosmos, somewhat as a man harmonizes himself in each new state with his previous experience and bodily state, but with the decisive difference (among others) that the man must hope, and may easily hope in vain, that the internal and external environment will continue to make it possible for his bodily harmony to survive, whereas with God there is no such problem. First, there is simply no *external* environment. (Plato saw deeply into the meaning of this in the *Timaeus*, but his thought on this point was too simply profound for most philosophers since his time.) Second, the 'internal environment' is here under a radical control not rivalled even by the influence of a fully-conscious man over his own nervous system. Why? No mere mystery. It follows from the concept of the divine essence that the divine experience sums up with unique adequacy all the value of the entire actual world, and hence each thing can look to it for guidance and inspiration. Analogously, a man's brain cells are constantly sensitive to his thoughts and feelings, which, compared to cellular experiences, are doubtless sublime and quasi-divine. Incomparably more must all things be sensitive to the unique beauty and richness of the divine experiences. Thus God needs only to continue adapting Himself to the world, with His unique adaptive skill and power. The world is then bound, for that very reason, to adapt to Him. (The leaders to whom men adjust themselves are those who at least create the illusion that they are in harmony with men and things.) The foregoing is a bare outline. But it perhaps suffices to justify Fitch's contention that the divine essence, perfection, is itself the supreme essence, the Form elevated above all other forms as such.

Must such a form be more than a mere form, *must* it be exemplified? One could fill a volume (we have been doing so) with reasons for an affirmative answer. If the form connotes the sole self-intelligible kind or order, and if the order of everything else is intelligibly derivable from its self-ordering, then that is already a reason. Again, the exact intersection of universality and individuality can hardly fail to be a logically distinctive locus in the intellectual world. Necessity of actualization is not obviously any *more* distinctive. All other individuals are contingent, true, but then equally all are lacking in the universal relevance of their defining characteristics. All others must be known a posteriori—of course they must, since they can only be defined a posteriori. All others have to 'fight their way into existence' (Peirce) against competitive possibilities; but the divine essence, the capacity to harmonize with and adapt to *any* situation, for just that reason is noncompetitive. It could not be generated or destroyed; an alleged contingency of its existing would have no intelligible objective reference.

I conclude: Fitch is essentially right. The divine essence, compared to others, is the perfect essence; and everything about this perfection is congruent with its actualization being necessary, and incongruent with its being even possibly unactualized.

Like Scholz, our Yale logician regards existence as an attribute of attributes. In discussing this we need to recall once more our distinction between existence and actuality. The inclusive mode of reality is actuality. This is, as Fitch says, not an attribute in the same sense as other things are attributes. Yet it is a sort of attribute, and precisely not an attribute of attributes either. It is rather an *attribute of everything except attributes*, whereas (ordinary) attributes are attributes of some only of the things which are not attributes. Everything except an attribute (or a mere abstraction) is an actuality (or class or system of actualities). Being actual is the same as being wholly definite (conforming to the Law of Excluded Middle as to predicates) or as being wholly particular or concrete. What has concreteness is just any and every concrete thing. Exemplified universals or properties are not literally concrete, concreteness is just not *their* attribute.

'Existence' is the fact *that,* among the actual things there are one or more which exemplify ('somehow concretize', to speak metaphorically or loosely) a specified attribute (including individually distinctive attributes, characteristics definitive of a given individual, such as being the son of So-and-so, or even as being 'this man'). If an attribute of something is whatever may be said about it, then one may call existence, or non-emptiness, an attribute of the essence actualized. But here 'about' has an extremely vague meaning, and 'attribute' a rather Pickwickian one. It is the exemplifying actualities which really 'have' the attribute, not it which has them. Actualization is the fact that something has the attribute. To, or in, the attribute itself this having (being had) is (in ordinary contingent cases) simply nothing.

To be *necessarily* had by some suitable actualities, however, is very different and is indeed an essence of an essence, an attribute of an attribute. Logically-guaranteed actualization is not just actualization. A man *assured* of posthumous fame could perhaps rest content, even without any actual fame in his own lifetime. And his satisfaction in the guarantee (so far as he believed in it) would not require that he knew any particular persons who would acclaim him or build upon foundations he had laid. Analogously, it is nothing to the divine essence (though something to God in His full actuality) by what actualities it exists; nevertheless it is everything to the essence that, since its existence constitutes possibility as such, it could not fail of actualization. Deprive it of this self-grounded necessity and it loses all its intelligibility and cannot perform any of its assigned roles. Here, in no Pickwickian sense, is indeed an attribute of an attribute. Without existential necessity, we may have an idol, we cannot have deity. It follows, *nota bene,* that sheer empiricism is antitheism built into a methodological principle. It simply begs the central religious question, and that is all it can in consistency do, so far as *that* question is concerned.

As to 'maximal imperfection', to which Fitch refers, I do not see that this has any clear meaning, unless it means the same as 'bare nothing'. And very likely that is truly 'the most deficient and imperfect entity in the world'. It also is necessarily unexemplified in actuality, because it is the total denial of actuality, whereas the divine perfection is (in a certain manner) the maximal assertion of it. Classical theism makes this assertion absolute in a sense which runs into totally opaque antinomies; neoclassical theism avoids these by requiring only that the divine actuality be supreme and all-inclusive with respect to whatever is actual and that the divine potentiality account for all that is possible but not actual, by being both the ground of its possibility and that which would fully inherit its richness were it to become actual. Thus all possibility of rivalry with another is made logically impossible. And this exclusion of rivalry, as a great man saw almost nine centuries ago, is the very principle which justifies worship.

22. *Conclusions*

We have in Part Two considered or mentioned the responses of some forty-four philosophers to the type of argument that Anselm invented. At least twenty of these, including a dozen modern writers, appear to have known virtually nothing of the structure of the Proof as presented in *Prosl.* III-IV and the *Reply*, or in Descartes's *Replies*! About fourteen, half of them modern, have had at least a partial understanding of such a structure, in some cases (Descartes, Spinoza, Cudworth) probably not derived directly from Anselm; but of the modern thinkers discussed in Part Two, only Malcolm and Hartman pay explicit attention to the remarkable difference between Anselm's two accounts, in *Prosl.* II and III, and deal with the obviously pressing problem of their relationship. One is moved to ask, how careless can we be?

About half of the forty-four may be said to have accepted the Proof, or at least to have seen something in it besides a mere sophistry (including Findlay, who sees it as implicitly a forceful disproof).

Of sixteen refuters of the Proof, three medieval and thirteen modern, few in their refutations so much as mention either of the two principles upon which *Prosl.* III and a number of later passages turn, but about which nothing is said in *Prosl.* II. And only Findlay shows much understanding of these principles. Yet among the critics here considered are some of the most influential: Thomas, Hume, Kant. Let us add one more, Bertrand Russell, who in his book on Leibniz and in his *History of Western Philosophy* makes it plain that he follows Leibniz and others in accepting the Gaunilo legend as containing all that there was to Anselm's reasoning.

Thus we have seventeen refutations (counting those by Esser and Lehmen) by philosophers, mostly very famous, scattered over nine centuries. With a solitary exception, these refutations take little or no account of what Anselm said in the latter two-thirds of the four-page statement of the Proof, or in most of the sixteen-page rebuttal of Gaunilo. Is there in the whole history of controversy a parallel case of casual reading of a hotly-controverted text?

One writer (Hocking) both defends and attacks the Proof: defends in relation to his own version and attacks in relation to one which he attributes to Anselm, any resemblance of either version to the historical Anselm being negligible. Hocking's teacher Royce was similarly remote from the *Prosl.* III reasoning (as was Royce's teacher Lotze, who nevertheless

went through the usual motions of refuting an unidentified
or misidentified argument).

Have not philosophy departments in universities everywhere
some responsibility to teach students the absurdity of these
procedures? No one has to publish a refutation of Anselm;
but if he does publish one, can it be less than his intellectual
and scholarly duty to know and say whether or not he is dealing
with the actual writing and reasoning of Anselm (or Descartes
—for he too has been carelessly read, his refuters and even
defenders often blandly ignoring his replies to some of the very
objections still being made in our own time), rather than a
feeble caricature, conveniently susceptible to refutation?

Since Malcolm challenged his colleagues to take *Prosl.* III
duly into account, at least a half-dozen replies have already
appeared. As we saw in Part One, Sec. 23, these all leave something to be desired. Perhaps the replies do succeed in showing
—hardly so clearly as Findlay and others had already shown it
—that classical theism cannot legitimately employ the Proof.
However, since no other form of theism is considered, except
vaguely and incidentally, the question, 'Is the trouble
with the Proof or with the type or types of theism it has been
used to support?' remains unclarified. The scholarly world,
after a little delay, is grudgingly catching up to Anselm and
Descartes; but alas, the subject now stands at a different point.
(Professors, if intellectually ambitious, are busy people.
Who can say whose fault it is if we cannot meet our responsibil-
ities? Perhaps it is that of those who want education to be
cheaper than cosmetics, power and luxury in automobiles,
smoking, or drink.)

And what about defenders of the Argument? Do they give
evidence of having read the two brief texts? As we have seen,

often not, especially in modern times. Leibniz and Hegel are striking examples. It is as though, for some reason, men recoil from Anselm's touch, almost as much when pretending to accept his Proof as when harshly rejecting it. Could the reason possibly be that there is an intuition that this Proof is a dangerous weapon? It turns against classical theism and classical pantheism, though both have sometimes used it; it turns against unqualified empiricism so obviously that empiricists have never used it. However, if our analysis is right, there is one doctrine it does not turn against, and that is the theism which has learned to free itself from the Greek overidentification of the divine with one side of the contraries, one-many, absolute-relative, necessary-contingent, being-becoming. If this conclusion is at all correct, then Anselm, without knowing it, had in principle transcended all the older forms of theism and skepticism alike and had furnished mankind with an instrument which we are only now in a position to use correctly.

Empiricism, however, has been right all along in this, that the a priori knowledge of God is at most only an understanding of His purely abstract aspect; while all that is concrete in His reality is to be known, so far as it can be known, through observation, scientific or personal. The God of our world now, and through the geologic ages, is revealed to us partly, perhaps, through Scripture, religious tradition or ritual, partly through science, certainly not through any proof. Proofs can only show that there is a divine actuality for these more concrete or experiential means to reveal, thus giving us an infinitely bare yet balanced, seemingly consistent, and intelligible *outline* which all our life and aspiration can joyously fill with contingent, more particular values, meanings, and surmises.

This book has presented the following contentions. Contrary to almost universal belief, the essential principles of Anselm's Proof are first stated not in *Prosl.* II, but in *Prosl.* III. They are: we can conceive something as such that its nonexistence is inconceivable; not to be conceivable as nonexistent is greater than to be thus conceivable; therefore, the concept of the greatest conceivable must be of something whose nonexistence is inconceivable.

The relevant objections are: (a) it is a mere assumption that 'greatest conceivable' and 'inconceivable as nonexistent' are themselves (consistently) conceivable; (b) a greatest conceivable must be either a greatest quantity or else a reality wholly lacking in quantity, in either case a dubious conception; (c) an absolutely greatest being must be incapable of receiving value from, or of being intrinsically related to the world, and therefore of being the loving and conscious God implied by religious attitudes; (d) the Proof appears to be an obviously illicit transition from abstract essence or idea to concrete actuality, or from the logically weaker (less definite) to the logically stronger (more definite); (e) and consequently (Findlay paradox), if the proposed definition of divinity implies such an illicit transition, it must be judged illogical or contradictory.

All of these objections, except perhaps (a), become inapplicable if one adopts the 'neoclassical' version of 'none greater (is conceivable)', taking it to mean, 'none greater—except itself'. 'Exists necessarily' then means the same as is 'somehow actualized in any possible state of affairs'. The particular *how* of actualization, or the particular actuality concretizing the abstract essence formulated in the definition, is contingent. The necessity that the essence be actualized is due to the absolutely infinite range of variability in its possible hows of actualization, or (the same thing) to this range's being strictly coordinate to that of possible states of affairs. Since no such state would exclude God, He exists 'no matter what'—in other words, absolutely necessarily. This neoclassical interpretation not only dissolves the Findlay paradox—for the affirmation *that* divinity is somehow concrete implies nothing whatever as to *how* it, or anything else, is concrete, and hence is a purely abstract statement—but also removes many other, and more familiar, antinomies of religious metaphysics. It implies neither a greatest possible quantity nor a reality without quantity; the God it describes can receive value from, be relative to, and know and love the world. He need not be 'immutable, yet active', free yet wholly necessary. Such antinomies are no longer inescapable.

Whether or not new logical difficulties may be expected to arise from the new doctrine, so that objection (a) remains perhaps in force, is the residual question, upon which historical controversies concerning Anselm (or Descartes) throw no direct or obvious light. For in these controversies the possibility of a neoclassical point of view was entirely overlooked, as it was by Anselm himself. But since the old difficulties disappear, the fair initial presumption in favor of there being some intelligible religious truth justifies a new inquiry into the possibility of a tenable theism. In particular, Kant's rejection of the other theistic proofs calls for radical re-examination.

Finally, the possibility of arriving at a correct estimate of the status and content of metaphysics in general depends in substantial degree upon a proper understanding of Anselm's discovery that the character of being *not conceivably surpassed* (by another) must be one of the three: nonsensical, contradictory, or necessarily (somehow) actualized. Between a theism which can solve the abstract-concrete paradox inherent in 'necessary being', as traditionally conceived, and a positivistic rejection of the logical possibility of any theism at all, a philosopher must, it seems, make his choice. And since every basic categorial question is connected with this one, Anselm has thus defined our task, in some respects, more sharply than anyone before him and almost everyone after him. Does he not therefore deserve at long last to be paid the minimal compliment of supposing that when he took a number of pages to state his case he needed those pages and had not said all he knew in the first two paragraphs? Granted that in this opening passage, about which so much has been said, there appears to be a notable fallacy, we have but one way to find out whether or not this initial fallacy is essential to the Proof as set forth in subsequent passages. That one way is to read—and reflect upon—those additional passages.

How painfully the fragility of human 'reason' is illustrated in this history! However, the hopeful side of the story is that the one right way is now open before us.

Bibliography

[Only writings consulted are included. For a much more extensive list, see the work by Koyré mentioned below.]

I. Anselm

Anselm, Saint. *Basic Writings (Proslogium, Monologium, Gaunilon's: On Behalf of the Fool, Cur Deus Homo.)* Translated by S. W. Deane, with an introduction by Charles Hartshorne. Second Edition, La Salle, Illinois: Open Court Publishing Co., 1962.

Patrologia Cursus Completus. Series Secunda. Tomi CLVIII-CLIX. S. Anselmus. Edited by Abbé Migne (Paris, 1853).

Hasse, F. R. *Anselm von Canterbury,* Leipzig, 1843. 2 volumes. Translated and abridged by W. Turner (London, 1850).

Rigg, J. M. *St. Anselm of Canterbury.* London, 1896 [a profound study].

Copleston, Frederick, S. J. *A History of Philosophy* (London, 1950). [A curious fact about this history, one of the better ones on Anselm's Argument, is that it gives a more literally correct account of the principle of *Proslogium* III when expounding Bonaventura's version of it than when expounding Anselm directly. Also curious is the total absence of the principle from this author's shorter *Medieval Philosophy* (London, 1952)].

II. The Proof

Barth, Karl. *Fides quaerens intellectuam Anselm's Beweis der Existenz Gottes,* Zürich: Evangelischer Verlag, 1913. [A very thorough, detailed study of the Argument as Anselm intended it. (English translation: New York, 1960).]

Baumgarten, Alexander Gottlieb. *Metaphysica* (1750), *pars* IIII, 803-845, esp. 809-811.

Broad, C. D. "Arguments for the Existence of God," *Journal of Theological Studies,* 40 (1939), 16-30, 156-167. [Total neglect of *Prosl.* III.]

Cook, A. A. "The Ontological Argument and the Existence of God," *Proceedings of the Aristotelian Society* (London, 1918), NS, 18.

Daniels, P. A. *Quellenbeiträge und Untersuchungen zur Geschichte der Gottesbeweise im XIII Jahrhundert, mit besonderer Beruchsichtigung des Arguments im Proslogion des Hlg. Anselm.* Münster, 1909. (Beiträge zur Geschichte der Philosophie des Mittelalters, VIII, 1-2) [An invaluable collection of medieval Latin texts referring to the Argument, with a penetrating analysis of them as indications that the author accepted or rejected Anselm's Proof, and a careful discussion of the philosophical beliefs which determined this acceptance or rejection.].

Davies, A. E. "The Problem of Truth and Existence as Treated by Anselm," *Proceedings of the Aristotelian Society* (London), NS., 20.

Engel, S. M. "Kant's 'Refutation' of the Ontological Argument," *Philosophy and Phenomenological Research,* 24 (1963), 20-35.

Esser, M. *Der ontologische Gottesbeweis und seine Geschichte.* (Bonn, 1905). "Finden sich Spüren des ontologischen Gottesbeweises vor dem Heiligen Anselm?" *Jahrbücher für Philosophie und spekulative Theologie,* 29 (1910).

Findlay, J. N. "Can God's Existence Be Disproved?" *Mind,* 57 (1948), 176-183. [One of the most original and penetrating of the criticisms of Anselm's Argument.] Also published in Findlay's *Language, Mind, and Value.* London: Allen and Unwin, 1963, in the preface to which occurs the following characteristically lucid passage, the objectivity (and generosity) of which speaks for itself.

I still think it [the article] makes a valid point: that if it is *possible*, in some logical and not merely epistemological sense, that there is no God, then God's existence is not merely doubtful but *impossible*, since nothing *capable* of non-existence could be a God at all. Kant, who at times suggested that the existence of anything was a synthetic and *a posteriori* matter (though perhaps establishable only by a non-sensuous intuition) should have seen that his views constituted a *dis-proof* of the existence of God, not left Him a flawless ideal to which some noumenal reality *might* correspond. Professor Hartshorne has, however, convinced me that my argument permits a ready inversion, and that one can very well argue that if God's existence is in any way *possible*, then it is also *certain* and *necessary* that God exists, a position which should give some comfort to the shade of Anselm. The notion of God, like the notion of the class of all classes not members of themselves, has plainly unique logical properties, and I do not now think that my article finally *decides* how we should cope with such uniqueness.

Guéroult, M. *Nouvelles réflexions sur la preuve ontologique de Descartes.* Paris: Vrin, 1955.
"La vérité de science et la vérité de la chose dans les preuves de l'existence de Dieu." Cahiers de Royaumont, Philosophie no. II. Paris: Editions de minuit, 1957. [I owe this item to my friend the learned bibliographer of Descartes (among other capacities) Gregor Sebba.]

Hartman, Robert S. "Prolegomena to a Meta-Anselmian Axiomatic," *Review of Metaphysics,* 14 (1961), No. 4, 637-675.

Hartshorne, Charles. *The Logic of Perfection.* La Salle, Illinois: Open Court Publishing Co., 1962. (The long second chapter presents ten forms of ontological proof and defends them against twenty objections. See especially sections IV, XI, XII.)

Henrich, D. *Der ontologische Gottesbeweis.* Tübingen: J. C. B. Mohr, 1960. (Probably the most thorough account of modern forms of the Argument, but with meager and misleading references to Anselm.)

Herrlin, Olle. *The Ontological Proof in Thomistic and Kantian Interpretation.* Upsala and Leipzig, 1950. Acta Universitas Upsaliensis 1950:9. (Excellent on Aquinas and Kant; vague on Anselm)

Jalabert, J. *Le Dieu de Leibniz.* Paris, 1960.
[Ch. V (pp. 69-92) of this excellent work has a fine summary of the Argument and its history from Anselm to Leibniz. The Thomistic view is well explicated on pp. 72-76. The best possible case for Leibniz's use of the Argument, and in general for its use in classical theism is presented in this chapter. The Findlay paradox is of course entirely missed, and

in my opinion all genuine contrast between necessity and contingency is destroyed. But like Leibniz himself, Jalabert will not have it so.]

Johnson, J. P. "The Ontological Argument in Plato," *The Personalist*, 44 (1963), 24-34.

King-Farlow, J. "Existence and Proving Gods," *Darshana, An International Quarterly* (Moradabad, India), 1 (1961), 46-58. [Discusses and revises the Thomistic criticism of the Proof.]

Kiteley, M. "Existence and the Ontological Argument," *Philosophy and Phenomenological Research*, 18 (1958), 533-534. [Relates the Argument to the "homological fallacy."]

Koyré, A. *L'Idée de Dieu dans la philosophie de St. Anselme.* Paris, 1923. [Particularly good on the relations of Anselm to Neoplatonism, and on the structure of the Argument.]

Malcolm, Norman. "Anselm's Ontological Arguments," *Philosophical Review*, 69 (1960), 42-52. [A vigorous defence of the "second argument" of Anselm. It provoked the following replies: R. E. Allen, "The Ontological Argument," *Philosophical Review*, 70 (1960), 56-66;

Raziel Abelson, "Not Necessarily," *Ibid.*, 67-84;

Terence Penelhum, "On the Second Ontological Argument," *Ibid.*, 85-92;

Paul Henle, "Uses of the Ontological Argument," *Ibid.*, 93-101; G. B. Matthews, "On Conceivability in Anselm and Malcolm"; *Ibid.*, 102-103.]

Nakhnikian, G. and Salmon, W. C. "Exists as Predicate," *Philosophical Review*, 66 (1957), 5.

Rescher, N. "The Ontological Proof Revisited," *Australasian Journal of Philosophy*, 37 (1959), 138-148.

Tillich, Paul. "The Two Types of Philosophy of Religion," *Union Seminary Quarterly Review*, 1 (1946). [Particularly good on the medieval period. Stresses the connection of the Proof with direct experience of deity.]

Zabeeh, Farhang. "Ontological Argument and How and Why Some Speak of God." *Philosophy and Phenomenological Research*, 32 (1961), 206-215.

Acknowledgments

The author cordially thanks the following publishers and journals for permission to quote—in sections or parts of this book as indicated in brackets—from the following books or articles:

(all items except the first are in Part Two)

Evangelischer Verlag, Zurich—*Fides quaerens intellectuam*, by Karl Barth. [I, 1]

The Macmillan Company—*Critique of Pure Reason*, translated by Max Müller. [10] Also "The Ontological Argument in Royce and Others," in *Contemporary Idealism*, ed. by C. Barrett. [14]

Macmillan & Co., London—*Descartes's Philosophical Writings*, translated by N. K. Smith. [5]

Scribner's—*The Realm of Truth*, by George Santayana. [14]

Benziger Brothers, Inc.—*Summa Theologica*, translated by the Fathers of the English Dominican Province. [4]

University of California Press—*The Rise of Scientific Philosophy*. [16]

Oxford University Press—*Essay on Philosophical Method*, by R. G. Collingwood. [11, 15] Also *The Works of Aristotle*, translated by H. H. Joachim et al. [1]

University of Chicago Press—*From Descartes to Kant*, by T. V. Smith and Marjorie Grene. [5]

George Allen & Unwin Ltd.—*Language, Mind, and Value*, by J. N. Findlay. [Bibliography]

Dover Publications—*The Philosophical Works of Descartes*, Translated by E. S. Haldane and G. R. T. Ross. [5]

Mind—"Can God's Existence Be Disproved?," by J. N. Findlay. [17] Also "Existence, Predication, and the Ontological Argument," by Jerome Shaffer. [20]

The Review of Metaphysics—"Prolegomena to a Meta-Anselmian axiomatic," by Robert Hartman. [18]

The Monist—"Aquinas on Saying That God Doesn't Exist," by G. B. Matthews. [4]

Philosophy and Phenomenological Research—"Kant's Refutation of the Ontological Argument," by S. M. Engel. [10]

The Chemex Corporation—Pamphlet by Dr. Peter Schlumbohm. [Frontispiece]

Index of Names

Abelson, Raziel, 110, 112, 116, 122, 309
Aegidius of Rome, 154
Albertus Magnus, 154
Alexander of Hales, 154
Allen, R. E., 110, 113, 115, 116, 309
Aquinas, St. Thomas, 13, 21, 26, 49, 52, 55, 127, 154-164, 170, 211, 230, 249, 283, 298, 308, 309; *Summa contra gentiles,* 160 f.; *Summa Theologica,* 159 f.
Aristotle, 27, 30, 55, 56, 57, 93, 122, 141 ff., 149, 161, 166, 247, 252, 282, 289
Armour, Leslie, 123 f.
Arnauld, Antoine, 200 f.
Augustine, St., 27, 30, 31, 36, 146, 149, 251

Barrett, C., 241 n.
Barth, Karl, 11, 13, 21, 36, 53, 106, 151, 168, 177, 238, 261, 283, 306
Baumgarten, A. G., 208 ff., 306
Berg, Jan, 265-267; "An Examination of the Ontological Proof," 265
Bergson, Henri, 43, 227
Berkeley, Bishop George, 242
Boëthius, 250 f.; *Consolations of Philosophy,* 250 f.; *De Trinitate,* 252
Bolzmann, L., 280
Bonaventura, St., 76, 87, 154, 155, 170, 306

Index of Topics

limitation, 169
limiting concept, 95
linguistic theory of necessary truth, 24
logic, v; modal, 274; pure, 58
logical, constants, 44; questions, 24 f.; strength, 42, 58; weakness, 42, 58
logically true, 5
logicians, 189, 232, 258
love, essential to self, 75; universal, 148

machines, thinking, 173
mathematicians, 86
mathematics, 24
matter, 196, 204; prime, 170
maximal being, 8, 27, 29
maximum, absolute, 215, 217, 262; actuality, 217
meaning, cognitive, 79; postulates, 3, 4, 96, 98; religious, 169
metaphysica generalis, 285; *specialis,* 285
metaphysical, i, iv, 78, 196, 283
metaphysician, metaphysicians, classical, 181, 184
metaphysics, 24, 28, 58, 98, 104, 106, 120, 159, 186, 242, 250, 252, 286;
    creationist, 215
method, 207
minor premise of the Proof, 59
modal, argument, 102; and temporal status, 128; classifications a priori,
    54, 60; coextensiveness, 58; coincidence, 229; equivalence, 148; logic,
    reduction principle of, 273 f.; statement, statements, 12, 161; status as
    predicate, 144; terms, 152; uniqueness of idea of God, 134
modality, modalities, 7, 61, 232, 233; existential, 210; real, 8; temporal
    aspect of, 145
monads, 195; interaction between, 194
monism, extreme, 243
monists of India, 147
Monologium, 53
monopoly of power, 201
mysticism, 249
mystics, 65

nature, presumed perfect regularity of, 202
necessarily, actualized somehow, 84; existing, 6; nonempty class, iii, 50, 290
necessary, all things as, 184; being, 19; defined, 43, 80; distinctive meaning
    of, 173, 175; existence, 33; proposition, 41; the, as abstract, 51 f., 143;
    truth, 3, 6